Great Commission

Disciple-Making

A Practical Guide to Growing as a Disciple Maker

By James A. Lilly

Recommendations

Being a faithful disciple and making disciples are two fundamental Kingdom of God responsibilities that Jesus assigns to everyone who would follow Him. With his book *Great Commission Disciple Making*, Jim Lilly has given us a comprehensive practitioners' handbook of transformational and reproducible Disciple-Making. This book provides a valuable collection of resources for people committed to God's Kingdom coming where they live, as it is in heaven.

> Jerry Trousdale, Director of International Ministries
> Cityteam Ministries, Author of *Miraculous Movements*

Jim has not just written about Biblical Disciple-Making. He is a successful practitioner. In this book he has taken us back to Scripture of how Jesus taught the twelve disciples to make disciples and to see the gospel spread throughout the known world. He begins with the premise that the Great Commission commands us to make disciples and not simple converts. He then gives us the step by step principles that Jesus gave to the Twelve beginning with looking for the Person of Peace, to discovering for themselves about who He was "Great Commission Disciple-Making" is a must read for anyone who wants to obediently follow Christ in the fulfillment of the Great Commission. Without it we will never reach the goal.

> Richard Williams
> Regional Vice President, Cityteam Ministries

It has been a great blessing to know Jim and Cindy Lilly. They are living examples of humble, prayerful, loving, generous, and hard-working followers of Jesus. Their lives and fruitfulness invite a careful watching and listening to all of us. With this book, Jim has made a significant contribution to the amazing renewal of biblical discipleship occurring globally. *Great Commission Disciple-Making* is a helpful manual for today's disciple-makers. Thoroughly helpful, the appendices alone are worth getting the book and sharing it enthusiastically.

> Dr. Edward N. Gross, Coordinator of Strategic Alliances with CityNet Ministries, Philadelphia, PA, Author of *Are you a Christian or a Disciple?*

Jim Lilly is grappling with the key issue of our time. If we are ever going to get serious about the last command of Jesus, we have to break out of our historically fixed methodologies into simpler less complex systems of Disciple-Making. Jim's practical journey through multiplicative disciple-making strategies provides not just an "ought to" but a "how to" learning experience.

> Roy Moran, — Spiritual Literacy Catalyst, Shoal Creek Community Church
> Author of *Spent Matches*

Jim's book creates a framework for a powerful discipleship experience. Throughout the process of discovery, he is constantly asking probing questions that allow us to enter a dialogue with the Lord that opens up the scriptures and illuminates our path. I heartily recommend this valuable piece of work.

Graham Cook, — author and conference speaker, Brilliant Book house

Since I have been part of DMM for the last 10 years, I highly recommend this book for those who are practicing DMM or want to learn. It is for those who are more about making disciples than just making converts, those who care more about disciple-making than filling church buildings or pews. It is for learners and for pastors who are more about finishing the Great Commission task than increasing their weekly church attendance. *Great Commission Disciple-Making* provides clear guidance from the Bible on how to make disciples through the Discovery Process of being obedient disciples, which is so transformative. I encourage all of you to learn through what Jim wrote.

Dr. Aila Tasse — Founder Lifeway Mission International
Cityteam International (East Africa)

I heartily commend to you Jim Lilly, and the powerful lessons the Lord has taught him and his wife Cindy. I will always be grateful to Jim for introducing me and coaching many of us in this simple pattern. First, it has helped me build stronger community deeper in God's Word, with my family and loved ones. Secondly, it has given me a practical way to be fruitful and multiply disciples in obedience to the Great Commission of Jesus our Messiah. The structure of DBS and DMM is the essential DNA of the Church which because of its simplicity leads to reproducibility. I strongly believe this is the best opportunity we have to cooperate with Jesus as we make disciples and He builds his big, beautiful Somali Church.

Michael Neterer, SALT Director, Arrive Ministries
Somali Adult Literacy Training

This is a very comprehensive manual full of spiritual technology necessary for reaching the ends of the earth. It has all the nuts and bolts for a Disciple Maker's tool box presented through the Discovery Process to catalyze a Disciple-Making Movement. It is designed to unfold many small but significant gems of knowledge and understanding of the dynamics of sparking a Church Planting Movement, such as the difference between multiplication and replication, and so on. You can feel passion dripping out of every page. *Making* to anyone who wants to improve his performance by upgrading his discipling skills.

Dr. Victor Choudhrie, author of *Greet the Church in Your House*, and trainer of house church leaders since 1992, whose network of churches in 2012 baptized one million new believers in India.

If your desire for discipleship demands action, obedience, and reliance on the Holy Spirit, this book is for you. If spiritual growth for you means knowing Jesus more instead of knowing more about Jesus, this book is for you. Jim Lilly is one of those people who will lead you in this path toward knowing Jesus more, loving Jesus more, and serving Jesus more. It won't be through memorizing facts to pass a one-hour exam. True discipleship demands obedience. This book will walk you along the path to obedience to the Savior.

David Cross, —Vice President of Information Technologies, Pioneers

Our purpose and goal as a Christian is to advance the Gospel of Jesus Christ to the ends of the earth and our commission, our orders is to make disciples. Sounds so simple, right? However, it seems as though we have complicated this over many years and the results have been staggering. Jim Lilly is a spiritual giant, a leader in this powerful movement in recognizing that making disciples rather than converts is the key to Kingdom expansion. He teaches that we are to do **what** Jesus told us to do and **how** Jesus told us to do it. This book is a practical approach to the foundation of disciple-making from an authentic man who lives it out daily as a leader both in his home and city. It has been an honor and a privilege to be a part of DMM in the Twin Cities and to work with Jim, a true man of God, and his wonderful wife and partner Cindy. If you are serious about being a part of what God is doing in this generation, I highly recommend that this book be part of your foundation.

David J. Engman, Founder/Pastor, Breakthrough Ministries, Minneapolis, MN

Contents

Acknowledgements

The general outline for this book comes from courses that I and other Cityteam members have taught. Contributors to the development include Dave Hunt, Jerry Trousdale, Mustapha Sandi, Richard Williams and David Watson.

Of all the people who have helped with the production of this book, foremost is my wife Cindy, helpmate and co-laborer in this work. She forbore months of my inattention and distraction as I wrote this. Then she took up her very able correction pen to make extensive editorial changes. Because she deeply understands every part of this material, she could not only make it more readable, but make it convey more clearly the message that needed to be told.

Next, I need to thank those who spent the time to edit this manuscript: Dan Servatius whose walk with the Lord through many difficulties has been an encouragement to me; Julia Warneke, Tim Lovestrand, and my sister-in-law Lonnie Ulmer who pointed out many statements that were unclear or confusing; Gregory C. Benoit volunteered to do the final print edit. Jennie Lodien and Gary Albright did the cover design pro bono. Romeo Garcia, my longtime friend in this discipleship journey, helped with the initial chapters by challenging me to look at what I wanted to say from the outside-in rather than the inside-out.

The concept of using scripture-based Discovery Studies to teach disciple-making came out of the cooperative work of a group of men and women who, besides being involved in their own ministries, have been working to implement Disciple-Making Movements (DMM) in the Twin Cities. This group includes Tom Mouw, Mike Neterer, Randy Torpen, Phil Bickel, Dave Engman, Jay Perske, Sergio Amezcua, Paul and Roxane Kuivenen, and my wife Cindy. The experience of John King who is part of Final Command with discovery based training gave us reasonable confidence that this method of training would work.

This journey of discipleship for me started under the unseen guidance of the Holy Spirit, but took concrete form with a breakfast with Dave Hunt in San Jose, California. This came about due to the suggestion of David Cross who is a missionary with Pioneers. Dave Hunt was one of the key people working with Cityteam in East Africa and was involved with the amazing Disciple-Making Movement in Sub-Saharan Africa which Jerry Trousdale describes in his book *Miraculous Movements*. It was Dave who visited our home city and, together with David Cross, launched DMM in this region of the United States.

Richard Williams, who has become both a good friend and my supervisor with Cityteam, spent hours teaching, coaching, and mentoring me. He even sent Ed Gross during the difficulties of getting started with the first iDisciple training here. Ed's series of talks on first century discipleship released an energy that made our first training the largest that Cityteam had sponsored to that date. The trainer who brought discipleship most deeply into my life was Ricardo Pineda, who introduced me to the Great Shemah in Deuteronomy 6. These people continue to be my support for all of the work that I have been able to do, both here in the United States and abroad.

There are two other men who have provided me with inspiration and technical understanding about disciple-making movements. First, Jerry Trousdale ventured to come to our first training when it seemed questionable whether there would be enough people to have a seminar. Jerry's experience and gentle compassion for seeing people becoming disciples of Jesus has been infectious in my life. Jerry also provided valuable critique and suggestions for this book. The next person is David Watson, who God used to lay the foundational understanding of DMM in Northern India and to spread the message and training to all parts of the world. Like Jerry, David gave useful input about the history of DMM. I have been honored to get to know both of these men and to continue to receive input from them.

Graham Cooke and Bill Johnson were responsible for breaking me out of the routine Christian life that I had been living for a decade. They opened up a different dimension to the Kingdom of God than I have ever seen before. When I heard them speak at a Lutheran Conference in St. Paul, Minnesota, I realized that there was much more to understanding and experiencing the kingdom of God.

All of my discipleship understanding is built upon a foundation of Christian community experience and teaching. I am indebted to Larry Alberts who was the first person to disciple and form me. Larry was the leader of the Body of Christ Community in Grand Forks, North Dakota. This was my initial fellowship, with whose members I still feel covenantal bonds of gratitude and love. The teachings of Steve Clark, Ralph Martin, and the other leaders of the Word of God in Ann Arbor, Michigan established my understanding of community and the Christian Life. Ern Baxter, Charles Simpson, and Bob Mumford's teachings challenged me in all areas of my life. John Wimber's teachings on healing taught me that the miraculous is the natural work of the Holy Spirit with whom we can actively participate. Next, Bill Gothard and his Institute of Basic Life Principles, with its focus on the sufficiency of the Bible, planted roots in me that have found new life in "Discovery Bible Studies." God used Tony and Collette Rolland to mentor our family life and prayed for a fatherhood anointing.

Finally, I need to mention the many Godly men and women whose lives have intertwined with mine. They include a meat cutter who did not finish grade school, pastors, housewives and homeschooling mothers, carpenters, school teachers, farmers, college and seminary professors, businessmen, retirees, even a former Hitler youth.

Forward

The goal of this book is to serve as a practical training guide to help people engage in the process of being and making disciples—the Great Commission.

Discovering the truths about discipleship directly from the Bible has more impact than the finest teachings any human can give. For this reason, the training focuses on a series of fifteen passages from the Bible that present key teachings of Jesus and his disciples about fulfilling the Great Commission. In order for the training to be most effective, it should take place in a small group. Jesus set the minimum size for a small group as two or three gathered in his name (Matthew 18:20). When you have completed the lessons in this book, you will find some practical guidance for taking the next steps in Appendix 1.

This book will answer two main questions. The first is **"What does it mean to be a disciple of Jesus?"** During forty years of listening to and participating in discussions about discipleship, it was not until I heard Ed Gross speaking about First Century Discipleship that I finally could say that I understood what it means to be a disciple of Jesus. We will look at some excerpts from Ed's book *Are you a Christian or a Disciple?* to see what he learned about first century discipleship. Jerry Trousdale's *Miraculous Movements* and David and Paul Watson's book *Contagious Disciple-Making* relate their experiences in developing and applying

the DMM process in India (Watson) and in Sub-Saharan Africa (Trousdale) with amazing testimonies and great practical wisdom.

The second question that will be answered is, **"What is required to make a disciple of Jesus and what is our role in that process?"** This is the heart of the Discovery Process. Fully understanding the Discovery Process will involve learning how to facilitate a Discovery Group yourself. This book will provide insights that will change the way you look at the world. Consider how you can form a small group which will examine these passages, learn them by memory, apply them obediently, and share what they have learned with others. It is in this group that you will experience the full potential of living as disciples of Jesus.

The final goal of this book is that you and the other members of your Discovery Group reach out to invite believers to become disciples, who can reach not-yet believers in your community, and finally go wherever Jesus and his Holy Spirit direct you.

In order for this to be a complete resource for disciples who will make other disciples, there are six appendices:

Appendix 1: **Great Commission Outreach Guidelines** gives guidance to help transition your Discovery Group into a missional one that actively reaches those "people of peace" whom God is preparing to gather the harvest in their fields (Luke 10:2, 6).

Appendix 2: **The Standard Discovery Series** provides complete lists of discovery passages to use in discipling groups of people, starting from a simple interest in God, to Jesus, then to becoming churches.

Appendix 3: **Discovering Discipleship Scripture Questions** are provided to aid in studying the fifteen discovery passages.

Appendix 4: **Prayer Guides** give a format to develop a plan to pray for a community of people and guidance in learning to pray the scriptures.

Appendix 5: **Discovery Group Questions** are to be used as an outline for a discovery group.

Appendix 6: **Video Training Resources** can be used both to introduce people to disciple-making movements and to explain each of the components of DMM.

Appendix 7: **Topical DS Series** that can be used as introductory studies to familiarize people with the Discovery Process as well as address common issues in peoples' lives.

My Journey to DMM:
The road that has brought you to this point of becoming a disciple-maker is part of your own unique story. My experience included a couple of promises from God and then more than thirty years of doing other things, not knowing what I was waiting for. There were two separate conversations with God that prepared me. When I speak of conversations with God, I mean those times when I wrestle with questions that culminate in coming to clarity of understanding that can best be described as God speaking to me with a non-audible voice.

The first of those two conversations took place off-and-on over several weeks. I had been studying world missions in the light of fulfilling the Great Commission. The amount of money that the church was spending on missions was and still is less than ten-percent of their total income. The size of the job to accomplish the Great Commission could drain all of the coffers of all of the churches and still not be accomplished using the methods that we had been using. It did not occur to me to ask if there were other ways. I simply thought that it was impossible unless God intervened.

One day in frustration I cried out to God, "How can the Great Commission be fulfilled? What we are doing is not able to even keep up with the birth rate. Even if we spent all of the church's money and efforts to send out missionaries, the way we are doing it, it is impossible to fulfill Jesus' last command." God spoke to me and said, "When you see Asia and Africa sending missionaries into the entire world, then you will know that the Great Commission will be completed." There was no promise that I would see it, but if I did, I would know that Jesus' command would be fulfilled.

It was about ten years later that I heard stories of Korea sending out missionaries. Another ten years later, I heard that house churches in China were talking of sending out missionaries to other countries. I was excited, but what about Africa? Every time I ran across an article from Africa, the story was always about how much help the church in Africa needed; "help us, send to us, and give to us." After a while I thought, not in my lifetime would I see Africa sending out missionaries to complete the Great Commission.

The second conversation occurred a few years later. Jesus said, "the gate is narrow and the way is hard that leads to life" (Matthew 7:14). One of these narrow gates occurred when I had to make a very difficult personal decision about the direction for me and my family. Would I remain with one fellowship which would leave my family's friendships intact or go with another that might mean relocating? I bargained with the Lord saying that all I needed was to be able to worship and grow in knowledge of Him. God impressed upon me as I wrestled with the decision, "Jim if you stay, you can love me, worship me, and grow closer to me, but I cannot fulfill the call I have for your life."

The call: what is the call for the life of a follower of Jesus? Is it to stay in a safe and comfortable place? Is there more to this life than loving, worshipping, and growing closer to God? This is what motivated me at the time and still is the joy of my life. But God was saying that he was calling me to something more. Not unlike Gideon, I put out a challenge for God to act sovereignly and give me a sign, which he did in less than 24 hours.

I told my wife all that had happened, and together we made the decision to take a new course. We did not know what that would look like, but it marked a new direction. We will learn later about the varieties of ways that Jesus calls people to become his disciples. Since Jesus calls each disciple personally, the way he has led you to this point will have been different than ours.

In the following years of fruitful work, of raising our family and serving in our local church, there was always an expectation that there was something more that God had for us.

Our transition into disciple-making began with my work as an evangelist. After 30 years of church work, I began going out on the streets and door-to-door. The more successful I became at seeing people repent and pray to receive Jesus, the more frustrated I became with the lack of lasting results. It was exhilarating to see the joy that came when people confessed their sins to Jesus and received his forgiveness. I could see the Holy Spirit move in their lives. But when I followed up with them, none of them was interested in learning more about Jesus or changing the direction of their lives. They had been burdened with sin, but now were forgiven. They now had the assurance that they would go to heaven. What was the matter with what I was doing? If Jesus had called me to be a fisher of men, then this was catch-and-release. It was great sport, but it was not advancing the kingdom of God in a perceptible way.

In my frustration, I searched the gospel accounts to see what Jesus had to say about evangelism. It was not a word in his vocabulary and he said nothing good about making converts. Rather, he said, "make disciples." But, I asked, "Where are the instructions?" In March 2012, while I was teaching a "Share Jesus without Fear" course in Salinas, California, Cindy and I were invited to a Saturday iDisciple Awareness Training in San Jose, CA. The seminar was an introduction to Disciple-Making Movements (DMM). During our first discovery study on Luke 10:1-11, we immediately saw how Jesus' disciples made disciples. The instructions had been there all along, we just had not seen them before.

Jerry Trousdale's book *Miraculous Movements* had just been released. Cindy read different parts to me as I was preparing to teach my course on evangelism. We both realized that making disciples was possible and that this was the only way that the Great Commission could be completed. What Jerry documented in Africa moved it beyond theory by showing that hundreds of thousands of non-believers, and especially Muslims, were becoming disciples of Jesus and leading others into the same relationship. Churches were springing up in some of the most hostile places on the earth.

As we were driving back to Minnesota, Cindy suggested that we start praying for God to begin a Disciple-Making Movements in our own city and state. Our prayers matched up with those of David Cross with Pioneer Missions, who gave us a few weeks of DMM training. As our training was ending, David invited our mutual friend Dave Hunt from California to meet with anyone that we could round up with a few days' notice. Two dozen people attended that meeting, twenty of whom I did not know.

My qualifications to lead this initial training effort were availability and willingness. I was simply open to try to coordinate an iDisciple Basic Training when everyone else was too busy. Why did God choose Cindy and me? It was probably because we were asking God to start in our state and city. I have learned that, when God answers the prayer of a disciple, it frequently includes the active involvement of the person who prayed!

For the initial training, Cityteam was bringing four trainers, and we had booked a room that would comfortably seat 60. However, a week before the training, only a dozen people had registered. Like our initial meeting with Dave Hunt, where many unexpected people showed up from unanticipated places, our first training was filled with more than 80 people.

In December 2013, Cindy and I and our oldest granddaughter Natasha went to Sierra Leone to see what was happening within that nation. After reading *Miraculous Movements,* we wanted to see how Discovery Groups functioned as they matured.

The high point of our trip to Africa was attending the Mega-Fest Church Planters Conference in the city of Bo. According to several presenters, Sierra Leone's Christian population had grown from less than 10-percent to about 30-percent in eight years. There are many works underway in this nation, but 5.7-percent of the population who have become Christ followers can be directly attributed to one disciple-making movement.

We had no idea how impactful these eight days of intense church planting strategy and training would be in our lives. The theme of the conference was "To the Ends of the Earth." It wasn't until the end of the second day that I realized that what I was hearing from speaker after speaker had a common theme. "We are deeply indebted to European and American missionaries and indeed we are poor, yet we have the two most important things we need to fulfill the Great Commission: we are disciples who have the word of God, and we know how to make disciples. First, we are going to North Africa, which is the most resistant place in the world to the gospel, and then we will go to Europe, and afterwards to the ends of the earth."

Suddenly, the promise that God had made to me 35 years earlier came back to mind. We met Chinese missionaries in Africa later on that trip, but I was hearing these 1,500 church planters commit themselves to fulfilling the Great Commission. More than 500 of these church planters came from Muslim backgrounds. So what you will be introduced to here has the potential to include you in an amazing adventure with God as he works among men.

More recently, our experience with teaching people and applying the Discovery Process to our own lives has convinced us that the Disciple-Making Discovery Process can change the course of history. I believe that we are capable of fulfilling the Great Commission in a single generation.

Introduction to Disciple-Making Movements

Becoming a disciple of Jesus will introduce you to a new world of people and experiences. You will be transformed so that, everywhere you go, you will find yourself meeting people whom God is touching with his Holy Spirit. You will lead some of these into a disciple-making relationship with Jesus that is similar to your own. This is the power behind what is called disciple-making.

What is a disciple? Is it possible to actually be a disciple of Jesus? Don't we need a human agent to disciple us? These are important questions. The early implementers of DMM started with one question that led to others: "What did Jesus tell us?" Next, they asked how that could apply to us today.

This book is intended to present what these men and women discovered and are applying around the world.

> [Jesus'] divine power has granted to us all things that pertain to life and godliness, through the knowledge of him who called us to his own glory and excellence. For this very reason, make every effort to supplement your faith with virtue, and virtue with knowledge, and knowledge with self-control, and self-control with steadfastness, and steadfastness with godliness, and godliness with brotherly affection, and brotherly affection with love. For if these qualities are yours and are increasing, they keep you from being ineffective or unfruitful in the knowledge of our Lord Jesus Christ.
> —2 Peter 1:3, 5–8

In the above passage, Jesus grants us access to all things pertaining to life and godliness. And Peter affirms some of the disciplines necessary to be effective disciples of Jesus.

The church and the world

The church throughout the world is experiencing challenges that have never occurred from so many directions at once. Two hundred years ago, Europe was the bastion of Christendom, but now it has the fewest professing Christians of any continent in the world. Canada and the United States are witnessing a decline of church membership and attendance. If this continues, within the next 35 years, the Church in America will be reduced to a similar size to that of Europe.

In the Middle East, hundreds of thousands of Christians are being driven from their homes, and thousands are being killed. The times are violent, and the violence comes closer to each of our lives every day. The forces of evil are being released both within the church and without. Within the church, there is the abandonment of the Biblical understanding of God's righteousness. Outside the church, not only is radical Islam threatening us physically, but our society itself is increasingly morally, politically, and socially hostile. It is obvious that business as usual will not reverse these trends. Something different is needed.

Certainly these are alarming signs that don't require great spiritual maturity or prophetic gifting to recognize. But God has not been caught off guard. He is doing something old yet quite new. He is doing something that sounds familiar but can make us uncomfortable. The Holy Spirit is restoring the call to make disciples of Jesus. He is equipping us to do this by very simple means. Wherever there is an attack of Satan, God is counterattacking with unstoppable force. He is not committed to military might, political negotiations, or media blitzes. These can only slow the moral decline and restore a shadow of the previous status quo.

God is doing something much greater and more powerful than anything that armies, politicians, or businesses can accomplish. He is teaching those who will listen how to become and make disciples. Jesus' last words in Matthew 28 were not meant as good advice leading to personal fulfillment or putting more people in pews on Sunday. They were designed to conquer Satan and win back the world for Jesus who is reconciling us to the Father.

This book is written for all those "who have obtained a faith of equal standing" (2 Peter 1:1) and have embarked on, or desire to embark on, the pursuit of being disciples of Jesus. It is for those who are willing to exercise the disciplines so as to be able to make other disciples who also will follow Jesus. This is the Great Commission!

This is a time of radical change and rapid decline of the Christian church in the United States and the collapse of the church in Europe. There are physical, moral, and political attacks upon the church throughout the world. These are discouraging times for many Christians. Nevertheless, there are some exciting things happening in the world as we look around us. The numbers of evangelical Christians is estimated at 180 million in Africa, 150 million in Asia, 120 million in South America—while North America is credited with 100 million and Europe with 6 million.

In 1949, when Mao Zedong came to power in China and expelled all of the foreign missionaries, there was a great lamentation in the West that this marked the end of Christianity in China. God surprised us all. Today, China has produced a church that numbers between 60 and 120 million and is sending out missionaries to other lands.

India had been very resistant to the spread of the gospel, maintaining about two-percent Christian population from 1950 until 2005. Now, according to one mission group, the number of believers in Jesus has almost tripled and is about seven-percent of the population. India is the second largest and fastest growing country in the world. One 25 year-old movement in India headed by Victor Choudhrie baptized over one million new believers in 2012. Victor Johns heads another 30 year-old movement of more than 100,000 indigenous churches and six million believers in one of the most resistant areas in the country. Joy Punnoose heads a group of tens of thousands of new believers and church planters in another difficult area. There are many other smaller church planting ministries, as well.

As mentioned earlier, there are now more evangelical Christians in Africa than any other continent. We will learn about the hundreds of thousands of Muslims who have become followers and disciples of Jesus across Africa. Thousands of them are now making disciples and working to plant churches in some of the most hostile areas of Africa.

So what is the secret to this rapid growth? One thing it is not: It is not the application of western missionary or evangelism methods. That is not to say that early western missionaries have not laid an essential foundation, but the rapid expansion is something entirely different.

How does this rapid growth happen? If we discover it and apply it, will it have similar effects in the US and Europe? We have discovered it! It is found in the pages of the four gospels. It was there all along. The amazing growth has come because normal believers simply decided to obey and do what the gospels tell us. They have started doing what eleven men who followed Jesus did. When Jesus said to his disciples, "Having gone, make disciples," they went and made disciples. And Jesus built his church, which is why you and I profess Jesus as our Lord today.

There are areas in the US where we are already seeing some initial success, but there are many questions that remain. This is the point where you and I can enter into an adventure. My hope is that your life will be profoundly changed and that your relationship with Jesus will deepen. As you enter into the Disciple-Making Process, your vision and ability to fulfill Jesus' final command will increase. My life and the lives of thousands of people who are living as disciples of Jesus give testimony of the transformation. A deepening relationship with Jesus comes from moving from being a believer and follower of Jesus to being his disciple.

What are Disciple-Making Movements (DMM)?

David Watson has described DMM as:

A methodology for starting Church Planting Movements. It focuses on developing self-replicating leaders who make self-replicating Disciple Makers.

Disciples and potential disciples are trained in a simple inductive Bible study called a Discovery Study and in an evangelism process called a Discovery Group. This allows them to learn on their own what the Bible says, encourages them to obey the Bible and to share what they learn with others around them. They are also encouraged to engage in meeting the needs within their groups and communities.

In situations where there are no disciples or potential disciples, leaders are trained to look for persons of peace, those God has prepared to receive the Gospel, and then begin this process with them.

The strategy for DMM is found in Matthew 28:16-20. The tactics for DMM are found in numerous verses, including Luke 10, Luke 9, Matthew 10, Mark 6,

Deuteronomy 6, John 6, John 14 and John 15.

All success points in DMM are defined by reproduction. Without reproduction there is no success. Leaders must reproduce leaders. Disciples reproduce disciples. Discovery Groups reproduce discovery groups. And, churches reproduce churches.[1]

We will start by presenting an overview of DMM and the framework in which it operates. I hope that this overview will make clear to you that making disciples has a higher priority than making converts, nominal Christians, or even believers in Jesus. The first goal is that each reader would live as a disciple of Jesus. Making other disciples follows naturally from this first step.

DMM was originally developed as a tool to plant churches among non-literate people in northern India. It differs from other Church Planting Movement (CPM) methods because it emphasizes fulfilling the final command of Jesus to "make disciples," rather than focusing on planting churches with a secondary interest in making disciples. There is a strong emphasis on Jesus' teachings to determine methodology, to do what Jesus said to do the way he said to do it. While churches often result from the application of DMM principles, success is measured by a sustainable and reproducing fellowship of disciples rather than a fully functioning church; our goal is "a Jesus option" in every location. That is, whether it is a church or a small discovery group, everyone in every neighborhood, town, village, or rural area would have a place within walking distance where they can learn about God and his son Jesus.

The core of the application of this Jesus-focused disciple-making is the Discovery Process. It is a very simple five step process, designed to replicate, multiply, and produce spiritual growth in the participants. The intention is that each disciple will learn to work with Jesus to make other disciples.

Do what Jesus said to do the way he said to do it.

To begin, you might have to "unlearn" some of what you have incorporated into your current Christian life. We will take a look at what Jesus said about many things. I know that, in my initial encounter with scripture and obedience-based discipleship, there were things that I struggled with, even after I saw them in Jesus' words and actions in the Bible. This book will lay a framework that should help you reconcile some of your preconceptions to this Jesus-focused Disciple-Making that we will see in the Bible.

One of the first things to start our journey is the reality that, if Jesus is to be your Rabbi, if you are to be his disciple, then his teachings and words are the center of everything that you study, seek to understand, and believe. All scripture is authoritative to a disciple of Jesus, but it is not all equal. Jesus' words are paramount and all of the words of the Bible are interpreted by Jesus' teachings in the gospels. What did Jesus have to say about the Old Testament law and stories? How do the epistles apply and reflect what Jesus taught?

Introduction to Disciple-Making Movements

I will frequently refer to three books which are important for you to read for background information. The first, *Miraculous Movements* by Jerry Trousdale, documents the impact that DMM has had in Africa from 2005 until 2012 using a combination of testimonies, commentary, and explanation. In my conversations with people who have read Trousdale's book, several have described it as reading another chapter in the book of Acts.

This book chronicles some of the amazing stories about the first seven years of the application of DMM to sub-Saharan Africa. Like no other book, it tells story after story that illustrates each part of DMM. As you read, it you will be inspired and challenged with the realities and possibilities that exist by the simple application of Disciple-Making Principles. Additionally, you will be instructed in many of the basics of DMM. It should leave you with the hope of adding your own story to the continuing unfolding of the Holy Spirit's work of making Disciples who can complete the Great Commission.

This book will provide understanding and vision to your pursuit of living as a disciple who will make disciples. What you learn from Jerry Trousdale will greatly augment our work here.

The second, *Are you a Christian or a Disciple?* by Edward Gross, lays out a theological framework for Disciple-Making. Dr. Gross' focus has been on first century discipleship. Understanding what the Bible meant by the word disciple is helpful in understanding what the Disciple-Making Process is all about.

Ed Gross' book will give you an opportunity to examine each part of your life as a believer, and it will challenge you to realign each of them with what it means to be a disciple of Jesus. Whereas *Miraculous Movements* and *Contagious Disciple-Making* are externally focused, *Are you a Christian or a Disciple?* is internally focused. It will give you the opportunity to make adjustments in your inner character and orientation. This book relies on years of careful and well-documented research to present its challenges and conclusions.

Since the first step in making disciples is to become a disciple, Dr. Gross's book is a critical resource in the foundation of the Disciple-Making Process.

The last of the three books, *Contagious Disciple-Making* by David Watson and his son Paul, gives the thoughts of the man whom God used to launch DMM in the late 1980s. David and his son are international leaders as well as DMM practitioners and trainers. David introduced DMM around the world. Practitioners of discipleship and evangelism ministries find that the Watsons' insights and advice have expanded the understanding that they have been seeking.

The Watsons write about the issues that need to be addressed around the world. They cover both the basics and the advanced components of guiding the start and growth of Disciple-Making Movements. What you read in *Contagious Disciple-Making* will support and add to your implementation and understanding of what you read here. It also provides concepts and areas to develop beyond what is presented in this book. The Watsons' book provides material to study and implement which will move you into the realm of guiding and training large movements.

Inductive Bible Studies

The core of the Disciple-Making Process is an inductive Bible study. This type of study requires the participant to draw conclusions based only on the information found in a specific passage. In a traditional inductive study, the individual group members are asked to answer three questions about the passage:

- "What does it say?"
- "What does it mean?"
- "What does it mean for my life?"

The inductive Bible study is designed to guide both individuals and small groups to discover the basic truths about God, his kingdom, and man's relationship to both. It uses just one source, God's truth as written in the Bible, without any distraction from outside sources.

For use as a Disciple-Making Process, this basic inductive process has been modified to include practical application—"I will" and "we will" statements. The first question is changed to "what is this passage about?" The last two questions are changed to include a discovery approach to theology ("What do we discover about God?") and anthropology ("What do we discover about man?"). These modified questions are designed to lead to a trans-formation of our thinking and understanding of God and our role in his creation.

Use of this book

This book is designed to be used in support of a series of 15 discovery studies as outlined in the Study Guide on the next page. Some of these studies can be combined, but plan on thirteen or fourteen small disciple-making group meetings.

Terminology

Most of the terms will be explained in context when they are used, but there are a couple of common words that have special meaning that you should be aware of. The first is the word **engage** or **engagement**. By this is meant making contact and establishing relationships with people that you are trying to reach. Since ongoing relationships are essential in making disciples, you will need to think beyond an access ministry.

The second is the word **catalyze.** In our context, this means causing something to happen with people without becoming enmeshed in the following and ongoing activities. For instance, catalyzing a disciple-making group or prayer ministry means to provide vision, organization, or training to someone within the group while maintaining a position outside the group. Literally, the word means to cause or speed up a chemical reaction without being consumed in the reaction.

STUDY GUIDE FOR DISCIPLE-MAKING TRAINING

This book is designed to supplement small group Discovery Studies of 15 different passages. Discovery Studies are inductive studies and have been described on the previous page. They include the additional components of memorizing the passages, applying them in practical ways to our lives, and telling other people about the passage that we have learned. It is these three additional steps that turn the inductive study into a Disciple-Making Process.

The ideal group size is four to eight people, but as a minimum a group of two people is sufficient. For a group of six people, plan on spending 90 minutes together. The meeting times will follow the format laid out in Appendix 5 and explained in the next two chapters.

Discovery Studies: Discovering Disciple-Making (see Appendices: 2, 3, and 6)
Following is the list of Discovery Studies and the page where each is found. The other columns give chapters which are recommended, and training videos that you can download.

Scripture	Description	Page	MM	CDM	CD	Video
Luke 10:1-11	Introduction	50	Intro-2	8	1,2	2a,3,5a,7
Luke 10:1-11	Disciple-Making Process	55	6	11, 15	15	5b,6,9
John 14:15–27	Obedience	63	-	7	3,11	5c, 7
John 1:35-51	"Come and See"	63	-	-	-	5d
Matthew 23:8–11	Our Role: "Be Brothers"	77	-	-	-	-
Deut. 6:1-15	Heart of discipleship	81	-	11	13	5e
Luke 11:1-13	Focused prayer	91	3	12	-	8
Matt. 9:35-10:16	Discipling Believers	97	5	13	-	-
Acts 16:25-34	Person of Peace	110	-	14	-	10
Matthew 28:1-10; 16-20	Great Commission	118	-	10,17	15	-
Matthew 16:13-21	Church Foundation	130	-	18	-	12b
Discussion	Cultural Adaption	139	10	5,6		5f
Philippians 2:5-8	Culture: Jesus Model	139	7	2,16	6	11
1 Cor. 9:19-23	Culture: Philosophy	139	-	-	-	-
Acts 17:22-27	Culture: Application	139	-	-	-	-
2 Tim. 2:1-7; 14-16	Replication: Concern	146	-	-	-	12a & c
John 15:1-11	Fruitfulness	150	-	-	-	1

Page: —Discovery study is on this page
MM: —*Miraculous Movement*, Trousdale
CDM: —*Contagious Disciple-Making*
CD: —*Are you a Christian or a Disciple?*
Video: —Appendix 6

Chapter One
Context of Disciple Making Movements

Kingdom Circles — An Illustration of Cultures and Traditions

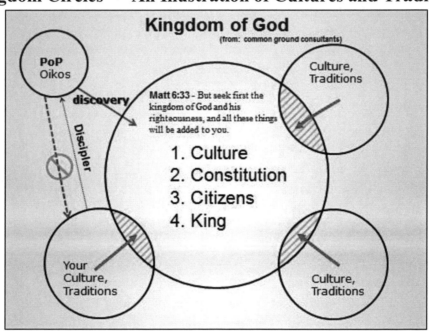

Figure 1.1 — Kingdom Circles *(adapted from Common Ground Consultants)*

PoP – Person of Peace (Luke 10:5–6) – The laborer prayed for in Luke 10:2).

Oikos – Greek word for household; PoP's social network; harvest field; Gentiles in Acts 15.

--⊘--▶ Do not bring the PoP or his Oikos into your church or culture (Acts 15:19).

Discipler — Disciple Maker who coaches the person of peace to facilitate a Discovery Study.

➡ The discovery process allows this Oikos to modify their existing culture to bring it into the kingdom of God according to what they learn from the Bible (Revelations 7:9).

The things inside the Kingdom Circle are the parts of your culture that form your identity, but are not explicitly mentioned in the Bible. These include all your additions to the simple model of church. Things outside the circle are those parts of a culture that need to change before they can be incorporated into the kingdom of God.

Kingdom is Encompassing

The Kingdom is the central message of the gospel. John the Baptist came proclaiming "repent, for the Kingdom of Heaven is at hand." After he was arrested (Mark 1:14–15), Jesus took up the same proclamation.

Jesus did not come proclaiming salvation, Christianity, the church, and happiness. He followed John the Baptist's message: "Repent for the Kingdom of God/ Heaven is near, or at hand" (cf. Matthew 4:17, Mark 1:14–15). This is the central truth of Jesus' message. The Kingdom is bigger than any of these, while including them all: salvation, the church, happiness, and persecution besides

Understanding God's kingdom is a lifetime pursuit. It can be said that only by understanding Jesus can we understand the kingdom. Only by being in Christ can we be in the kingdom. Jesus encompasses it all. Disciple-making is about inviting people to Jesus and his kingdom.[2]

A kingdom has certain characteristics. It has a king, citizens, constitution, and culture, and it has laws and rules. The culture or nature of the kingdom of God is eternal, invisible, spiritual, and unshakeable. Jesus made it clear at the outset that you do not have to become a Jew to be in the kingdom (Luke 2:9–10; 4:25–28 — Jesus' ministry reached beyond the Jews from the beginning). Furthermore, when he sent out his disciples, he expected them to understand and be able to proclaim the Kingdom of God. Therefore, understanding this diagram and what it represents is important in the Disciple-Making Process.

Personal Assignment 1:

Take some time to answer:
Who is the king (1Corinthians 14:27–28)?

Who are the citizens (Ephesians 2:19, Romans 12:5)?

What is the constitution (Luke 5:1, 11:28)?

What is the culture (Romans 14:17; 1 Corinthians 4:20 and all of Jesus' Kingdom Parables)?

Read Acts 15: 1–20, the "Council of Jerusalem." Then draw your own version of the Kingdom Circles using one small circle for the Gentiles and another for the Jews. Next, write an explanation of the question and final decision that the council reached. Finally, write an explanation in the space below that you could tell someone who is interested in learning about Jesus, a potential person of peace.

Repentance

It is necessary to repent or to change the direction of your life, to enter the kingdom. That means that your priorities, desires, actions, and thoughts need to line up with the kingdom's. The Greek word for repentance "metanoia" (μετάνοια) literally means a change of mind or nature. "Do not be conformed to this world, but be transformed by the renewal of your mind" (Romans 12:2). Repentance in this sense means much more than being sorry for or merely avoiding things that are grossly bad or evil. It means a realignment of your life in every area to conform to the Word of God.

This definition of repentance describes much of what it means to be obedient as a disciple. Biblical discipleship is ongoing transformational repentance which prepares disciples to enter and participate in the Kingdom of God. It is implemented by responding to the things that the Holy Spirit reveals in the group discovery of passages of the Bible, with "I will" and "we will" statements that produce a change in the way we relate to the world.

Family is Foundational

Discipleship is not organizational. Everything about the kingdom of God and being a disciple is relational. Our rabbi Jesus is the Son of God, and God in his trinity is relational. We love one another, care for one another, correct one another, help one another, and learn from one another. We are family because we are disciples of Jesus.

As disciples of Jesus, our identity is in God's family. (We are children of God, brothers and sisters.) We must learn to live our lives openly before one another. That means that we talk to each other, confessing our sins, sharing our joys, our sorrows, and our difficulties. Like members of a family, we need to learn to handle conflicts and direct confrontation without becoming so offended that we break off relationships. Jesus was very direct with people, including his disciples. Having a teachable spirit means that a disciple will seek to learn from every encounter, especially when it would be easy to take offense at either the message or the method of delivery (Ephesians 4:13–15).

Discipleship is focused on Jesus

Being a disciple means doing *what* Jesus taught us to do the *way* that he told us to do it. Since the entire record that we have of Jesus is contained in the words of the Bible, we will focus on learning and internalizing the words of the Bible. As Jesus said, "The one who loves me is he who makes my commandments his own and obeys them" (cf. John 14:21).

This means that we start where Jesus started. Jesus worked with men who were well grounded in all of the Old Testament. Knowledge of the Old Testament forms the foundation upon which we build our understanding as disciples. These stories connect us to Jesus' heart and those of his disciples. We want to make them part of us as well, to engrave them on our hearts.

Once we have laid in a solid scriptural foundation of the Old Testament, the four Gospels become the core of Disciple-Making. Jesus encouraged his disciples to draw close to God until finally, as we see in Matthew 16:15–18, Simon Peter learned to hear directly from God the Father. Only in the gospels do we find this orientation.

Did the Apostles make disciples of Jesus or disciples of themselves? The word disciple does not appear in the Bible after the book of the Acts of the Apostles. Does that mean that the Apostles did not make disciples of Jesus? Did they ignore the teachings of Jesus in fulfilling the Great Commission? In practice we tend to look at just the epistles as the Apostles' teaching. We forget that the four gospels also represent the apostolic teachings of Matthew, Peter (Gospel according to Mark), Paul (Gospel according to Luke), and John. The teaching Paul used to train people how to be disciples was probably similar to that in the gospel of Luke. Peter's disciple-making training materials probably were similar to the gospel of Mark.

Disciple-making revolves around the gospels. If we accept the four gospel accounts as examples of the disciple-making training used in the early church and look back at Jesus' words, we can see that many of the teachings of the Epistles are rooted in them. The Epistles are applications from the Apostles' understanding of what they observed or learned as disciples of Jesus.

The Epistles are founded upon the teachings of Jesus, but are centered on church formation. They are supplemental to the Gospels for Disciple-Making. By this I mean for example, that Paul particularly took effort to clarify gospel truths to correct people who had ignored, misunderstood, or misapplied the teachings of gospels. For example, Paul clarifies Jesus'

statement in John 14:6 that "no one comes to the Father except through me," saying "For by grace you have been saved through faith. And this is not your own doing; it is the gift of God, not a result of works, so that no one may boast." (Ephesians 2:8–9).

The writers of the epistles were establishing and supporting all of the necessary functions of the church, including government and culture. What the Law did for the Hebrew people, the epistles are doing for the church.

The Law — The Torah — had at least three functions. Its main focus was to provide a means of being reconciled to God and define man's relationship with Him. The second function was to establish basic moral guidance. The third function of the Law was to define a unique people; to set a group apart and give them a coherent identity and governance. The Epistles serve the latter two functions for the church.

Jesus replaced the first function of the Law because he has fulfilled the law (Matthew 5:17, John 19:30) by becoming the new Adam who reconciles us to his father through himself (1 Corinthians 15:45). There is no need of ritual sacrifice and ceremonies. The veil separating mankind from God has been torn and separated. Jesus is the eternal, heavenly, Holy of Holies. We abide in Jesus and he abides in us and so we have full entrance to the presence of God as adopted sons and daughters. Being a disciple of Jesus brings us more deeply into this reality.

Context of Disciple-Making Movements

The driving question for the development of the Disciple-Making Process is how can we replicate Jesus' disciple-making process? More than twenty years of experience demonstrates that the Discovery Group Process which will be described in Chapters 3 and 4, replicates very closely how Jesus taught his disciples.

Five Fold Strategy of Jesus

Looking at the overall process that Jesus used in his Disciple-Making Process, there appears to be five distinct steps:

1. Jesus modeled being a disciple of his Father (See page 29)

2. Jesus discipled a group of people at different intensities (multitude, the Twelve, the three).

3. Jesus sent out the Twelve to the Lost Sheep of the House of Israel (Matthew 10:1–16).

4. Jesus sent out the Seventy-two (Seventy) disciples produced by the Twelve to the surrounding non-Kosher Jews, Samaritans, and gentiles (Luke 10:1–11).

5. Jesus sent out the disciples to the ends of the earth once they were empowered by the Holy Spirit (Acts 1:8).

This is the general format that is followed in this book. We will look to Jesus as the model disciple. The first step as you live as his disciple is to reach other believers and bring them to Jesus so they too can become his disciple.

Through this you will multiply the number of disciples to reach neighbors, friends, and family. Finally, as the Holy Spirit directs, you will begin reaching beyond the confines of your personal world and some will go to the "ends of the earth."

History of DMM

The modern history of "Disciple-Making Movements" (DMM) dates only from about 1989. However, the original DMM process that we seek to copy was implemented by the eleven men that Jesus sent out from a hillside in Galilee, plus the extra one disciple of Gamaliel that Jesus picked up on the road to Damascus. These twelve men successfully made disciples without external logistical support, Bible colleges and seminaries. And the hundreds of millions of followers of Jesus today are living proof that the process worked.

There has always been a cost to consider when embarking on the journey as a disciple of Jesus. The first group of disciples, along with their amazing success, experienced much affliction,

deprivations, and suffering. In the end it cost all but one of the disciples their lives. And John, who died a natural death, lived the last several years in exile separated from the people he loved. What was so precious to these men that they felt their suffering was a price worth paying?

The Eleven were simple, unlearned, unpolished men, although Paul, the disciple Jesus met along the road to Damascus was highly educated. From this we learn a couple of important things. First, the Disciple-Making Process must be simple enough to learn and use, so that even unpolished and uneducated people can be taught to use it. Second, it must be rich enough so that brilliant and highly educated people can find a framework to grow in knowledge and understanding of God.

Developing the modern DMM process as described by David Watson was one of questioning everything previously done with contemporary missions. The question he asked himself was, "What must we stop doing to be successful?" If something was compatible with what Jesus did, you will find it in the DMM process. This means that there are some techniques and similar orientations that can be found in all successful mission organizations and ministries. But what these organizations most have in common is what they are *not* doing that the less successful ministries *are* doing. For instance, they do not build buildings, they do not impose their doctrines and practices, and the missionaries do not have a visible presence in the indigenous work.

What must we stop doing to be successful? Watson David

There are some fundamental differences that separate the DMM process from almost all other evangelism or mission techniques. The concept that people can actually become disciples of Jesus directly using the Bible, rather than becoming a disciple of a mature Christian, is one difference. The role of the Disciple Maker

as a brother or sister rather than a teacher is also different. There are several other significant differences that we will look at a little later.

What is attractive to mission agencies who are adapting this approach? Usually it is the simplicity of the process, the focus on families and natural social groups and the mentoring of those who are not yet believers to invite others into the Discovery Process. This results in rapid multiplication and a focus on the scriptures which leads to fidelity to the Bible.

DMM was developed in India in the late 1980s and early 1990s. However, many of the principles can be found in the writings of Henry Venn and Rufus Anderson, who wrote in the mid-nineteenth century (excerpts found in *To Apply the Gospel: Selections from the Writings of Henry Venn*, 61–63, 1971), in *The Planting and Development of Missionary Churches* by John Livingstone Nevius, (NY: Foreign Mission Library, 1899), and in the writings of Roland Allen in the early twentieth century.[3]

Following are some excerpts from an article written by David Watson who has been one of the key people in developing and introducing DMM around the world.

History in India

David Watson tells of his experience with the initiation of DMM in India:

None of us, in our wildest dreams, ever thought we would witness what was happening. We had no plans for seeing hundreds and thousands of churches

started. We didn't think it was possible in the places we were trying reach, for they had demonstrated great resistance to the gospel. We were doing everything we could think of in hopes that something would get started.

Context of Disciple-Making Movements

Six men that I had worked with had been martyred over the last 18 months. The Indian government expelled our family from the country. There were 80 million Bhojpuri living in an area known as "the graveyard of missions and missionaries." There were only 27 evangelical churches in the area. They struggled to survive. Less than 1000 believers lived among the Bhojpuri at that time. . .

[I told God] I cannot believe that you [God] would call someone to do a task without telling them how to do it. Show me in your word, how you want me to reach those people. If you show me, "I will" do it.

This was my covenant with God. God upheld his part. Over the next year, he led me through scripture and brought my attention to things I had read, but never understood — at least in this context. Patterns emerged and new thoughts about church, making disciples and church planting came to life.

I prayed for five Indian men to help develop these ideas in North India. I met the first one at a secret forum gathered in India to discuss evangelizing Hindu peoples. His name was Victor John. . . .

"I believe what you're saying," he told me. "I can see it too." Over the next year three other men emerged to work with me. [Finally] I got a letter from someone I didn't know in India.

"Brother David," it began, "You don't know me, but I feel God telling me that I should become your disciple." But God didn't give me the man I prayer for. You see, a woman wrote the letter I got that day.

Over the next few years we struggled as we implemented the things God taught us. Our first church planted with this new methodology didn't happen until two years after I met Victor.

All of a sudden, we saw eight churches planted in one year. The next year, there were 48 new churches planted; the year after that, 148 new churches; then 327; and then 500. In the fifth year, we saw more than 1000 new churches planted!

A formal survey of the work among the Bhojpuri showed that our team actually under-reported the number of churches planted in the area! Things were exploding and are still exploding!

A couple of years ago I sat down with Victor John, "I am a millionaire," he said.

What do you mean?

He grinned, "This year, we baptized the one millionth Bhojpuri into the Kingdom. In God's economy, that makes me a millionaire."

I couldn't stop the tears — Over one million new brothers and sisters over 12 years — over 40,000 new churches.

I had no idea that people would look back on what God did with my failure and call it a "movement." I never dreamed he would make me a millionaire.[4]

Summary:

In 1990, David Watson, working with five others, searched the scriptures in order to build a church planting model based on Jesus' life and teachings in the Gospels. What they developed automatically adapted itself to the local Indian culture.

Lesson: De-culture Western Christianity; that is, separate the Euro-American cultural overlay from the gospel, by starting where Jesus started, making disciples.

Took two years to plant first church: 8 churches➔ 48 churches ➔ 148 churches ➔ 327 churches ➔ 500 churches ➔ >1000 churches.

Lesson: go slow to grow fast

David Watson's "Critical" components of Disciple-Making

When David met with Bhojpuri leaders who were planting at least 50 churches a year, he discovered the following attributes among these most effective team leaders:

- **Persistent Prayer**: An average of three hours of *personal* prayer a day, three hours of *team* prayer a day, *personal* fasting one day a week, and *team* fasting and prayer one weekend a month.

  "Many of these leaders maintained secular jobs while engaged in their church planting. They got up to pray at 4 A.M. and were at work by 10 A.M."

- **Obedience-Based Disciple-Making:**

Do what the Bible says — *share* what the Bible says with others. Hold each other accountable in the *context of community.*

We teach every church planter and every believer in our ministry something very simple: If the Bible says "Do it," then you must do it. If the Bible says "Don't do it," then you don't do it. We also tell them they must pass everything they learn to someone else as soon as possible — the same day if they can. This cycle of hearing, obeying and sharing develops mature believers and fuels the movement among the Bhojpuri.

We noticed an interesting side effect of obedience-based discipleship. In most Bhojpuri churches, members from the highest to the lowest castes worship together.

You cannot have a movement if you do not obey God's word.[5]

- **Person of Peace:** God is preparing people to come to him, our job is to *find that person* and let the words of the Bible and the Holy Spirit speak to him

History in Sub-Saharan Africa

One of the important questions to ask about any methodology is this: is it portable to other cultures, nations, languages, and peoples?

Even as the one millionth Hindu-background believer was being baptized in India, a bold experiment was about to commence in Sub-Saharan Africa. David Watson was invited to present the concepts of DMM and train several groups of

leaders in several nations in Sub-Saharan Africa. A few of these people began to consider using obedience-based disciple making materials.

The question was asked:

"If we bring people to the scriptures from Muslim and Animist background, will they too become disciples of Jesus, who make other disciples and facilitate the growth of churches?"[6]

Serious efforts to reach Muslims had been underway for many years, starting with prayer and engagement ministries, sometimes called access ministries. Literally hundreds of groups and organizations had been involved in these efforts, sometimes cooperating and other times competing.

In 2003, "Final Command Ministries" was founded by Jerry Trousdale and Claude King, along with prominent African colleagues Younoussa Djao in Cote d'Ivoire and Shodankeh Johnson of New Harvest Ministries in Sierra Leone. In March of 2005, Final Command assigned them to Cityteam to accelerate the launch process. Eight months later, this work in West Africa was joined with a Cityteam work in Ethiopia that was coordinated by Dave Hunt. The East Africa partnership eventually included more than five nations with 50 indigenous leaders and organizations. Jerry initially served as the overall director of the work in Africa under Harry Brown's leadership. However, in keeping with the concept of leaving early, Younoussa Djao from West Africa eventually became the continental director of the entire work.

Jerry Trousdale tells the story of the results of this collaboration over the seven years ending in 2012 in the book *Miraculous Movements*.

The stories in *Miraculous Movements*, and the companion book *Father Glorified* by Pat Robertson, are so amazing that not a few people have asked me if they are true. My wife Cindy and I visited Sierra Leone in 2013 and had the opportunity during a commissioning ceremony to see three of the people mentioned in the books: the blind man ("Zamil"), the man who met the imam under the tree ("Koinet"), and the illiterate woman ("Nadirah"). Their Disciple-Making work in Sierra Leone has resulted in hundreds of new churches. These two books are amazing and encouraging. As Jerry Trousdale writes:

Cityteam and our partner organizations are seeing changes as increasing numbers of churches are being planted among Muslims in Southeast Asia, Central Asia, the Middle East, and Europe, but our longest and deepest involvement with Islamic regions has been in Africa. Therefore, over the last seven years, for us and for a few hundred African ministries with whom we partner, the changes among African Muslim peoples as resulted in the following: [This data was for 2011]

- *More than six thousand new churches have been planted among Muslims in eighteen different countries;*

- *Hundreds of former sheikhs and imams, now Christ followers, are boldly leading great movements of Muslims out of Islam;*

- *Forty-five different unreached Muslim-majority people groups, who a few years ago had no access to God's Word, now have more than three thousand new churches among them;*

- *Thousands of former Muslims are experiencing the loss of possessions, homes, and loved ones, but they are continuing to serve Jesus;*

- *Multiple Muslim communities, seeing the dramatic changes in nearby communities, are insisting that* someone must bring these changes to their community also; and

• *More than 350 different ministries are working together to achieve these outcomes.... In recent years, we have concluded that "Disciple-Making" is a more accurate term than "Church Planting" to describe the core biblical principles at work in these rapidly multiplying movements.*[7]

In a nutshell, Disciple-Making Movements spread the gospel by making disciples who learn to obey the Word of God and quickly make other disciples, who then repeat the process. All the principles that we are seeing at work are clearly outlined in the pages of scripture. The result has been more than one million new believers in sub-Saharan Africa in ten years. About 40 percent of these come from Muslim backgrounds.

History of DMM Around the World

When people speak of Church-Planting or Disciple-Making Movements, they are talking about at least 100 churches that were produced by four generations of mul-

tiplication within four years. This defines both the start of a movement and when it stops.

Illustration of Multiplying Movements

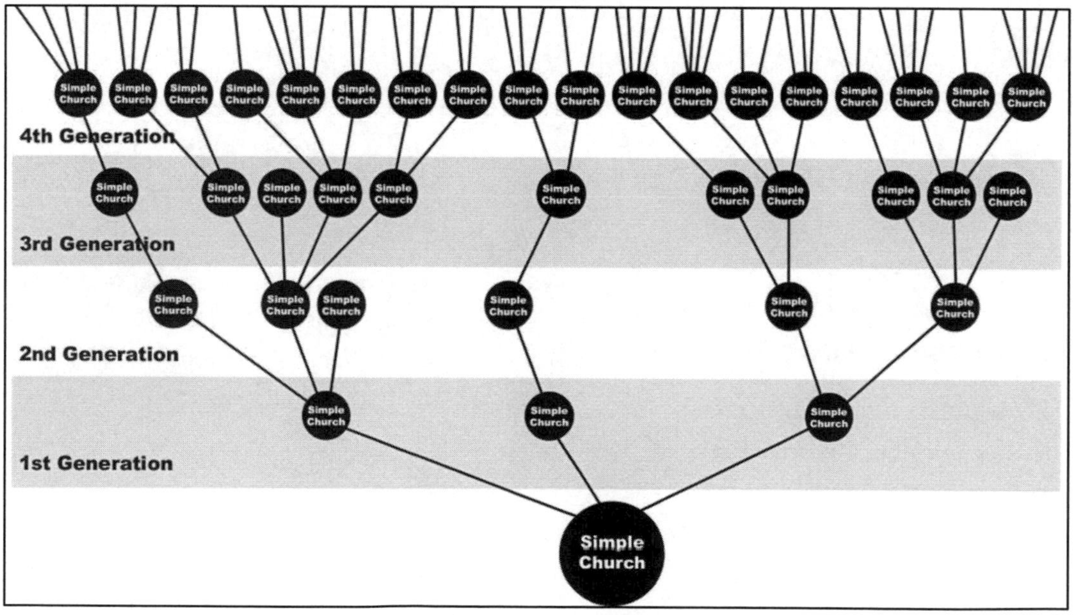

Figure 1.2 — (Derived from Act Beyond - beyond.org) — *Illustration of the multiplication of Discovery Groups or Simple Churches to the fourth Generation.*

Subsequent to the work in India and Africa, which today are each estimated to have produced more than a million believers, other smaller movements are occurring

elsewhere. In Southeast Asia, God has used DMM to start seven Church Planting Movements with about 4,000 total congregations and another 12 emerging Church

Planting Movements (second and third generation churches, but as of 2015 not yet a fourth). There is one movement in California which started in 2007 and has more than 1,000 Discovery Groups or churches, to the seventh generation. This one movement has also spawned emerging movement in Nicaragua and Honduras. In four years, each of these two produced more than 400 Discovery Groups or churches and more than four generations. Haiti became an official movement by the end of 2015, having grown to more than 100 simple churches with one at the fourth generation.

There is also a nascent movement that originated in the Philadelphia and New Jersey areas that has exceeded 40 groups and is composed of homeless people living on the streets and in the shelters of more than five cities in three different states.

The Church in China

The largest of all church planting movements in the world has been occurring in China for more than 40 years, where one estimate is that 30,000 new believers are added every day. Believers in underground home churches are estimated to number in the millions, with the usual range given between 60 million and 120 million.

All of the movements in China share a common commitment to obeying and telling the Word of God. While the focus is usually on planting churches, there is an increasing emphasis on making disciples who can and do make disciples.

While the rapid expansion in numbers is what usually grabs people's attention, there is an equally important growth going on within the lives of the people involved in these Disciple-Making Movements. The reading, memorizing, discussing, practical application and telling of the words in the Bible has the ability to produce deep spiritual growth and spiritually mature believers and disciples of Jesus.

What about the Church in North America?

In John S. Dickerson's 2013 book *The Great Evangelical Recession,* he looks at the current demographical trends, and he outlines a bleak future for the Christian churches in America. Some of the major themes include rapidly increasing social hostility, internal political divisions, declining financial giving, the abandonment of the church by young adults, and the loss of membership with the passing of the older generation. The illusion presented by the rapid increase in size and numbers of mega-churches covers up the rapid decline in overall church membership and the overall number of churches.

Dickerson looks at the fact that about 70-percent of youth raised in the church are abandoning it by the time they are 30, and he sums up this part of the puzzle:

> We are failing at discipleship. That is, we are failing at the core command Jesus gave to His followers. Paraphrasing Jeff Schadt, "many parents rely too heavily on the church to do discipleship..."

Many churches have failed at Disciple-Making not only for lack of trying, but because they do not know what being a disciple of Jesus means. We don't know what a disciple is because we ourselves have not been disciples in the sense that those who followed Jesus were disciples.

This book will guide you to discover and apply some of the basic concepts necessary to become a disciple of Jesus similar to those used by Jesus and the twelve original disciples. My hope is first to see those who faithfully attend church become disciples of Jesus through discovery and obedient application of the words of the Bible to their lives. Next, I hope to see that these people would aspire to raise their children as disciples of Jesus through the same process. Finally, it is my hope that they would begin making disciples of their neighbors, friends, and extended family members. This is what has been happening in the places around the world that have seen rapidly reproducing disciple-making movements.

What is so different about Disciple-Making Movements that produces such amazing results? The church of the west has been expending great efforts at mis-sions since the nineteenth century without seeing anything comparable to this. We have had prayer efforts, we have sent missionaries, and we have translated the Bible into thousands of languages. Yet until these movements began, there were only six identified movements among resistant peoples until 1950. Now there are more than 100.

Much of this book is focused on explaining the processes that make it all possible. But there are some significant philosophical differences between DMM and the evangelism approach which has been the primary method used until now. Understanding DMM requires significant shifts in our paradigms.

Take a few minutes to compare the two lists that follow. Many of my own challenges in initially understanding and accepting DMM were in failing to recognize that it is not just another method of evangelism. These two processes have different goals. DMM results in disciples of Jesus, not merely converts, and it results in the planting of new churches, not just increased church membership.

From Evangelism Toward Discovery-Based Disciple-Making[8]

Western Evangelism	Discovery-Based Disciple-Making
• Outcome: Salvation: Go to Heaven	• Outcome: Kingdom Living
• Contact: Individuals	• Contact: Groups and Families
• Initial goal: Believe	• Initial goal: Obey
• Evangelize to Belief	• Disciple to Christ
• Start at the Cross	• Start at Creation
• Process: Teach and Preach	• Process: Facilitate
• Method: Persuade	• Method: Discover
• Impact: Make a convert	• Impact: Produce a Disciple of Jesus who makes other disciples.
• Focus: Come and Join a Church	• Focus: Go and Start a Church.

Evangelism is an integral part of Disciple-Making Movements, but embracing discovery-based Disciple-Making requires expanding our vision to accommodate a much larger goal, the fulfillment of the Great Commission.

Shifting our understanding of salvation from simply forgiveness of people's sins to the concept of Kingdom living adds greater depth to our expectations. Paul summarizes this as

> He has delivered [i.e., saved] us from the domain of darkness and transferred us to the kingdom of his beloved Son, in whom we have redemption, the forgiveness of sins. - Colossians 1:13–14:

Changing our vision from saving an individual to bringing households into the kingdom of God allows us to see more of the harvest fields, as we see in Acts 16:30-32

> Then he brought them out and said, "Sirs, what must I do to be saved?" And they said, "Believe in the Lord Jesus, and you will be saved, you and your household." And they spoke the word of the Lord to him and to all who were in his house.

Saving belief grows out of a relationship of obedience to Jesus as Lord. The word "Lord" implies obedience by those under the lord's authority. This critical discipline is key in understanding discipling people to Jesus.

> Because, if you confess with your mouth that Jesus is Lord and believe in your heart that God raised him from the dead, you will be saved.
> — Romans 10:9

Why should we start at Genesis? Consider that God had a purpose for starting at the beginning. He revealed his plan and purpose incrementally to mankind. Since this was God's approach, it makes sense to follow his example. The Old Testament provides the foundation that Jesus built upon.

> In the beginning, God created the heavens and the earth."

— Genesis 1:1

Everyone then who hears these words of mine and does them will be like a wise man who built his house on the rock."
— Matthew 7:24

Why "facilitation" in place of "preaching and teaching?" Is "facilitation" Biblical? These are two important questions. The goal of Disciple-Making Movements is to complete the Great Commission. A person of peace can be easily coached to facilitate others in the Disciple-Making Process. The words of God are read aloud and the Holy Spirit does the teaching. In John's account of the call of the first five disciples, two of them each invited (facilitated) one other to come follow Jesus before they had received any teaching (John 1:35–51).

Go therefore and make disciples of all nations..."
— Matthew 28:19

But the Helper, the Holy Spirit, whom the Father will send in my name, he will teach you all things and bring to your remembrance all that I have said to you.
—John 14:26

But you are not to be called rabbi, for you have one teacher, and you are all brothers."
— Matthew 23:8

For where two or three are gathered in my name, there am I among them."
— Matthew 18:20

Discovery of truth in the words of the Bible is by the revelation of the Holy Spirit. Jesus promised that the Holy Spirit will teach us. There is no greater persuasion than having the Holy Spirit speak to a person personally.

Why do we speak of "disciples not converts"? Flipping the question, why did we ever settle on making converts when, as we have just read in Matthew 28:19, Jesus told us to make disciples?

The underlying concept of DMM is discipling people to Jesus, rather than converting people and then discipling them. If you consider Jesus' relationship with his disciples, you will see that this is what he did. Discipleship started well before any of them had a full knowledge of who Jesus was. Jesus sent out the Twelve and the Seventy-two to proclaim the kingdom of God and heal the sick before Peter's revelation and confession of faith

Simon Peter replied, 'You are the Christ, the Son of the living God.
— Matthew 16:16

Disciple-Making Movements are about fulfilling the Great Commission. Jesus said that he would build his church once he has prepared a foundation of disciples. It is this purpose that drives everything about DMM. We will look at this more closely in Chapter 10.

And I tell you, you are Peter, and on this rock I will build my church, and the gates of hell shall not prevail against it.
— Matthew 16:18

DMM is not theory. There are millions of people from all sorts of religious backgrounds who are living as disciples of Jesus and making other disciples. There are disciple-making movements in many parts of the world that are continuing to replicate by making new disciples and seeing new churches grow. Discovery-based Disciple-Making is another tool for an evangelist, but one with a different purpose: accomplishing the Great Commission by making disciples of all nations.

Roy Moran, who developed the prototype of the two column chart shown above, pointed out that, according to the 2013 Global Status on World Missions out of Gordon Conwell Seminary, the cost of each baptized convert using traditional evangelism and western missionary methods as of that date was $710,000. The cost of a baptized disciple using the DMM model in the same period was $0.66. The sheer economics of fulfilling the Great Commission makes DMM a more viable option.

Supplemental Reading

Miraculous Movements by Jerry Trousdale
- Introduction
- Ch. 1 — "Jesus' Counterintuitive Disciple-Making Strategy
Ch. 2 — "Pray the Lord of the Harvest

[1]"All Things in Christ", by T. Austin Sparks, *Searching Together, Christ Alone,* Quoir Publishing, vol. 41:03–04, 2015

Chapter Two
Living as a Disciple of Jesus

The goal of this book is for you to put into practice what you learn. With the information, training, and experience that you gain here, you should be able to actively participate in completing the Great Commission.

Bringing people to live as disciples of Jesus starts with Genesis and progresses through several passages in the gospel accounts. The process is designed to develop a deep relationship between disciple and Jesus.

What makes this process successful? First, when we seek to discover the truths of God in the Bible, the Holy Spirit will be faithful to teach us all things and to bring to mind all the words of Jesus (that we have memorized) (John 14:26).

Second, the process is simple enough that anyone can do it with very little—if any—special training.

Third, people remain focused on what is in the Bible and are not allowed to introduce outside materials.

Fourth, the Holy Spirit working through the Bible is the teacher—not a leader, pastor, or participants. That translates into "no

teaching or preaching allowed" when a group is studying and discussing the scriptures in the Disciple-Making Process.

As we go along in this study, you will be challenged to discover for yourself what God wants to teach you in the Bible. There will be many times that you will be left with a question which you will have to resolve in a dialogue with God. These are the type of good questions that Jesus led his disciples into and left them to resolve with God. When God gives you an answer to these questions, you will find that you are changed in a way that will change the world around you. When we study Matthew 16, we will see an example of this.

While you can read this book on your own, putting it into practice will require you to gather a small group of like-minded people. Look for people who have an interest in living as disciples of Jesus and who are willing to try to commit to memory, actually obey, and share what they are learning with others. Invite them to one meeting. Watch the eight-minute video by Act Beyond (see appendix 6) and do a discovery study of Luke 10:1–11, then ask them if they would like to meet again (see: 1. Implementation Assignment: Introductory Discovery Group).

Start with Prayer

The foundation of everything that a disciple does is prayer. It would be a poor foundation to the process of Disciple-Making if it were anything else but prayer.

First, ask God to identify what group or groups of people he wants you to reach out to. This can be any group. For example, it might be the neighbors around your church or your home, coworkers or fellow students, an ethnic group of people in your city, students at a school or university, family or church members, or activity groups or clubs such as: bridge, skateboarders, or a bowling league. There is no limit to the number of harvest fields.

Personal Assignment 2:

In a notebook, on one of the first lines write the names of one or more groups (A, B, C, etc.) for whom God is giving you a heart and desire to reach. (See Figure 2.1)

Outreach Group A	Outreach Group B
Name of Possible Partner	Name of Possible Partner
Name	Name
Name	Name

Figure 2.1 — Prayer grid to put in your notebook

Next, think of people who may share an interest in reaching any of these groups that you can invite to participate with you in the process of making disciples. They could be people inside or outside the group you want to reach. Write their names in a list beneath each of the people groups. Take time in prayer to ask God to direct you as to how and when you should invite them to join you.

Jesus promises to be with us whenever two or three are gathered in his name (Matthew 18:20). The Disciple-Making Process is empowered when Jesus is with us. This group of fellow disciples will become intercessors and active participants to join you in making disciples among the lost.

Transformed Lives

One of the pitfalls that people fall into when they first grasp and begin to apply Disciple-Making principles is to see these principles as a new set of tools to be integrated into their existing work. However, the tools that Jesus most easily uses are the transformed lives of men and women who live as his disciples.

Personal Assignment 3:

The usual approach to presenting the Great Commission is to look only at Matthew 28:18–20. But the story begins earlier in verse 16. These two additional verses give some valuable insight.

> [16] Now the eleven disciples went to Galilee, to the mountain to which Jesus had directed them. [17] And when they saw him they worshiped him, but some doubted. [18] And Jesus came and said to them, "All authority in heaven and on earth has been given to me. [19] Go therefore and make disciples of all nations, baptizing them in the name of the Father and of the Son and of the Holy Spirit, [20] teaching them to observe all that I have commanded you. And

Living as a Disciple of Jesus

behold, I am with you always, to the end of the age."

In verse 16, take time to answer two questions, "Who went?" "Why did they go?"

To whom are the command and directions given in verses 18 through 20?

What does this mean to us today?

What kind of relationship with Jesus is necessary for us to be able to fulfill the Great Commission?

In verse 17 what was the response of the eleven?

How many doubted?

What are some of your doubts?

What do we learn about the interaction of obedience, doubting, and being disciples from this passage?

What things can we learn from Jesus' response in verse 18 to the eleven's action of obedience, worship yet doubting?

In verse 19, most Bibles translate the past aorist participle Greek verb (πορευθέντες, *poreuthentes*) as the command "go," making a separate command from "make disciples." In the Greek, however, the participle is literally "having gone." While there is a strong imperative connection with the two verbs, the fact is that there is only one command in this sentence: "make disciples." We will be led to different actions depending upon how we translate the passage: "Therefore, having gone"; or "as you go, make disciples, baptizing them in the name of the Father and of the Son and of the Holy Spirit," will lead to different actions.

If you understand verse 19 to be one command ("as you go, make disciples") instead of two ("go first, then make disciples"), what would you do differently?

In verse 19, who is to baptize new disciples?

What does this mean to us?

In verse 20, the Greek word translated "observe" is "Τηρεῖν" (terein) which means to continue to obey orders or commands, to obey, or to be keeping commandments. So, what are we to teach new disciples?

In practical terms, how will teaching disciples <u>to obey</u> all that Jesus commanded differ from just teaching <u>what</u> he commanded?

Jesus makes a promise in verse 20, what is it?

How have you or might you, experience the fulfillment of this promise?

From the entire passage, what are the conditions needed for the promise of Jesus' presence to be fulfilled?

We can summarize all of the law and our mission with three imperatives of an obedient walk with God:

- Love the Lord your God with all your heart, all your soul, all your mind, and all your strength.

- Love your neighbor as yourself.

- Make disciples.

If these are the three key commandments of the entire Bible, it is important that we understand them and consider how they apply to our lives. I encourage you to read Matthew 28:16–20 over again and ask yourself what it means and tells you, and how you should apply it to your life.

So here are a few rules about making disciples.

1st Principle: You must *be* a disciple before you can *make* one. Jesus spent more than 2-1/2 years forming these men so that they would be disciples who could hear from God (Matthew 16:14–19). The Great Commission was given to disciples, not to the multitude of followers, nor to the great crowds who believed in Jesus. You will find that making disciples is natural for a disciple. It is difficult or even impossible for those who are not. This may be why so few professing Christians have little more than a passing interest in fulfilling the Great Commission. "God hasn't called me to this. Isn't that the job of missionaries, evangelists, and pastors?" These are common responses of Christians to the call to make disciples. There is truth in what they say, but it is more a statement of their relationship with Jesus than a calling of God.

Therefore, if your ultimate goal is to make disciples, let your first goal be to live as a disciple of Jesus. Jesus sent the twelve (Matthew 10:1–6) first to the "lost sheep of the house of Israel." Do not overlook other believers in your churches and fellowships. Invite them to join you in living as disciples by applying what you learn here.

As you work through this material, you will have the opportunity to study and let the Holy Spirit teach you. As you respond in obedience to what the Holy Spirit shows you, Jesus' mission will become your own. Your understanding of the Bible and relationship with Jesus will both change and deepen. Making disciples will not only be something that you go to do, it will become part of all the activities of your life. When you are at work, in the grocery store, out to eat, even in church, you will find that the Holy Spirit brings people to you. These are the people you can bring to the scriptures and who Jesus will make disciples.

2nd Principle: Becoming a Disciple Maker is by invitation. We will see in John's account of the calling of the first five disciples that two were directed toward Jesus by another rabbi, two were called by other disciples of Jesus, and only one was actually directly called by Jesus (John 1:35–46). Whatever the initial reason you decided to follow Jesus as a disciple, Jesus will confirm that to you and use you to invite others.

If you read through the sixth chapter of John, you will see that the road of Disciple-Making requires ongoing commitment

as Jesus challenges his disciples. Many disciples forsook him because his teachings were hard to accept. For these disciples, to accept Jesus' teaching meant to both believe and apply it to every area of their lives. To continue as his disciples, they had to know that Jesus had the words of eternal life and there was nowhere else to go (John 6:68). The same applies to us today.

Jesus said that it was better that he go to the Father so that He would send the Holy Spirit (John 14:12–26). I trust that the Holy Spirit working through the words of the Bible will reveal to you the words of life.

Disciple-Making is a process and a lifestyle. It takes time and continues for a lifetime. Once you have accepted the call to live as a disciple, start looking for people to invite into the same type of discipleship relationship with Jesus that you experience (John 1: 41, 45). Disciples make disciples even if they have doubts, as long as they walk in obedience. Everything flows naturally out of your life when you are a disciple. Disciple-Making is caught, not taught.

3rd Principle: Prayer is intimately involved in every aspect of being and making disciples. Paul commands us in 1Thessalonians 5:17 to pray without ceasing. We will take some time to discuss prayer a little later, but start now by committing yourself to consistent prayer as best you are able. Begin now by asking God to show you how to pray.

Seek to pray alone and together with others. Wherever and whenever you find people with a common heart, mind, and interest—pray! Whenever you feel a moving in your heart for something—pray! It is the Holy Spirit who is present at these times. When the Holy Spirit is present and gives us a burden, he will direct our prayers, and if he directs our prayers, he is present to fulfill those prayers. "Seek the Lord while he may be found" (Isaiah 55:6).

First Century Discipleship

Definitions of words are tremendously important. **What does it mean to be a disciple?** Jesus told us to make "disciples." He never said to make converts. To be a disciple of Jesus and accomplish what Jesus said to do requires doing it *the way he said to do it*. This means imitating Jesus. The classical instruction method is by:

- Telling and showing how;

- Doing it with the disciple;

- Watching and coaching the disciple; and

- Allowing the disciple to function on his own while maintaining a relationship as mentor/coach.

As disciples, we should:

- **Study** and understand the scriptures and also learn from what others discover from it.

- **Apply** what is learned to our lives with someone to hold us accountable and help us.

- Be **mentored** by another disciple.

- **Submit** continually to God.

So where did the idea of discipleship develop? The first record of a teacher having disciples was about 400 BC among the Greeks. Most of us are aware that Socrates had many disciples; the two most famous were Plato and Xenophon. The practice of discipleship traveled throughout the Grecian world. It reached its zenith among the Jews of Israel.

Commentators have reflected on Paul's use of the phrase "in the fullness of time" in Galatians 4:4 and Ephesians 1:10, saying that "the fullness" can be seen in the political environment of the first century Roman Empire. This included such things as a single multi-nation government, relatively safe land and sea transportation, a highway and navigation system, common language, and common currency. But it also included the development of a system of rabbis and disciples based on the Greek model—but with a unique focus, the memorization and training in the Torah.

According to Ed Gross, there were more than 800 rabbis who had disciples and were contemporaries of Jesus. Two of them, Gamaliel and John the Baptist, are mentioned in the Bible. Several of these rabbis had more than 1,000 disciples.

Ed Gross quotes Michael Wilkins in his book *Are You a Christian or a Disciple?*:

> From its very earliest use (in Greek literature), "mathetes" (disciple) was not simply a learner or a pupil in an academic setting. In fact, Herodotus, in whose writings the noun occurs for the first time in ancient Greek, uses the term to indicate a person who made a significant, persona, life commitment.

> Socrates speaks similarly of disciples of the Spartan culture: "All these were enthusiasts, lovers and disciples of the Spartan culture; and you can recognize that character in their wisdom by the short,

memorable sayings that fell from each of them.

Ed Gross goes on to summarize:
Discipleship in the ancient world was a common phenomenon. It primarily involved commitment of an individual to a great master or leader . . . Jesus' form of discipleship was misunderstood, even by some of his closest followers. But Jesus patiently taught his disciples what it meant for them to be his kind of disciple, his kind of follower."

So, what did it mean to be the disciple of Jesus? D. Thomas Lancaster wrote:

"In the days of the Master, the disciples of the sages had four major tasks to perform:

a. To memorize their teacher's words. *The oral transmission process was the only inter-generational communication practiced among the sages . . . .*

b. To learn their teacher's traditions and interpretations*. A disciple learned how his teacher kept the commands of God and interpreted the scriptures. Every detail about the teacher was important . . . . To a disciple, these were like gems and pearls meant to be gathered and treasured.*

c. To imitate their teacher's actions. *A disciple's highest calling was to be a reflection of his teacher. He sought to act, to speak and to conduct himself the same way in which his master conducted himself.*

*d.****To raise up disciples.*** *He created a new generation of students and transmitted to them the words, the traditions, interpretations, teachings, actions and behaviors of his master.*

"Many authors, while repeating the previous four characteristics of a disciple, would add one more mark of official disciples in their relationship to their teachers. It was foundational to all the rest, but absolutely necessary to be singled out and established as its cornerstone. . . .

*e.****To submit completely to the will of the teacher.*** *1st century rabbinic expert David Bivin wrote, "A special relationship developed between rabbi and disciple in which the rabbi became like a father. In fact he was more than a father and was to be honored above the disciple's own father.*[9]

Jesus Modeled Disciple-Making

As we study several passages in the gospel of John, we see that Jesus modeled being a disciple for us. We need only look at Jesus' example to understand what he expects from us as disciples.

Obedience
If you keep my commandments, you will abide in my love, just as I have kept my Father's commandments and abide in his love. —John 15:10

Share from Memory
And the word that you hear is not mine but the Father's who sent me.
—John 14:24b

Know all the Old Testament
Do not think that I have come to abolish the Law or the Prophets; I have not come to abolish them but to fulfill them.
—Matthew 5:17

Imitate and Conform

So Jesus said to them, "Truly, truly, I say to you, the Son can do nothing of his own accord, but only what he sees the Father doing. For whatever the Father does, that the Son does likewise.
—John 5:19

Make Disciples

So Jesus said to the Jews who had believed him, 'If you abide in my word, you are truly my disciples,
— John 8:31

By this all people will know that you are my disciples, if you have love for one another.
— John 13:35

By this my Father is glorified, that you bear much fruit and so prove to be my disciples.
— John 15:8

Disciple-Making is modeled and not merely taught. What Jesus taught his disciples he also modeled for them.

Scriptural examples of these five disciplines of Jesus disciples:

The five critical disciplines that were presented in *Are you a Christian or a Disciple,* are not enumerated in a list in the scripture, but they are found individually in the commands of Jesus to his disciples and are affirmed by Jesus' disciples in how they lived. Rearranging to put the most important discipline first we have:

Obey Jesus in everything.

If you love me, you will keep my commandments."
— John 14:15

Teaching them to [obey] all that I have commanded you." *My edit from the Greek.

— Matthew 28:20a

Know from Memory all Jesus' commands and teachings so they can tell others.

Have you understood all these things?" They said to him, "Yes." And he said to them, "Therefore every scribe who has been trained for the kingdom of heaven is like a master of a house, who brings out of his treasure what is new and what is old.
— Matthew 13:51–52

Know Old Testament and learn and accept Jesus' understanding of it.

You have heard that it was said to those of old, 'You shall not murder; and whoever murders will be liable to judgment.' But I say to you that everyone who is angry with his brother will be liable to judgment; whoever insults his brother will be liable to the council; and whoever says, 'You fool!' will be liable to the hell of fire.
— Matthew 5:21–22

Conform their life to that of Jesus in everything (thoughts, dress, actions, speech, etc.)

A disciple is not above his teacher, nor a servant above his master. It is enough for the disciple to be like his teacher, and the servant like his master.
—Mt 10:24–25a

Do not be conformed to this world, but be transformed by the renewal of your mind, that by testing you may discern what is the will of God, what is good and acceptable and perfect.
— Romans 12:2

Jesus mission to reconcile the world becomes our mission (2 Corinthians 5:18)

Personal Assignment 4:

Jesus gave us a couple of qualifiers that other rabbis could not. These are extremely important in the Discovery Disciple-Making Process. Read the following verses and answer the questions

Make disciples after model of Jesus — This is Jesus' final command

> Therefore [having gone] make disciples of all nations… Baptizing… teaching them to [obey] all that I have commanded you, and behold, I am with you always, to the end of the age."
> — Mt 28:19–20

> And behold, I am with you always, to the end of the age.
> —Matthew 28:20b

> For he has said, "I will never leave you nor forsake you.
> — Hebrews 13:5b

> For where two or three are gathered in my name, there am I among them.
> — Matthew 18:20

> But the Helper, the Holy Spirit, whom the Father will send in my name, he will teach you all things and bring to your remembrance all that I have said to you.
> — John 14:26-27

> But you are not to be called rabbi, for you have one teacher, and you are all brothers. And call no man your father on earth, for you have one Father, who is in heaven. Neither be called instructors, for you have one instructor, the Christ. The greatest among you shall be your servant.
> — Matthew 23:8–11

> For the kingdom of heaven is like a master of a house, who brings out of his treasure what is new and what is old.
> — Matthew 13:51–52

Know Old Testament and learn and accept Jesus' understanding of it.

> You have heard that it was said to those of old, 'You shall not murder; and whoever murders will be liable to judgment.' But I say to you that everyone who is angry with his brother will be liable to judgment; whoever insults his brother will be liable to the council; and whoever says, 'You fool!' will be liable to the hell of fire.
> — Matthew 5:21–22

Conform their life to that of Jesus in everything (thoughts, dress, actions, speech, etc.)

> A disciple is not above his teacher, nor a servant above his master. It is enough for the disciple to be like his teacher, and the servant like his master.
> —Mt 10:24–25a

> Do not be conformed to this world, but be transformed by the renewal of your mind, that by testing you may discern what is the will of God, what is good and acceptable and perfect.
> — Romans 12:2

Jesus mission to reconcile the world becomes our mission (2 Corinthians 5:18)

Who is to do the discipling (teaching)? Who is to be our teacher?

As a Disciple Maker, what is our role in the discipleship process?

Based on these passages, what would the Disciple-Making Process look like?

The entire Discovery Disciple-Making Process is based on this: if we gather in groups of at least two and obey Jesus' words in the Bible, Jesus will ask the Father to send the Holy Spirit who will help us remember and teach us all things (John 14:21).

The Discovery Process is the application of the promises of the scripture. It has been tested and found true by millions of people around the world. This is what makes this Disciple-Making Process exciting personally. You can become a disciple of Jesus, rather than a disciple of a godly man who points you to Jesus. The

Holy Spirit really does show up to teach, change, and transform you.

The goal, therefore, is to live as a disciple who makes disciples. This process starts with the Discovery Study (DS) which is the third and core step of the Discovery Process (see figure 4.1).

Implementation Assignment:

Contact people whom you identified (see Figure 2.1) and discuss what you have learned about being and making disciples (Matthew 28:16–20). Invite them to one meeting to look at this passage and discuss becoming disciples who will make disciples.

Supplemental Reading

Are you a Christian or a Disciple? by Ed Gross.

- Ch. 1 — "A Life Changing Question"
- Ch. 2 — "Where Christian was Coined"

Contagious Disciple-Making, by David L. and Paul D. Watson

- Ch. 8 – "Disciple-Makers Make Disciples, Not Converts"

Chapter Three
The Discovery Process: How it Works

Discovery Study (DS)

Discovery Studies are the core of the Disciple-Making Movements Process. Typically, individuals prepare ahead of time by learning the passage so that they can tell it in their own words and apply it to their own lives. There are five steps in this inductive Bible study process:

1. Write the passage as it is written in the Bible, including verse numbers.
2. Write the passage in your own words.
3. Write out one or two "I will" statements.
4. Write what you discover about the passage, about God, and about man.
5. Write out your plan to share the passage with someone.

There are several formats to use for written Discovery Studies; the two-page four-column (Figure 3.1) and the three-column method (Figure 3.2) are the most common. There are also the one page, four-quadrant portrait layout (Figure 3.3) and three-column landscape layout that you can use for shorter passages (Figure 3.4). You will want to choose only one to introduce to a discovery group.

Purposes of the Written Study

There are three main purposes in doing the Discovery Study.

First, is to commit a passage of scripture to memory in our own words, so that we can tell others. Second, to gain a deep understanding about what we can learn from the passage.

Written Discovery Study

Four-Column Discovery Study			
First Sheet		**Second Sheet**	
His Words Passage as Written	**In My Words**	**Applica-tion** I will . . . We will. **Sharing Plan** • Who will you tell? • When? • Where? • How?	(Page #) **Discoveries** • About God • About man

Figure 3.1 Two Page Four Column Study

Three-Column Discovery Study		
Left Sheet		**Right Sheet**
Passage word-for-word from the Bible by hand	**Passage in my words** that you can share with others	(Page Number) **Application** I will . . . We will . . . **Plan to Share** I will tell . . . when, where, how . . **Discoveries** about God and Man

Figure 3.2 Two Page Three Column Study

One-Page Short Passage Four-Quadrant Study	
His Words Passage as Written	**My Words** To tell other people
Discoveries About God About man	**Application Sharing Plan**

Figure 3.3 One Page Portrait Four Quadrants for short passages

One-Page Short Passage Three-Column Discovery Study		
Passage word-for-word from the Bible by hand	**Passage in my words –** that you can share with others	**Application** I will . . . We will . . . **Plan to Share** I will tell . . . , when, where, how **Discoveries** about God and Man

Figure 3.4 One Page Landscape Three Columns for short passages

We ask three questions:
- What is happening in the passage?
- What do we learn about God's character, nature, and purposes?
- What do we learn about man?

N.T Wright described the last two as *Theology*, learning about God, and *Anthropology*, learning about man.

Third, decide what one or two practical things you can do to start applying this passage to your life.

The question asked is:
- If this passage is true, what changes will I make in my life to conform to it?

We do not assume or require that members of the Discovery Group of non-believers accept the Bible as true. We simply expect that they will compare their lives to what they have learned and make at least one small practical change the following week. As they continue in this process step by step, the Holy Spirit will move them to understand that the scriptures of the Bible are true.

During the Discovery Study, normally everything is done orally. If a group wants to write out the passage during the meeting, an extra time of 30 to 45 minutes will have to be allocated.

Write out the passage by hand

In the first column, write out the passage by hand exactly as it is written in the Bible. This does a couple of things that aid in the memorization process. First, the process of writing something down engages different parts of the brain. There are three mental operations involved. There is the reading process. Then there is a transcription process, where the brain interprets and directs the hand to write. Last, there is the checking process where the brain compares what the hand has written with the original text. In each step, the passage is being embedded in the mind.

The second thing that happens by writing the passage word-for-word is that it forces you to look at each word individually. Words or phrases are noticed that were missed or skimmed over in the normal reading process. This can give deeper understanding or other insights into a passage. This also aids in anchoring the passage in the memory.

For instance, as I wrote out a study of John 15, "I am the **true** vine and my Father is the vine dresser. Every branch **in me** that does not bear fruit is taken away," the fact that Jesus called himself the "true" vine, and the fact that he referred to every branch "in me" were two details that I had not noticed before, which gave new depth of meaning to me.

Choosing a Written Format

The order of the next two or three columns is optional and can be adjusted to fit your personal preference. Normally, you write it out in your own words, and then in the next column write out at least one "I will" statement. The other three steps are normally completed in the discovery group.

If you choose to use the four column option (see figure 3.1), you will normally write out your discoveries in the fourth column.

If you write out your discoveries before your group meets, be sure to leave room to write out the discoveries of others in your next group meeting. We will look at this more deeply in the next chapter.

Write the passage in your own words

The next step in the written study is to write out the passage in your own words. I normally try to do this without looking at the original passage, as it aids my memorization. My wife Cindy, on the other hand, refers back and forth as she rewrites it. Remember, the purpose is to be able to tell the story in your own words, not to make the process difficult. Depending on your creative versus literal thinking, you can write the passage close to the original text or weave it into a colorful story. I have heard dramatic presentations given in dialogue style as well as in heartfelt literal presentations. Each person should select a style with which he is comfortable. This is what you will share with other people that God brings into your life.

The model for learning the passage in your own words can be found by comparing stories in Matthew, Mark, and Luke. Each writer told the stories differently. They did not have Jesus' words memorized as we like to do; rather, they knew Jesus' teachings deeply and shared from that understanding in their own words. The goal for us then is to be able to replicate the same process. We do this not only by committing the words to memory, but also by engrafting them deeply into our lives. The result is that we will be able to accurately convey the stories in a meaningful way to the people we meet (Deuteronomy 6:6).

"I will" and Discovery steps

The next two steps, the application and the discovery step, can be done in any order. The process of discovery is often omitted in your private study and completed during the group discussion of the passage.

This is often preferable, but again depends on your personal learning style as well as the cultural norms of your group.

The Application — "I will . . ." step

The application step requires looking at the passage and at the question "How can I apply this to my own life?" Is there something that I can change in my personal life, the way that I relate to God, the way that I treat others? At first, it may be difficult to come up with something that is practical and measurable, something that you can report to your Discovery Group the next week.

For example, I once had a woman in a training seminar tell me that the Luke 10 passage about the sending of the Seventy-two made her feel that she should pray for people to be healed. I asked her, "Who will you pray for?" She said, "I don't know." I then asked her, "Do you know someone who is sick?" "Oh," she replied, "Yes I do. My mother-in-law has been sick." I asked, "When will you see her next?" She said, "My husband and I visit her every Monday." I asked her, "Can you pray for her then?" "Yes," she said, "And I will!" Praying for the sick in general is difficult to measure. Your "I will" statements need to be practical and measurable.

The other thing to remember is that we are trying to learn to be obedient, one step at a time. Look at the way God deals with us. If he were to bring everything before you and say, "Change!" you would be overwhelmed; the task would be impossible. God has placed all of us in families for reasons, one of which is to learn how the training process works. An Olympic ath-

lete started life as a baby, he began to crawl, and he received encouragement from his parents and siblings. When he learned to walk, the parents told everyone with great pride, "The baby took three steps on his own."

This is what obedience-based Disciple-Making is all about. It is a resolution to change a direction or part of your life and begin with a small *measurable* step. These steady changes fulfill what Jesus meant when he said, "Repent for the Kingdom of heaven is at hand" (Mark 1:15). Being a disciple of Jesus is a life of continuous *metanoia*, the Greek word for repentance, which means a change of mind, action, and direction.

Take a few moments to write out an "I will" statement. Then ask yourself, "In a week, can I specifically report whether I did it or not?" When you are in a group and someone shares his "I will" statement, ask yourself, "When he reports the next time we meet, will his report mean anything specific?"

During the first few meetings with your own Discovery Group, evaluate how practical each of the "I will" statements is.

The Discovery Step

The final step in the process which, as I have said, can come before the "I will" application, is discovering what the Holy Spirit wants to show you in a passage. Sometimes when I am struggling to commit a passage to memory, I will complete the Discovery Step before I write the passage in my own words. This helps me understand the passage and makes it easier for me to put it to memory.

The Discovery Process – How it Works

Group learning is broader and deeper than that of any one individual.

Most people complete the Discovery Step when they meet. Just as important as tracking each other's "I will" statements is recording your group's discoveries. The group's discoveries will augment your own; group learning is broader and deeper than that of any one individual.

In some cultures, people are trained to believe that there is just one right answer. If people come with their list of prepared discoveries, they may argue if someone proposes something different, or they may not be open to hearing what others have to say. So how you handle this step is both a personal and cultural question.

There are three general questions to ask in this step.

1: "What is this passage about?"
You may need to do some additional reading to put the passage into context. When a passage includes a transitional word or phrase such as, "therefore" or "after this," it is usually good to read what happened before so that you can put it into context. Remember the old adage: "When you see the word *therefore*, ask yourself what it's there for."

When I explore a passage and am perplexed by it, I often ask God, "Why did you give me these words? Why did you say it?" Each and every word in the Bible has a purpose. Sometimes another person in the Discovery Group may have an insight that will help you understand it. If it still bothers you, ask God, and his Holy Spirit will reveal it to you in time. These are the "good questions" that God can use in your life. The very act of pursuing a question with God may bring you into a process of personal transformation.

2: "What have you discovered about God?"
For some passages, God's character, personality, purposes and expectations, commands, and promises are clearly revealed. For others, the answer may be more difficult to find. It is even possible that there may be nothing that we see about God. One of the benefits of meeting with a group of people to search the passage is that someone may look at it from a very different perspective and be able to point out something that you had never seen.

3: "What have you discovered about mankind?"
Sometimes, we learn something about human nature, pride, ignorance, or how we relate to God or each other. You may uncover sins to be avoided or examples to follow. It is easier to see in others the faults that encumber you, faults that because of your nearness, you don't see. All of these discoveries will influence your understanding and should influence your actions.

Discovery Study — Oral Method

DMM was originally developed for use among non-literate people in northern India. Its use in much of Africa is also primarily among oral cultures. There are many immigrant communities in literate nations who cannot read nor write the language of their host countries, and may also be unable to read and write their own language.

Sociologists have noted that, with widespread video media use, we are moving into a post-literate era. While most of the new generation of young adults can read, they do not do so for entertainment or recreation. Their preferred method of communicating is oral and visual.

Most of what we are studying here is oriented toward people who can read. In practical application, there may be occasions where you may need to know how to guide a Discovery Study among illiterate people.

In general, oral learners develop memorization techniques that those who grow up in literate cultures do not. The result is that they are much more able to memorize large segments of scripture than those who read and write. The main challenge is getting the scripture to them in an oral form in the language they think in — their "heart-language."

The easiest way to do this is to have a literate person read the scripture in the native language of the hearers. If the Bible is not available in that language, then having a bilingual person translate it will work. The person reading needs to have a good grasp of both languages. Also, it is important to use a translation that is easy to read.

Another option is to use audio recordings. There are many organizations that are engaged in this undertaking, and audio recordings of the Bible are available in hundreds of languages. For example, I have a few friends in Uganda working with the Ambassador Institute who have made audio recordings of large segments of the Bible in the local dialects. They use these in training people to be able to tell the Bible stories orally.

With the widespread availability of smart phones, Bibles are available in more than 700 languages—many of which can be both read and listened to. There are numerous resources available.

Five Step Oral Study

The Oral process covers the same materials as in the three and four column written study, but is all done orally:

1. LISTEN — Listen two or three times to the passage being read.

2. REPEAT — Each person tells the story until he is able to tell the story in his or her own words. Other members of the group are to supply missing parts and correct errors.

3. DISCOVERY — What is the passage about and what do you discover about God and man?

The SPECK Method

One mnemonic device to use in oral studies is the SPECK method.

"S" stands for sin to avoid;

"P" stands for promise to rely on;

"E" stands for example to follow;

"C" stands for command to keep; and

"K" stands for knowledge of God and man.

Is there a sin to avoid, a promise to rely upon, an example to follow, a command to keep, or something that we can know about God or man in this passage?

4. What will you do if the passage is true? These are the "I will" and "we will" statements.

5. What is your plan to share with someone else?

6. Do you know someone whom your group can help

Discovery Group Process — Five Core Elements

Discovery Groups follow a process that moves logically to achieve the goal of forming a group of disciples of Jesus. These disciples in turn are able to fulfill the Great Commission by making more disciples.

The following five steps seek to accomplish a Disciple-Making Process that conforms as closely as possible to that used by Jesus.

1. Opening Questions:
Community/Relationship Building

Learning to know and trust each other is essential to achieving unity in action and prayer.

There are three simple questions to ask:

- "What are you thankful for?"

- "What challenges do you have?"

- "How may we help you?"

Over time, the answers to these questions will reveal insights and understandings among the Discovery Group members. The relationships of the members will grow in both practical and spiritual ways. When the Discovery Group is made up of non-believers, the final question is meant to be practical and is important in developing trust and fostering unity.

It is important to understand that the time together is not meant to be a counseling session, but simply an opportunity for people to open up their lives to one another. If there are deep personal needs, the facilitator should make arrangements to meet with the person at another time. While there is no expectation that non-believers will pray, in a group of believers prayer is always appropriate. I usually have everyone write down the challenges and needs for prayer of each person in the group. When I am facilitating a Discovery Group, I like to have different people volunteer to pray for someone else's needs. We take time at the end of our group time to pray for those needs. The record of each person's needs in these Discovery Groups becomes part of intercessory prayer.

The quality of conversation that can happen within a family or any social group when these three questions are asked and time is spent listening to the responses is amazing. Recently, we had six of our grandchildren (ages six to twelve) spend a couple of days with us. At the dinner table, I asked the three questions. We learned more about each other and our relationships within the families than we had ever heard at one time. The eight year old told her entire family about how much fun it was when "Poppy" asked those three questions.

I have used these three questions to open conversation with store clerks, in business meetings, and at church socials. What is one thing that you are thankful for today? What is the greatest challenge or problem that you are facing? If the person seems open, I will ask if I may pray for their need. An opportunity to pray with someone invites the Holy Spirit into the situation. We will learn about *Shemah* statements later, but these kinds of open-ended questions also serve the purpose of discovering people's openness to learn about God.

2. Review Questions:

Encouragement and Accountability

There are three questions in this step:

- With whom did you share last week's passage?

- Did you apply what you learned since our last meeting, and how did it go?

- How have you experienced God since the last time that we met?

These accountability questions should encourage people to fulfill their commitments. Statistics suggest that a person stands less than a 10-percent chance of fulfilling a commitment made only to himself. But that same person has more than 90-percent chance of fulfilling a commit-

ment if he makes himself accountable to another.

Successful completion of commitments by one person encourages other members of the group. It can be very exciting when there is a supernatural response to a commitment. During a training session that I gave in Africa, a woman was prompted by what she discovered to try to reconcile with a neighbor who had not spoken to her in two years. The neighbor's response was overwhelming when the woman appeared at the door with a special dish. The neighbor cried and asked for forgiveness for the broken relationship. In the following conversation, the neighbor asked to receive Jesus and learn to follow him.

Finally, this time is an opportunity for the group to listen to each other's fears and difficulties in following through on their commitments. Giving advice and assistance are appropriate at this phase of accountability. With groups of believers, it is also appropriate to ask God's help in prayer. One of the most important factors in living in the kingdom of God is finding the moral support to persevere in our commitments. Discovery Groups of friends who are pursuing the same goals can make a significant difference in each other's lives in supporting each other.

I have witnessed father's groups that have changed entire families. Men simply challenged each other with the words of scripture and encouraged one another through this accountability process.

I am reminded of the parable of the Sower and the seed in Matthew.

And as he sowed, some seeds fell along the path, and the birds came and devoured them. Other seeds fell on rocky ground, where they did not have much soil, and immediately they sprang up, since they had no depth of soil, but when the sun rose they were scorched. And since they had no root, they withered away. Other seeds fell among thorns, and the thorns grew up and choked them. Other seeds fell on good soil and produced grain, some a hundredfold, some sixty, some thirty. He who has ears, let him hear."

— Matthew 13:4-13

The support of a Discovery Group whose members are learning to live as disciples of Jesus can move the seed of God's word off the pathway and keep it from being devoured. It can remove some of the rocks and soften the ground with understanding. It can pull up the weeds and concerns of this world that seek to choke out the new life. In short, these types of open, sharing, caring, and obedient groups can greatly increase the chance that the seed sown in their members will produce an abundant harvest.

In a culture or society that has no foundation or is hostile to the words of the Bible, a Discovery Group provides the social context to live as a follower or disciple of Jesus. This is especially true in the midst of harassment or persecution. In hostile societies, greater strength and protection is found in supportive groups. Persecuting a group is more difficult than a single individual. A recent incident in India occurred when a secret group of believers was discovered in a Muslim village. Several Muslim leaders challenged them, but together the small group was able to defend their decision to follow Jesus. The Muslim opposition was unable to refute them, whereas a single individual would have simply been threatened and beaten.

Here is the actual report from David S., a missionary doctor friend of mine:

This [group of believers] came to the notice of some opposition. So last Sunday [June 7th] a group came to the believers and interrogated them and tried to accuse them. But the believers could give good testimony and reason to believe in Jesus. So the opposition felt defeated and did not do anything.

But still, the oppositions warned that on the coming Sunday the 14th, they will come again with a larger group, including a few Muslim scholars and priests to interrogate the believers. Their objection is that the believers are manipulating their religion.

Monday the 15th of June — Brother Ali reports that he encouraged these brothers last Wednesday [June 10th] and they spent an extended time in prayer. He gave them literature explaining the truth about Jesus which they distributed all over the village. This evidently impressed their critics so that no one came to oppose them on Sunday as they met for prayer.[10]

3. Group Discovery Study (Read, Reread, Retell, Details)

The heart of Disciple-Making is allowing God's words to permeate every aspect of our lives. In a literate culture, the Discovery Process starts by everyone reading silently while one person reads out loud the words of the passage. This simultaneously engages different parts of our brains, producing visual to auditory translation, comparison, and communication within the brain. During the rereading, one person reads aloud while everyone else closes their Bibles and listens. The intent is that each of us will listen to understand. There is a scriptural reason, as well. We know from Romans 10:17 that *faith comes from hearing, and hearing through the word of Christ.* By reading the Bible passages out loud, we are actually hearing God speak through each other.

The next step is to retell the passage by memory in your own words. The goal is that the group learns the passage together. An example of this is a relative of ours who has a Jewish background. One of the things that he had to do for his Bar Mitzvah was to memorize large segments of the Torah in Hebrew. I was amazed when he told me this and asked him how it was possible. He said that it is really very simple and easy. He and his group of initiates would follow the same process used here: Read it, say it out loud, say it by memory while others in the group listen and correct it based on what they remember.

This process dates back more than 2,000 years. It is probably similar to the process that Jesus and his contemporaries used. When you engage in this process, in about twenty minutes you will have a good grasp of as many as a dozen verses. Initially, many people are apprehensive at the thought of committing a passage to memory. They see it almost as an "examination" or test to say the passage out loud by memory. But with experience, people quickly discover that it is a great way to learn. Remember, our goal is to learn together because together, we learn faster, better, and deeper.

Once everyone has had an opportunity to engraft the passage into their mind, we begin the process of discovery by looking at the details. The first item is to discuss the meaning of the passage. Next, we will look for what it teaches about the nature or person of God and about human nature, as well.

The three questions to ask in the discovery study are:

- What is the passage about?
- What do we discover about God?
- What do we discover about man?

Sometimes it is useful in understanding the passage to read some of the preceding text. But during the study, we want to confine all attention and remarks to the current passage. That means no preaching or teaching. It is useful to get in the habit of challenging each other with the question, *"Where does it say that in this passage?"* (Or use a similar phrase.)

No preaching or teaching; only discovery

A comment may seem to be off the mark because the speaker is including his own preconceptions, extraneous doctrines or teaching. These are the things that need to be excluded. However, often it can be that this person is looking at the passage from a very different perspective. It is these different viewpoints that give a deeper understanding of the passage. So use a challenge question, withhold judgment, and then respond once the group hears the individual's explanation of the insight. If there is a deep insight, be sure to capture it in writing.

The Discovery Process – How it Works

There are many examples of people interjecting extraneous doctrines, particularly with passages that they have heard explained to them over the years but have never stopped to examine. By being challenged to compare what we have believed against the scriptures themselves, we have the opportunity to adjust our thinking so that it more closely conforms to what God actually says. Learning to understand scripture *from* scripture rather than learning *about* scripture from what others teach us is one of the results of Spirit-led, obedience-based inductive study. This is an important part of the unlearning that is necessary to live as a disciple of Jesus. This was true also of Jesus' original disciples. How many times did he say to them, "you have heard that it was said . . . but I say to you."?

I remember the first time I experienced a case where a true discovery took place. One of the members of my group made a statement about God that to me and everyone else in the group seemed totally unconnected to the passage. I asked, "Where does it say that in this passage?" His unique perspective on the passage gave all of us a greater understanding of God. This commonly happens among people honestly seeking God. By this means, the members of a Discovery Group can learn some very profound things about the scriptures, God, and themselves.

The difference in these two examples is that, in the first, the person superimposed an interpretation upon the scripture that he did not find in the passage. The second person found something *in* the passage because he looked at it from his own unique perspective.

One of the most helpful dynamics is when everyone in the group shares what God is showing them. This type of group learning will be more complete than only studying as an individual. The individual written study that happens ahead of time is still important, as it allows each member of the group to develop his own thoughts about the passage.

There is reluctance for people to speak if they think they are in the presence of an expert. If a person brings in extra information, even if it is good, those who are not equally knowledgeable will remain quiet. By confining all remarks to the passage, everyone is on an equal footing. People learn that God speaks to them and, indeed, the expert learns, too.

A very practical reason to confine remarks strictly to discoveries about the passage being studied is that it allows the group to finish in a reasonable period of time. Being respectful of each other's time is important.

If a person often brings in extraneous materials, especially doctrines or teaching hostile or counter to what the passage states, you should discuss his actions face-to-face after the group. If there continues to be defiance, then ask him to leave the group.

The second question, "*What do we discover about God?*", is a challenge to not only look for direct references about God, but also discover his intent and action as revealed in this passage.

The third question, *"What do we discover about man?"* is similar to the first question about God, where people's initial response to the question about God is to look for specific references to him. However, when asked about man, we usually look at our own intentions, failures, successes, and actions rather than at the direct references. Once this happens, people begin to see interconnections between us and God. This opens up new perspectives on God's different characteristics, as well. For example, if the people in the story have done evil, we realize that God has a standard for good. If people are delivered, we realize that God is a deliverer.

Two things will occur during this three-step process. First, you will deeply understand the passage and begin to incorporate this new understanding into your life. And second, the Holy Spirit will begin to speak inwardly about deficiencies and the need to change how we understand God and the world. It is these changes in perception and understanding that generate the *"I will"* and *"we will"* statements.

4. Personal and Corporate Application

Hopefully, you will enter your group time with some of your personal applications written down in the *"I will"* format. Sometimes during the group discussion, God may point out something else. Whether you change or keep the same *"I will"* statement, this is the place where you will make a personal commitment. In this step, you are asking the group to encourage and hold you accountable.

One of the group's responsibilities is to visualize how they will know whether or not you have fulfilled your commitment. That is, the group needs to evaluate whether an *"I will"* statement is something that can be started within the next 24 to 48 hours. Second, how can the *"I will"* statement be reported as being done, partially done, or not done at the next meeting?

Another aspect is the spiritual growth of the Discovery Group itself. One of the goals is that each of these groups will, over time, take on patterns of behavior and understanding that conform more closely to those presented in the Bible. As these groups progress through more of the Bible, some groups may eventually become simple churches. These simple churches are able to provide more support for the lives of their members.

There are also three application questions for the group. Ask, "If this passage is true:

- How does it change our understanding of God?

- How does it change how we treat others?

- How does it change what we do?

These three questions should occasionally generate *"we will"* statements. This occurs when the group identifies that the way in which they relate to one another or others outside the group does not match the standard that God sets in the passage. In later Discovery Series when the concepts of church are studied, these *"we will"* statements can lead toward the development of a simple church structure or home fellowship.

There are six different Discovery Series that have been developed to guide groups of non-believers as they are discipled to Jesus. These six Discovery Series, developed by *Cityteam* and its partners, take about two years to complete (see Appendix 2). They have been extensively field-tested in different cultures around the world.

5. Concluding Questions: Outreach

The fifth and final step in the Discovery Process is to develop an outward focus. Jesus was always focusing his disciples' attention on the needs of people around them.

You cannot be a disciple of Jesus unless you develop a concern and care for others. Jesus came to seek and save the lost. This is part of his mission and character, and it should become ours, as well.

The two critical steps in the Discovery Process are *application* and *telling others*. They are the keys to personal transformation and maturity, and to multiplication and the spreading of the gospel.

The first question in this step:
"What other questions do you have about this passage?"
This question is intended to make sure that everyone in the group has a thorough understanding of the passage to be shared. It is not uncommon that, as the group discusses a passage, people in the group may realize that there are things that they did not understand.

The second question is:
"With whom will you share this story, when and how?"

Sharing the passage with other people is particularly important. It serves to embed the passage in the mind and heart of each member. Equally or even more important, it facilitates us reaching other people in a non-threatening way with the hope of the gospel.

One of the keys to success in this part is to have a fairly detailed plan before you leave.

- What is the name of a person whom you intend to tell?

- Where will you be when you tell him?

- How might the conversation go?

- What follow-up question might you ask him?

Even if the plan doesn't work out with that person, the work of preparing will increase the chance of sharing with someone else.

The Final Questions
These final questions usually require a group response, although individuals may respond, as well. Jesus demonstrated mercy numerous times by delivering people who were demonized, healing the sick, raising the dead, and feeding the multitude. These acts were examples of Jesus meeting people at their point of deepest need.

Whether the acts are small and short-term or large and ongoing, a Discovery Group needs a purpose and focus outside itself.

- Do you know anyone who needs help?

- What can this group do to help them?

These acts of service give Discovery Groups an identity and unity. Service opens doors to share what God is doing and can do. In fact, as we will learn a little later, these actions help the group to engage the people around them. Once the group selects a project of reaching out to meet a need, this time in the meeting can be used to discuss what has happened and to help with any other needs.

When I was teaching in Mexico, there was a lot of enmity between Evangelical believers and Catholics, Jehovah's Witnesses, Mormons, and Seventh Day Adventists. As an example, every few nights, someone would throw a bag full of rotting dead rats over the fence of the pastor. (I learned what the expression "smells like a dead rat" means — whoo, pretty bad!)

Over the years, walls of hostility had grown up between these believers and their neighbors. The result was that the Evangelical believers withdrew and did not talk to their neighbors. They had developed a reputation of not only being separate, but being aloof. Finding ways to interact with their neighbors can begin to bring down some of those walls of hostility and offer opportunities to introduce others to Jesus.

Prayer should be introduced to each group by discovery. Groups of non-believers would not be expected to pray until it becomes one of their *"we will"* statements.

However, if the Discovery Group is made up of believers, it is appropriate to pray for the individuals that each person in the group has decided to tell the passage he has learned. Jesus has promised to be with us to the end of the age, so include him in your planning and expect him to give you guidance.

When do you want to meet again?
When starting a new Discovery Group, the initial invitation should be for one meeting to see what a Discovery Group is all about. Unless the facilitator has a pre-established authority, or the meeting is part of a pre-established program, people will be more likely to commit to one come-and-see inquiry meeting. At the end of this first meeting, the facilitator should ask, "Do you want to do this again, and when do you want to meet?"

It is important that everyone in the group commits himself to continue meeting. If the subsequent meeting needs to be delayed or rescheduled, it is better to deal with it now rather than have people not show up later.

Once a pattern has become established, this question does not need to be asked every week, but periodically it is good to check with everyone.

Imitation is critical when learning

As anyone knows who has been involved in training for sports, music, or dance, proficiency comes after much practice of the basics.

A characteristic prevalent in Euro-American culture is the pattern of

grabbing an idea and integrating it into what we are already doing. Living as a disciple is about imitation, repetition, being willing to try, to fall short, to learn from mistakes, and then try again.

I remember one of my daughters when she

was four years old, watching figure skaters on the ice. She told us how beautiful they were and that she wanted to skate like that. So one beautiful sunny day, we rented some skates for her and she went out on the ice among these graceful skaters. The reality of beginning ice-skating is far from graceful. She felt more like an ugly duckling than a beautiful swan.

The reality of Disciple-Making is the same. It involves learning both what to do and how to do it. This means practicing the basics until they are mastered.

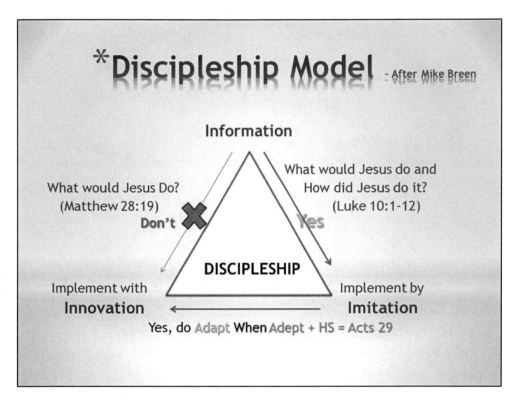

Figure 3.5 Disciple-Making Visual Model: "Imitation before Innovation"

I had a friend who was a state champion for his high school wrestling team. I was using the Disciple-Making Model (Figure 3.5) to explain to him the idea of imitation before improvisation. He completely understood the concept. *"I remember my coach teaching me a new move,"* he said, *"every time he would come by and see me 'improvising' he would say, 'Denny, what did I tell you to do? Well, do it the way I taught you* [imitate]*! Then, after a few days, he came by one more time, watched me, and then said, 'Denny, you have it, now let's see how you can improve on it.'"*

Improvisation before thoroughly mastering the process will not produce the desired results. However, once the process is fully internalized, adapting the process to meet specific circumstances is encouraged—but a person should never forget to practice the basics.

One of the stories of my adolescent years was about Vince Lombardi, the coach of the Green Bay Packers. Lombardi established that franchise as one of the significant ones in professional football. In the year of this story, the Green Bay Packers were ranked number one and their perpetual rivals, the Chicago Bears, were ranked near the bottom. However, Green Bay was routed in the Sunday exchange.

The next training day, Vince Lombardi gathered his humbled team together and said: "Gentlemen, football depends upon fundamentals and basics. That is what you forgot and is why you lost yesterday's game. So, we will focus today's practice on the basics." Then he had one of his players hand him a football and he said, "This, gentlemen, is a football[11]."

The lesson from all of this is: plan to practice the process exactly as presented until you fully understand it and can do it by instinct. Oh yes, never forget to review the fundamentals.

Small Group Acrostic — LOOP

A couple of good friends who have a ministry with The Navigators have developed a simple acrostic to help remember the essential steps of the Discovery Process. A more complete version is found in Appendix 5.

Live the Word

italics — do not start doing until second meeting

- What are you thankful for?
- *Whom did you tell? What happened?*
- *Did you complete your "I will"?*
- What challenges do you have?
- How can we help you?
- *How have you experienced God?*

Open the Word (Read, Reread, Retell, Details)

Read and reread and learn to retell the passage to others in your own words. Next, study the details.

- What is the story about?
- What can we learn about God?
- What can we learn about people?

Obey the Word

Based on what we have learned:

- How does this change how we see God?
- How does it change how we treat others?
- What will you do? ["I will"]
- What will we do? ["We will"]

Pass the Word On

- Do you have any more questions?
- Who will you tell? What is your plan to tell this person?
- Who will we help? What is our plan?

**1. Implementation Assignment: Introductory Discovery Group

Start a Discovery Group with the people whom you identified earlier, both to practice together and to form a supportive outreach group. The purpose of this group should be to participate with you in living as and making disciples. Look over the STUDY GUIDE FOR DISCIPLE-MAKING TRAINING, just before Chapter 1.

Invite the believers whom you identified in Chapter 2 (Figure 2.1) and others that you have thought of since, as being interested in engaging and making disciples to a one-time introductory meeting. In the meeting, have them read Luke 10:1–11 out loud and then watch the 6 or 8 minute video 2 — "Act Beyond Introduction" (video URL links are in Appendix 6). Discuss how they see the principles in the Luke 10 passage being implemented in the video. Next, watch Jerry Trousdale's "What are DMMs?" video 3 and discuss it. Ask them if they are interested in meeting again. Ask those that are to do the written discovery study below and watch video 7, Dave Hunt's video on the Bible study process.

If time permits, watch Part One of Ed Gross' series on First Century Discipleship, video 5a. (An alternative to Ed's series is to watch video 4, Disciple Definition, by Richard Williams.) Otherwise, start the next meeting with one of these videos. (Group members can watch any of these videos on their own, or the group can review them, if needed.)

Decide which members of this group want to meet again and if they would like to invite anyone else. Then select a time and place where you will meet. If there will be new people, you will need to decide if you want to repeat this information.

Written Assignment

Have those who want to meet again do a written Discovery Study on Luke 10:1-11 in a notebook using the four or three column format (Figure 3.1 or Figure 3.2). As a suggestion, start an index of passages that you study on the first page of each person's notebook. As illustrated in the figures, have them number each of the two-page studies consecutively. This index will be a help in the future, as you look back at your notes.

Appendix 3 has a list of detailed questions which may be useful as you begin to examine these scripture passages. Take a few minutes to look at them and decide if they will be useful to you.

Supplemental Reading

Miraculous Movements, Jerry Trousdale, Ch. 6, "Discovery Bible Studies and Obedience-Based Discipleship"

Contagious Disciple-Making, David L. and Paul D. Watson, Ch. 15, "Discovery Groups"

Chapter Four
Applying the Discovery Process

Where does Disciple-Making start?

The Disciple-Making Process used by DMM has three integrated parts as illustrated in figure 4.1. The disciple-making process is based on Luke 10 and Matthew 10. The Disciple Maker works with the person of peace as he or she facilitates the Discovery Group with his family or social group.

The core of the entire process is Discovery Study. Through the study and application, the result is what the Holy Spirit reveals to each member and the group.

Three Parts of the Disciple-Making Process

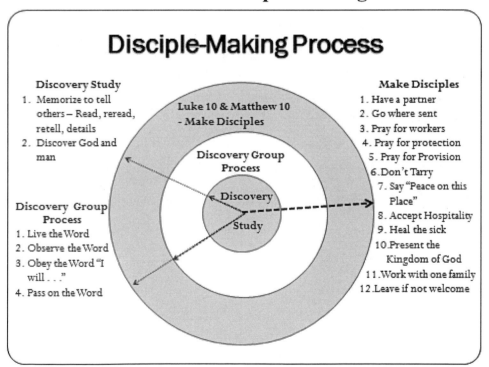

Figure 4.1 Illustration of three steps of the Disciple-Making Process

Applying the Discovery Process

Note: Appendix 3 has a list of questions that can be used to help you think through each passage in these Bible studies. Some people may find this useful as they prepare their own Discovery Study of the passage.

As you go through these studies, your first mission is that of Matthew 10. You need to find people among your Christian friends who will join you in living as disciples of Jesus. Using the model of Luke 10, the ultimate goal of this new group should be to make disciples of those who do not yet know Jesus and fulfilling the Great Commission.

Role of the Facilitator:

Every group should have a facilitator with several responsibilities. If you are training a group of believers to be Disciple Makers, this should rotate so that each person in the group has an opportunity to learn how to facilitate. With a group of non-believers, the facilitator is the person that you are mentoring.

The facilitator:

- Maintains order.

- Assures that all comments pertain to the passage during the discovery step, and that there is no teaching or preaching.

- Should use questions to engage everyone in the group and to assure that all the key discovery points are brought out. These are developed with the Disciple Maker in the coaching meeting.

- Sees that group members record a list of other's challenges, so that they can support each other between meetings.

- Tracks each person's "*I will*" statement and name of the person with whom they will share the scripture. Use this list for accountability during the next meeting.

- Is an active participant in all of the parts of the process as an equal.

Discovery Group Size

The best group size depends on the amount of time available. The facilitator needs to make sure that everyone has opportunity to share. In a training situation, the trainer also needs to assure that everyone has the opportunity to facilitate as many sessions as possible.

- In general, plan to spend 15 minutes per person to complete all five steps. So if there are four people in a group, allot one hour. If there are six people, allot 1-1/2 hours.

- The depth and breadth of sharing improves up to a limit of six to eight people. After this number, some people typically will be passed over during sharing and discovery time. Larger numbers mean that an occasional absence will not disturb the group interactions.

Training Process

How to train larger numbers of people

Having a combination of large group and small group times can improve the learning. Training groups of three to four people per small group provide an environment for fairly deep sharing, yet it also allows more people to have an opportunity to facilitate one or more groups. Becoming comfortable facilitating Discovery Groups is one of the more important skills that a Disciple Maker needs to develop.

I have found that the following 2-1/2 hour time schedule works well in a training session:

- Large group opening session — 45 minutes

- Small group Discovery Group — one

hour for groups of four

- Large group sharing and questions — 45 minutes

Large group times in the beginning can be used to give overviews and discuss questions and passages from the previous session. At the end, have a large group time in which each small group can have champions tell the passage in their own words, share a few of their main discoveries, and ask questions helps strengthen group identity and make learning more effective.

**2. Discovery Group Exercise: Luke 10:1-11

Jesus' teaching in this passage is key to understand the Disciple-Making Process that the disciples used. When Jesus told the disciples to make disciples in all the world, the process outlined in this passage is what they would have understood to be the method.

This will be your first full Discovery Group meeting. Check to see that everyone has completed at least the first two columns of the written discovery study.

From Appendix 6, find the URL and watch video 6, Dave Hunt's presentation on "The Discovery Group Process" and take some time to read through the process described below. Discuss this video and any questions that arise about the group process. This should prepare you for your first discovery group.

Next, discuss each step and read each of the three questions in each section before you start answering them. Chapter 3 provides an in-depth explanation of the

process, and there is a concise outline of the process in Appendix 5. You can read through the "Review Questions" in section 2 of this process, but this first meeting you will not be expected to answer them. You will, however, do this section the next time you meet.

Conclude your meeting time by watching video 5b of Ed Gross' series on First Century Discipleship (Appendix 6).

The Discovery Group Process

It takes four or five sessions before people become completely comfortable with the Discovery Process. So press on through the first few times. Understanding comes with hands-on practice.

If you want to include a written study, you will need to add 30 to 45 minutes to your meeting time.

1) OPENING QUESTIONS

• What are you thankful for today?

• What problems have you had today? Remember that this is not a counseling session. If counseling is needed, meet separately. *(Write down the items in your notebooks for ongoing prayer and future updates.)*

• Is there any way that we can help you?

2) REVIEW QUESTIONS
(Start this at second gathering.)
• With whom did you share the last passage?

• Did you apply what you learned since our last meeting and how did it go?

• How have you experienced God?

3) DISCOVERY STUDY
Luke 10:1-11

This part of the Discovery Process can be summarized as "Read, Reread, Retell, and Details."

Read and Reread the Passage Aloud

Read the passage aloud at least twice. The first time, have one person read it aloud while the others follow in their own Bibles reading silently. The second time, one person rereads out loud while the others close their Bibles and just listen. Read at a pace that allows each person to think about and begin to memorize each word of the passage.

Retell the Passage

Then take turns trying to retell the passage in each person's words, covering all of the main points with the group adding missing parts. The goal is to learn together and be able to share the passage with someone outside the discovery group.

At least two people should take turns saying the passage in their own words by memory. The more times you do this, the greater the learning of everyone in the group. Usually, if four to six people share the passage in their own words, everyone will know the passage thoroughly.

Once people are familiar with the passage and have put it into their own words, the group is ready to discuss the passage and share what they discover in it.

Details of the passage

This is a Discovery Process which means that no one is allowed to teach or preach. Participants are required to confine their remarks to the passage. Experience has shown that this keeps everyone on an equal status; i.e., there are no experts in the group. Knowledge of all group members increases together and everyone grows confident to share, which adds to the breadth of sharing. It also keeps extraneous doctrines from being introduced, and allows the group to finish in the allotted time.

Challenge question: "Where does it say that in this passage?" Everyone in the group should learn how to challenge each other with this or a similar remark. The facilitator should encourage people to ask this question. Initially, this may seem uncomfortable, but it will become part of the group culture in a few sessions.

As mentioned earlier, it is very common for different people to look at the same passage from very different perspectives. When they are challenged to explain how their views are connected to the passage, their response may become great learning times in discovery groups.

A second point is that, anytime a person has a discovery and can explain where they see that in the passage, the group needs to accept that as what the Holy Spirit is teaching that person. Each person's understanding of God will increase over time as they are exposed to what the Holy Spirit reveals through each of the other members.

Discovery Questions

Members of the Discovery Group should write down the group's responses to these questions in the notebook that they use for their journal.

• What happens in this scripture passage?

• What do we discover about God?

• What do we discover about people?

4) APPLICATION: *"I will"* change my daily life to reflect the reality that I have learned.

The goal of *"I will"* statements is to make small concrete changes in the life of each group member voluntarily in response to what the Holy Spirit shows him or her. While group members are expected to hold each other accountable, they are not permitted to set expectations for others in the group. As a friend of mine was fond of saying, "We should confess our sins one *to* another, not one *for* another." In other words, let each person choose what he will do without coaching or direction.

Having said this, the facilitator should talk after the meeting to the person who repeatedly refuses to make any changes in his or her life. These *"I will"* applications are an integral part of the Discovery Process. Anyone who continually refuses to participate should be asked to leave the group.

Both individual and group *"I or we will"* statements should be measurable and doable before the next group meeting. If they haven't been fully completed within one or two group meetings, have the person or group abandon it and move on to something new.

Application Questions

After discovering truths from God's Word, identify what difference this makes in each of our lives.

• If this scripture passage is true, how does it change how we see God?

• If it is true, how does it change how we treat others?

• If it is true, how does it change what we do?

5) CONCLUDING QUESTIONS
Outreach

As a group, discuss other people who may be open to start a study within their social network. Each person should develop and share a plan to do this. It should include the name of the person, where and how it might take place, and what follow-up questions might be asked.

Group Multiplication

When one of the members of the group finds someone who wants to learn about God, another group can start. Your group member will help their new contact start a study in their home or with their friends. Coach and encourage your group member to mentor the new "person of peace" (facilitator) to start a discovery group.

The members of your group should pray for and support each other with each prospective contact. Anyone in a group of believers may become the facilitator of new groups within their own social network or coach another person of peace to start a group.

Outreach Questions

• What other questions do you have about the passage?

• With whom will you share this story? And when and how will you share it?

• Do you know anyone who needs help?

• What do they need help with and what can we do to help them?

Final Question
• When do you want meet again?

Written Discovery Assignment

For the next meeting, have your group do a written discovery using three or four columns to study:

John 14:15–27: Obedience and the Holy Spirit, our instructor. See Appendix 3 for study questions.

Supplemental Reading

Contagious Disciple-Making, David L. and Paul D. Watson, Ch. 11 — "Be a Disciple Who Makes Disciples"

Are you a Christian or a Disciple?, Ed Gross, Ch. 15 — "Follow Jesus in Making Disciples"

Chapter Five
Learning Obedience

The first thing that separates a disciple from a believer, or from a follower, is obedience. There may be sorrow or remorse over past actions, behaviors, thoughts, or sins, but repentance itself is changing our way of thinking and the direction and actions of our lives. In other words, repentance means to obey and conform our lives to God's standards which we find in the Bible and as the Holy Spirit guides. God's grace is available to us as we respond in faith. These acts of obedience are to be expressed in practical and observable ways. As you do a Discovery Study on John 14:15–27, this will become apparent.

There are four goals for this chapter:
• First, that you will gain more experience and understanding of the purpose of each part of the Discovery Process.
• Second, that you will understand how obedience is connected to the Disciple-Making Process that Jesus taught.
• Third, that you will understand your role as a Disciple Maker.
• Finally, that you will learn some of things that are counter-intuitive to the many common approaches to Disciple-Making practiced today.

Review the Discovery Process

Personal Assignment 5:
Take a few minutes to review what you have learned so far:

What are the five steps of the Discovery Process?

1.

2.

3.

4.

5.

What is the role of the facilitator? (See Chapter 4.)

What is the one rule of the discovery study? (What *is* and *is not* permitted?)

What is the "challenge question" that everyone in the group should become comfortable saying?

What are some of the ways that you can handle a long passage during the actual Discovery Study? (Improvise ideas.)

Grace and Obedience

Let's start by looking at how most of us who have a Christian background grew up thinking about obedience. Most Protestant and many Catholic Christians understand that we are saved by grace and not by works (Romans 11:6). Occasionally, some have read into this that obedience is a type of attempting to be saved by works. This reflects a poor understanding of repentance in the salvation process.

Defining grace is very important. If we are saved by grace, then what does that mean? Here are some definitions suggested by a seminary instructor.

Martin Luther wrote, *"Grace, in the proper sense of the term, denotes God's favor and good will toward us which he cherishes in Himself."* (St. L. XIV: 98)

Martin Chemnitz wrote, *"The term 'grace,' as used in Scripture, often signifies favor, benevolence, and mercy, but sometime it signifies the gifts which are conferred by benevolence."* (*Examen*, p. 629)

The term "working definition" means a definition that can be used in practical situations. The previous two do not tell us how grace works or what it produces in us. They are definitions that come from external observation, not internal discovery.

There are many ways that God demonstrates his favor to us. I have been awed many times by God's favor as he has shown me a beautiful sunset or sunrise, but that kind of favor does not transform or empower me in an eternal sense. I have enjoyed God's mercy both before and after I was "saved" or "reconciled with God," but that mercy in itself did not save me. We need an operational definition of grace, a definition that can be used in place of the word that it defines, and which gives understanding of how it works.

When you study John 14:15–27 in this lesson, you will find in verses 16 and 23 hints for a working definition of grace that connects Jesus' mission to the transformation that we associate with "salvation" via the "grace" in Romans 11:6.

N. T. Wright discussed the importance of having a working definition of grace in a 2013 speech, a key concept of understanding salvation. He said that it wasn't that there was any one set definition of grace, but each person needs to grapple with it for himself. The unmerited favor of God is inadequate to explain how grace works. As a personal definition, Wright said that he defined grace as: **"God's presence in us to accomplish his purposes through us."** This is close to my own personal definition of grace as **"the power of God working in us and through us to accomplish his purposes for his glory."**

In other words, grace involves the abiding presence of the Father, Son, and Holy Spirit within us as we love Jesus and obey him. Just as Jesus loved and obeyed his father in heaven, so we can enjoy a similar relationship with the Triune God.

Ed Gross addressed the false dichotomy between grace and obedience in his book *Are You a Christian or a Disciple?*:

> *The pride of many Evangelicals is the Great Commission. Yet, in His Great Commission Jesus said, "Teach them to obey everything I have commanded." The prayer of many Evangelicals is, "Your kingdom come." But, the very next petition of The Lord's Prayer following that petition is, "Your will be done on earth as it is done in heaven." And how do angels in heaven do the will of God? Is it by hearing His command and altering it or by obeying it explicitly? We know the answer. The word "angels" means messenger. They are given a message to deliver or a mission to perform and they do it. When we do His will on earth like the angels do it above, we live like disciples. We obey explicitly. Evangelicals certainly will never do away with either missions or prayer, but, devaluing obedience in them both actually alters them, leaving us with something other than what Christ commanded about either mission or prayer. . . .*
>
> *How many Evangelical missionaries define their goal today in terms of new converts*

> *who obey everything Christ has commanded? If not, it is no small omission.* [12]

Ed has been greatly influenced by the writings of Dietrich Bonhoeffer. Following are a few of Bonhoeffer's remarks about obedience:

> *Humanly speaking, we could understand and interpret the Sermon on the Mount in a thousand different ways. Jesus knows only one possibility: simple surrender and obedience, not interpreting it or applying it, but doing and obeying it. That is the only way to hear his word. The only proper response to the word which Jesus brings with him from eternity is simply to do it. Jesus has spoken: his is the word, ours the obedience."*
>
> *"All along the line we are trying to evade the obligation of single-minded, literal obedience. How is such absurdity possible? What has happened that the word of Jesus can thus be degraded by this trifling, and thus left open to the mockery of the world? When orders are issued in other spheres of life there is no doubt whatever of their meaning.... Are we to treat the commandment of Jesus differently from other orders and exchange single-minded obedience for downright disobedience? How could that be possible?* [13]

This may be an issue that you will have to work through in accepting the call to live as a disciple of Jesus. As you search and pursue Jesus' words, the Holy Spirit will be with you to conform your thinking to the words of the Bible (Romans 12:1–2).

Reporting for Accountability and Encouragement

Let us look again at the Discovery Group Process. We did not do the second section of the Discovery Process in the first study called "Reporting for accountability and encouragement." Hopefully, by this time you have attempted and completed at least one "*I will*" and / or "*We will*" statement and you have made an attempt to share the passage that you studied with another believer. The passages that we are studying are intended to prepare followers of Jesus to become disciples who are able to make other disciples for Jesus. The passages in the "Discovering God" series (see Appendix 2) are designed to engage non-believers.

Let's review the three questions:

- Did you do what you said you would do?
  o What happened?

- Whom did you tell?
  o What happened?

- How have you experienced God since the last time we met?

This second step adds accountability, and it also provides an opportunity to encourage one another with results of our obedience. As we step out in obedience and apply what the Holy Spirit shows us, sharing the words of God that we have learned by telling others, Jesus will show up and accomplish amazing things. These stories are not only encouraging; they build faith and teach much about the ways of God.

The accountability and encouragement step is where things "get real." It is what gives impetus to the spreading of God's word. It brings transformation in the way that a person perceives God. It changes our lives and the lives of those around us. It is the step that extends and builds up the Kingdom of God. Without the application, we have a Bible study but have lost the Great Commission.

The application of the "*I will*" and "*we will*" statements and sharing the stories are the most challenging parts to get started and do consistently, but once they are established, they produce a new level of expectant life in the discovery group. As you facilitate groups or train others to facilitate groups, use the accountability and encouragement step to reinforce application and sharing of the passages.

One question sometimes asked is, "Should the group keep adding new '*I and we will*' statements to the list of uncompleted commitments?" There are two parts to the answer to this question. First, the accountability step should be a time when members examine why they were or were not able to complete the commitments made and what happened. Particularly during the first few meetings, the group should discuss what they can do to be more successful, or apply successes that one has had to the challenges of another.

Second, don't overburden each other with incomplete "*I will*" statements. After a couple of weeks, lay aside partially completed "*I will*" statements and move on to the new.

**3. Discovery Group Exercise: John 14:15-27

This study presents a portion of Jesus' teaching on obedience and the roles of the Holy Spirit in the Disciple-Making Process.

You should have completed a three- or four-column written discovery study before your group meets, unless your group has decided to take the time to write it out when you are together.

Once you have completed your written study, meet with your Discovery Group. Do the entire five-part Discovery Process, adding in the accountability and encouragement portion. The goal is to help each other obey what he believes God wants him to do.

Start by watching video 8, "Obedience," by Jerry Trousdale and video 5c of Ed Gross' series on First Century Discipleship. The URL links to both of these can be found in Appendix 6.

Group Actions

• Take some time immediately during the introductory questions to give thanks to God for the things that the group members share. (This is just for groups of believers; there is no expectation that non-believers would pray or give thanks to God until they are led by the Holy Spirit to do so.)

• Write down each problem that your group shares. If there is a practical way of helping resolve it, write that down, as well. If prayer is needed, write that down. Use this list to pray at the end of your time together. One of the most important things that you can do is to pray for the needs of the members of your discovery group throughout the week.

• The oral discovery study occurs after the group members have practiced saying the passage out loud in their own words and have discussed it. Write down as many of the group's discoveries as possible. This is for each person's reference as they go back and review what God has shown them.

• Next, write down all of the "*I will*" and "*we will*" statements, as well as the names of the people who each person proposes to tell about what they have learned. These are the practical commitments that people make and for which each group member will give a report the next time they meet.

• The last item is to identify a "group project" for the Discovery Group to reach out beyond itself, by meeting a need of others who are not involved in the Discovery Group.

This is an activity to help the group expand its influence. By reaching outside the group, new relationships are formed. If the Discovery Group consists of people who are not yet believers, who live in a society hostile to the gospel, this both reduces possible future hostility and increases the possibility of future multiplication. For your group of Disciple Makers, it should be an intentional action to begin engaging the people and groups of people you want to reach.

Written Discovery Assignment

For the following meeting, do a written Discovery Study at home on John 1:35–46 and Matthew 23:8–11 — Our role in Disciple-Making — in preparation for your next discovery group.

Supplemental Reading

Contagious Disciple-Making, David L. and Paul D. Watson, Ch. 7 — "Disciple-Makers Understand the Importance of Obedience"

Are you a Christian or a Disciple? Ed Gross, Ch. 3 — "What 'Disciple' Meant in the First Century"; Ch. 11 — "Ordinary People Achieving the Impossible"

Chapter Six

Purpose of the Discovery Process and The Counter-Intuitives of Disciple-Making

The Discovery Process tries to replicate the process that Jesus used to form his disciples. It is not exact, but it is the goal. There is no complete list of the steps that Jesus used with his disciples, but there are enough examples to form a basic framework of what a disciple was and did. Jesus gave specific instructions about our relationships in the Disciple-Making Process. He sent disciples out two by two. He gave instruction about prayer, about where they should go, and about what they should do.

Another feature of the Discovery Process is that it is designed to prepare non-believers to worship God. Let's look at the intended outcomes of each section and question.

1. <u>COMMUNITY: Opening Questions</u>

These first three questions are wonderful for getting people to open up and share their lives with one another, but they are also preparing people to be open to God. They quickly build a community bond with people in the group, and they initiate a bonding with God Himself.

The first question: **"What are you thankful for this week?"** This question prepares

people to worship God. When working with non-believers, don't mention prayer until the members themselves discover the need for it. However, for a group of believers, prayer should be an integral part of this step.

The second question:
"What are your needs or challenges?"
This prepares people for intercessory prayer. It is important to emphasize that meetings are not meant to be counseling sessions. Giving personal advice or counseling should happen outside the meeting.

The third question:
"Is there some way that we could meet any of these needs?" This teaches practical service and caring for one another.

At the end of this section, if the members of the group are believers, I often have them write down prayer requests for one another and then pray at the end of the meeting time.

2. <u>SHARE EXPERIENCES: Review Questions</u>

The first two questions in this section are what transform the Discovery process from a simple Bible study into a Disciple-Making Process. The accountability and encouragement that comes from each person successfully doing what he said he was going to do, builds camaraderie and confidence over time.

The first question is **"With whom were you able to share what you learned last week?"** It trains in evangelism as well as accelerating learning and spiritual growth.

The second, **"How did you apply what you learned last week?"** teaches obedience which leads to loving God (John 14:21).

The faithful completion of these first two commitments develops good habit patterns which facilitate spiritual growth as well as practical disciplines, which transfer to other areas of life.

Assuring that personal accountability happens requires that the facilitator maintain consistent standards of obedience, while encouraging members of the group to both set realistic goals and to follow through with them.

The Disciple-Making Process works with God's plan to prepare us for our role in the eternal kingdom of God.

Eternal Effect of Disciple-Making

Paul said in 1 Corinthians 6:3, "Do you not know that we are to judge angels?" What kind of training do we who were "made a little lower than the angels" (Psalm 8:5, NKJV) need to have to be qualified to judge angels?

When I was first struck with this question, it seemed impossible to me. I asked, "How can this be?" Then this passage came to mind: "God is Spirit and those who worship him must worship him in spirit and in truth" (John 4:24). Likewise, I recalled that angels are spirits without physical bodies. They do not have the ability to experience what we experience.

In Hebrew 5:8, I read that Jesus who was God incarnate "learned obedience by the things he suffered." I realized that, if God's incarnation afforded him a unique opportunity to learn obedience, then Jesus is offering us as disciples, who learn obedience, a transformational opportunity with eternal consequences.

This ties to my own experience, as I think of all the opportunities that I had to learn when I was young. As I matured, I found that everything I learned opened up opportunities and enabled me to do many things and enjoy more of life. I also found that those things which I could have learned, but did not, limited my abilities and opportunities. I live today with both those blessings and limits. If this is true in the physical life that we lead, how much more in the eternal?

When I consider that our heavenly father has offered each of us the opportunity to learn from the greatest of all teachers as his disciple, I am challenged and realize that it has eternal implications in terms of God's kingdom.

The third question, **"How have you experienced God since the last time we met?"**, trains people to be aware of God working in their lives and in the world.

The Discovery Process is centered on hearing from God through what the Holy Spirit shows us in the Bible. This third question leads us to recognize that God also speaks through many other means. This includes the events of our everyday lives, answers to prayer, words we receive from God directly, and the words that other people speak to us.

God was actively involved and speaking to people before a single word was ever written down in the Bible. Every story in the Bible itself came from God's direct intervention in people's lives. The Discovery Process seeks to establish a foundation of understanding the Bible. This question about experiencing God should help us increase our ability to hear God speak to us in multiple ways, and to see him at work in our lives and the world around us.

Support and Accountability

One of the strengths of a team is its ability to encourage its members. We can accomplish more, and even grow more individually as members of a team, than alone as individuals.

Accountability provides opportunities to support each other in fulfilling commitments. In my current Saturday morning Discovery Group, I am frequently challenged by other members to think differently as to how I can apply the scripture passage that we have been studying.

In leadership development training, it is a common statement that commitment without accountability will be completed less than 10-percent of the time, but where there is voluntary accountability, the success rate is about 90-percent. Accountability reduces the chance of forgetting commitments or making excuses that cause us to fail. It is an encouragement, not a discipline or a correction tool that the group

uses. Ultimately, we are accountable to God, but the support and encouragement of a team or group can help us fulfill what God wants for our lives.

Having each individual give an account of what he or she does also provides opportunities to encourage one another with past successes and give new ideas for future success.

Here is an example of an encouraging story. A high school student decided to share a particular passage that his family was studying with a friend who was very depressed. When he shared the passage, his classmate told him that he had been contemplating suicide. The passage itself led to a change in the classmate's life; he began attending church with the young man, and he went to a counselor. Stories like this one help us to realize that Jesus indeed "is with us even to the end of the age" (Matthew 28:20).

3. DISCOVERY: Bible Study

The Discovery Study has rightly been called the engine that makes the Discovery Process work. The words of the Bible have been given to us to reveal more about God's nature. The Holy Spirit teaches and reminds us of all things so that we can come to know more and experience more of God. It is this interaction among God's Word, the Holy Spirit, and our obedience that transforms us over time.

Reading and writing the Bible passage word-for-word causes participants to focus on each word of the passage. It helps them to not gloss over words in the text.

The first question, **"How would you say this in your own words?",** leads participants to understand scripture.

The second question, **"What does this teach us about God?",** leads to worship and knowledge of God. This is the step that develops both personal and group theology—the knowledge of God.

The third question, **"What do we learn about man from this passage?",** gives us insight into what God expects us to be as individuals, families, and the church.

If anyone makes a statement about anything that appears to be incorrect or is not in the text of the passage, then the facilitator or some other member of the group should ask that person, *"Where did the Scripture (this passage) say that?"* (Ignore minor mistakes). This trains the group to give Biblical guidance and correction. It is also the key to growing in proper—i.e., orthodox—understanding of the scriptures.

It is important to recognize that, when a group of non-believers first starts, they will not have a correct understanding of God. When God first created the heavens and the earth, "the earth was void and without form" (Genesis 1:2); and then, over the six days of creation, God brought increasing order and meaning. So also the Holy Spirit is at work during the Discovery Process. Over time, he leads the members of the group to a greater and more accurate understanding about God and each person's relationship with him.

When facing the initial errors and misunderstandings, the facilitator and mentor need to restrain themselves from giving the correct answer. Rather, they should use questions that cause people to examine what they think, especially the key one, "Where does it say that in this passage?" This challenges the speaker to show how his remark is based on the passage being studied. Over time, this will provoke a deeper learning and greater dependence and conformance to the Bible.

4. <u>OBEDIENCE APPLICATION</u>

"I will and we will statements" must be practical and measurable. It should be something that can be started in 24 to 48 hours and completed before you meet again.

As we said earlier, obedience and sharing are the key disciplines that transform good Bible studies into a Disciple-Making Process that can fulfill the Great Commission. As you learned in the last study of John 14, when we obey the Holy Spirit, we grow more in love with God. It is this process that eventually leads non-believers to entering the kingdom of God and that brings them into a living, eternal relationship with Jesus.

"I will change my daily life to reflect the truths that I have learned" is the transformational part of the Discovery Process for both the individual and the group as a whole.

The first of the three questions in this part of the Discovery Process is: **"If this scripture passage is true, how does it change how we see God?"** It is meant to start a discussion in which the members decide how to apply what they have discovered from the Bible study to the way that they think about God. Together, the group begins to form a unified understanding of God.

The second question, **"If this is true, how does it change how we treat others?"**, should lead to a discussion in which the members decide how to change how they behave toward other people, personally and as a group.

The final question, **"If it is true, how does it change what we do?"**, is the point at which individuals make their commitment to the group in the form of one or two "*I will*" statements to be completed before the next meeting. Again, the specific commitments are voluntary, but each member of the group is expected to find at least one concrete thing that he or she can change in his life in obedience to what they have read.

For example, when a passage presents a clear message to a group of Hindus that God is one, the group should commit to standards of practice that reflect their new understanding of God. This should affect how they relate to one another and to those outside their group. These commitments should be expressed in the form of "*we will*" statements. In our example with a Hindu Discovery Group, the statement might read, "We will only worship the one true God." In this collective commitment, the group of individuals becomes unified and begins to resemble ever more closely the "body of Christ" which Paul speaks of in Romans 12 and 1 Corinthians 12. Likewise, these "*we will*" statements can lead Discovery Groups to take on more and more characteristics of a church as they complete the "Discovering Church Planting" series.

5. OUTREACH:
Concluding Questions

The first question in this final series, **"What other questions do you have about this passage?"**, should ensure that each member of the Discovery Group is prepared to share the passage with understanding.

It is not unusual that, during the discussion, some members will develop new questions which they didn't have before. These questions may not have been answered during the discussion. It is important that each person is comfortable with his understanding of the passage.

The second question, **"With whom will you share this story, when, and how?"**, is preparation for evangelism.

If each participant develops a plan, he is much more likely to be successful in sharing with someone else. Choosing a person with whom they could share the story helps members of the group to think about who would be interested in it. The Holy Spirit has an opportunity to work here. Thinking through the process of starting the conversation and asking follow-up questions helps overcome the initial fears and hesitation.

This plan is a guide, not an inflexible recipe. What is important is that they share the story with at least one person each week. Like all plans, these verbal plans form a basis that the group members can start from as they reach out to others. As the members mature and grow more comfortable, the group may increase their commitment to share with two or three people each week.

Finally come a pair of questions: **"Do you know anyone who needs help? What can this group do to help them?"** This is the outreach and community engagement question.

New believers can quickly find themselves isolated from others in their community as their behavior and beliefs change. By staying engaged with non-believers in their community through service and by demonstrating love, the suspicions of outsiders are reduced and positive interest in the discovery group is generated.

During a three-day training that I gave in southern Mexico to a group of Evangelical Christians from several churches, they shared stories about the discrimination which a member of one of the churches experienced from his neighbors. This man had been thrown into jail for witnessing to people in a town about 30 miles away. It took several weeks and many requests before the federal police intervened to free him.

By having discovery groups reach out and demonstrate real care and concern for their neighbors, these walls of hostility should be less likely to develop. Where they exist, as in these communities, these acts of kindness are the best means of bringing them down.

When do you want to meet again?
This question calls for a commitment to continue meeting. It teaches that every step we take closer to God takes a decision on our part.

Last, **pray for the needs** of the discovery group members and the people with whom they will share and help. This is also is a good time to pray for healing and to allow the Holy Spirit to demonstrate himself among the group. This would *not* be an expectation for a group of non-believers until they had reached the point of wanting to pray for one another.

Counter-Intuitives - Though Biblically based, it is different

Almost all Christians find something about DMM that feels uncomfortable. My own challenges involved my understanding of salvation. In my training, I understood that salvation was always an individual interaction between a sinner and Jesus. The accounts in Acts of entire families being baptized seemed to me to be doctrinally unsound, a cheap form of salvation that could not be valid. I never considered that it was my thinking rather than the Bible that needed correcting. Furthermore, the idea of obedience-based discipleship seemed vaguely to diminish the idea of salvation by grace to me. For some people, thinking that the Holy Spirit will teach us and that Jesus himself will be with us seems impractical. But what do the scriptures teach?

One of the first challenges for Christians who become involved in DMM is to confront the forms, practices, and expectations they have been taught with what Jesus teaches us in the gospels. Living as a disciple means unlearning some religious ideas which hinder making disciples.

In some ways, it is easier to work with new believers because they don't have this obstacle to overcome. I recall my own experience as an atheist encountering for the first time the reality of God and his kingdom. I had just had an amazing experience with the power and presence of God. I did not wonder if this experience was correct doctrinally. I simply knew that I had experienced God. Thankfully, I had people who directed me to read the Bible.

The following list of "Counter-Intuitives" was developed by Jerry Trousdale and David Watson and first given by Jerry at a conference in December, 2006. An abbreviated list is found in *Miraculous Movements*.

Counter-Intuitives

In addition to the challenges to our own religious world-view that need to be addressed by seeking God in the scriptures, there are some counterintuitive things which make these movements grow. Let us take a look at some of them.

Go slow so you can grow fast — When speaking of rapid multiplication of discovery groups and churches, the normal assumption is that DMM is something like one-on-one evangelism of an individual, except that you are reaching a small group where you lead people to an encounter with Jesus, and then you move on to another group. It is actually the exact opposite. The fact is, the Disciple-Making Process is a long-term relational process with one or a few people.

The job of the Disciple Maker is to establish the first group (solid circle in Figure 6.1) by means of working through the person of peace, who in turn will facilitate this group and encourage the multiplication of other groups and mentor their facilitators (diagonal line filled circles) who in turn will mentor the facilitators of other groups (dot filled circles.) The Disciple Maker's goal is not to start hundreds of discovery groups himself, but to work through a few people who will faithfully carry on this process until literally millions of people are reached. David Watson shared in a conversation that the parts of disciple making movements that he continues to monitor and care for number over 2-1/2 million new believers. This is the fruit of 25 years of his work.

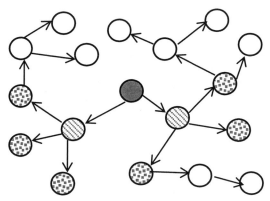

Figure 6.1 *Replication of multiple groups in a geographic area or among a people group.*

Typically, a Disciple Maker spends between two and four years meeting regularly with a new facilitator and mentoring him or her. The Disciple Maker will then maintain an ongoing, but not so intensive, relationship for perhaps a lifetime. How this works itself out will depend on the cultural setting, whether it is benign or hostile.

Focus on a few (one) to win many — Learning to mentor people is one of the essential skills of a successful Disciple Maker. Growth comes as the facilitator and members of his or her group find other people whom God is drawing to himself. This has at least two implications for you as a Disciple Maker. First, you must be prepared to spend time in developing this primary relationship. Second, if you want to be effective as a Disciple Maker, you need to be realistic as you assess the abilities and willingness of the person whom you are mentoring to put into practice all that you are leading him to discover

If the facilitator whom you are mentoring is not up to the challenge of "bringing in the harvest" within his social group, then an early exit is advised. That doesn't mean that you drop the person, but it does mean that you look to invest your available time with other people who are both willing and able.

Tim Miller speaks of looking for a "Saul of Tarsus" in *Poised for the Harvest, Braced for the Backlash.* Not many people will be an apostle like Paul. Most of us are more like Ananias of Damascus

> So Ananias departed and entered the house. And laying his hands on him he said, "Brother Saul, the Lord Jesus who appeared to you on the road by which you came has sent me so that you may regain your sight and be filled with the Holy Spirit." And immediately something like scales fell from his eyes, and he regained his sight. Then he rose and was baptized; and taking food, he was strengthened.
>
> For some days he was with the disciples at Damascus. And immediately he proclaimed Jesus in the synagogues, saying, "He is the Son of God."
> — Acts 9:17-20

Ask God to prepare you to reach one or two people like Saul as a person of peace. Likewise, ask God for a few faithful people like Timothy and Titus who can replicate disciples of Jesus. Mentoring people in the Disciple-Making Process is usually a long-term investment of your time; we want to spend our time as fruitfully as possible.

Share only when people are ready to hear. Walk away if the time is not right — This is simply the application of Matthew 10:14 and Luke 10:10–11. When leaving a group of people, you are not making a statement of "never," but rather "not now." Perhaps more prayer is needed, or an engagement effort needs to be modified, or God needs to bring a Disciple Maker with different skills or anointing, or perhaps more time is needed.

When or if to leave people after an investment of time and effort is one of the more difficult decisions that a Disciple Maker needs to be able to discern and make.

A new insider is more effective than a highly trained *mature* outsider — This is contrary to the evangelistic practice that is rooted in making converts and training them to a high level of knowledge and spiritual maturity before releasing them to make more converts (from their now likely estranged family and clan).

The discovery-based Disciple-Making Process capitalizes on the not-yet-a-believer's existing relationships to invite them into the same Discovery Process that the person of peace is going through. Of course, this requires the close and ongoing mentoring described in the first and second counter-intuitive in this list.

A lay church planter is more effective than a paid professional church planter — Sociologically, people receive more easily from others of similar education, economics, age, and cultural background.

Start with creation, not Christ — God began his story at the beginning. It was not an accident that he walked mankind through a process of discovering their need, who he is, what he offers, and what he expects. Why do so few people fully live their lives for Jesus after confessing their sins, asking him to forgive them and save them? Could it be that all they want is to be forgiven and go to heaven? Could it be that no one ever told them of the great work that God wants them to participate in by bringing his kingdom to Earth?

Starting with creation allows people to discover God's plan and the reason that Jesus came. The passages selected foreshadow who Jesus is and what his actions mean. When the members of the discovery groups arrive at the gospels, they will have acquired all of the pieces needed to assemble a full understanding of what Jesus offers us. In the Discovery Process, they have been living out genuine repentance in obedience to the guidance of the Holy Spirit. Entering into God's kingdom and accepting Jesus' gift of redemption is placed upon a solid foundation that will have equipped them to also make disciples of all nations.

Don't teach the Bible! Teach people how to discover truth from the Bible and how to obey (Matthew 28:19). What would be different in churches today if everyone in a congregation was actively searching the scriptures to discover God's purpose for their lives and their church, and was working to put it into practice? What kind of sermons would be preached if people in the audience would occasionally ask the pastor, "Where does it say that in the Bible?"

One of the powerful results of teaching people to search the scriptures and apply it is that groups of people engaged in this Disciple-Making Process grow in the knowledge of God's truth. They develop increasingly orthodox beliefs.

A good friend of mine, Emma May Hutchinson, was a missionary in Zambia until a few years before her death. She told me that the reason she started a Bible school to train pastors was that at least 90-percent of pastors and Christian leaders in that country held significant heretical beliefs and teachings. People followed the man, not the word of God.

The leader is a facilitator, not a Bible teacher — Training people to facilitate and not to teach is an ongoing challenge when Christians lead groups. It is usually not as difficult with non-Christians, but it still takes vigilance and repetition of instruction.

Let the lost lead Bible studies — For many trained Christians, this is a very difficult concept to accept. A quick reflection of how Jesus called and trained his disciples will make apparent that this is similar to what Jesus did. It works for two reasons. First, the Discovery Process confines the discovery group members to studying the passage, and no extraneous teaching or conjecture is allowed. Second, it works because the facilitator, though he is not yet a believer, is being mentored each step of the way. This is another reason for the strong focus on long-term mentoring.

Disciple to conversion — Unlike becoming a believer of Jesus, there is no standard definition of when a person becomes a disciple of Jesus. Is it when they start studying the Bible, when they start studying Jesus' teachings, or after they have accepted Jesus as their Lord and Savior? Whatever your thoughts, the process of discipleship begins once a person begins the Discovery Process. The intent is that they will continue growing in their understanding and personal experience of God throughout the discipling process until they eventually reach the place of personal repentance, surrender, and commitment to Jesus. At that point, they are believers in Jesus Christ. This is what the "Discovering God" series is about.

Prepare to spend a long time, but anticipate "miracle accelerations" — When Jesus says that he will be with us "to the end of the age," is that true? If it is and he is with us, can we expect to see miracles occur? The many years of experience with DMM in different parts of the world demonstrate that miracles don't always occur, but they do occur frequently. When they happen, the Disciple-Maker can expect to see several groups starting

and a significant openness by more people to engage in discovery groups.

I was recently in India touring various small village churches. I was told more than once that every place where there was a church in a predominately Hindu or Muslim village, it was because there was a very clear miracle in answer to prayer. Here in the U.S., one of the men whom we recently trained in turn trained another leader who started a discovery group in Texas. The leader that we trained was invited to Texas to visit the other man's discovery groups, where he prayed with a blind person who was then able to see. Within a few days, there were four active discovery groups, and now a church has developed. This is an example of miracle acceleration.

When miracles take place or questions arise, the Disciple Maker needs to be flexible to do some Discovery Studies that address the questions or manifestations of the Holy Spirit. It is the Holy Spirit who is at work. Our job is to assist him in his work.

Once the people in a discovery group have both experienced and discovered in the scriptures the power of the Holy Spirit or have any of their questions answered, return to the original study. The goal is to lay a solid foundation. Forgiveness and miracles without a foundation of understanding will not keep a person living as a disciple of Jesus.

The best time for a church to plant a church is when it's very young — Why? There is an enthusiasm generated when the Holy Spirit begins forming a group of people into a church. People are excited and open to participating in what the Holy Spirit is doing. They are open to try new things and to share them with others.

As the organization of a church solidifies, roles begin to be defined, equipment and sometimes a building is purchased and must be maintained. People become more preoccupied with the internal working of the church, and the time available to reach out diminishes.

Generally, the first two years of a church's existence is the most productive time to plant other churches. It is rare that a church older than five years will plant another church. This is the normal maturing process of a church. What it means for the Disciple Maker or church planter is that he needs to be aware and seize the opportunities to plant other churches that arise in the first months of a new church's life.

No mass evangelism so that the masses will be saved — Billy Graham's crusades produced hundreds of thousands of professions of faith yet, in spite of all the follow-up efforts, only two- to four-percent of them could be found in a church a year later.

In my experience of working with street evangelists trying to reach people with the gospel, I discovered that our effectiveness of moving people from prayer and surrender to followers was less than one-tenth that of Billy Graham's organization.

As David Watson described earlier, the work of five people in India who prayed and became disciples, and then found people of peace and mentored them over a few years, produced more than six million new believers and disciples of Jesus in less than 20 years. These groups of disciples and churches continue to double about every five years. In sub-Saharan Africa, nine years of work produced over one million new believers who are increasing by about 20-percent every year.

God is not a program. He is not a process, although he can use programs and processes. Our God is a relational God. It is part of his DNA: Father, Son, and Holy Spirit. He sent his son, who in turn sends us with that same calling: to reconcile the world to him and his father. It is about an eternal relationship that we have and can offer to others as disciples of Jesus (see 2 Corinthians 5:18 and John 17:25–26).

Obedience is more important than knowledge — Knowledge in itself does not change us, but obedience forces a change in everything about a person. Knowledge itself will *puff up* (1 Corinthians 8:1) rather than *build up*. As shown earlier, the steps of obedience to the revelation of God are actually acts of repentance, a conscious decision to change the direction of one's life to conform to God's desires. Repentance is required to enter into the Kingdom of God. It is in the Kingdom of God that we have access to more of the knowledge of God's purposes and ways and God himself. "He who loves me obeys my words and my father will love him and we will make our habitation in him" (John 14:23).

Don't focus on personal evangelism; focus on reaching the whole community through families. The Person of Peace is

the key. — Again, this can be a difficult change of mindset for those who have experienced the adrenaline rush of praying with an individual to receive Jesus. Consider that, in traditional conversion-focused evangelism, the act of a person receiving Jesus as Savior and Lord normally begins to separate them from their social community. Very quickly, they become an outsider to their family and friends. Furthermore, the new believer or convert is not equipped to guide his social group into a long-term relationship with Jesus that he himself doesn't have.

What happens when it is obvious that the Holy Spirit is at work in a person's life and he wants to surrender his life to Jesus? Since we are *co-laborers* with the Holy Spirit, our job is to *cooperate* with the Holy Spirit. So, yes, if that is the person's desire, then pray with him, but also immediately invite the person to lead his friends and family in a discovery study. Start mentoring him into a role of "laborer in the harvest" from the outset.

Focus on ordinary people, not professional Christians — Professional Christians are those people who are employed or supported to engage in Christian works such as church planting, or who are missionaries, pastors, or evangelists. If we are entering a different social culture, be aware that existing Christians in that culture are usually considered by the non-believing members as people outside the culture, and usually unacceptable. Remember that the professional Christian's job is "to equip the saints for the work of ministry" (Ephesians 4:11–12).

Buildings often kill church planting — As we have already mentioned, stewardship of physical assets consumes people's time and effort. It is important to understand and accept that, as a church grows, the acquisition of buildings is a normal part of maturing in non-hostile environments. Buildings can serve as training and equipping centers for DMM and can lend public credibility to a church. But the fact is that it may remove that church from direct church planting and move them to a supportive role.

Expect the hardest places to yield the greatest results — Remember that we are in a spiritual battle. When the devil digs in and gets aggressive, consider that this is a strategic stronghold for him. A victory for the gospel in this area can open up many other opportunities. So attack the strongholds with much prayer before physically engaging the people.

In Matthew 10 and Luke 10 Jesus tells his disciples to shake the dust from their feet if they are not received. However, spiritual opposition which is often encountered in spiritually hard places needs to be confronted with much prayer, seeking God and with varieties of tactics, and persistence. Indifference is to be met with departure. Hostility is part of the spiritual battle. Be encouraged when you encounter opposition (James 1:2).

Leave early! Here is the last one. It is counter-intuitive to all traditional missionary work. From the beginning, the Disciple Maker needs to be planning his exit. This was the mark of the early Apostles. It was effective then. In *Poised* *for Harvest, Braced for Backlash,* Timothy Miller writes:

> *Paul probably never knew exactly how long God would allow him to be physically present with a group of new disciples. The very nature of his ministry, therefore, necessitated a mode of foundation building that imparted to new believers something that would result in both their personal transformation and in the further advancement of the gospel, regardless of the disruptions and unpredictable circumstances, engendered by the release of power through him.* [14]

Again, recognize that it is Jesus who works through the Holy Spirit to build his church (Matthew 16:18). Our goal is to establish a foundation of scriptural knowledge, obedience, sharing, accountability, and mentoring so that the Holy Spirit can replicate and multiply without our direct involvement. This does not mean that the Disciple Maker abandons the work and relationships, but rather that he is not physically present. The relationship with those whom you mentor who have become your coworkers continues either with electronic and telephone communications or occasional physical visits. If you are working in a hostile environment, these meetings will most likely be in a remote location to ensure the protection of both him and the new church.

**4. Discovery Group Exercise: John 1:35–46 and Matthew 23:8–11

This will be your third Discovery Group study. Look at appendix 6. Take some time to watch video 5d: "First Century Discipleship," by Ed Gross. In your Discovery Group meeting, review what you have learned so far and then complete the Discovery Process focusing on John 1:35–46 and Matthew 23:8–11. These two passages define much of our role in the Disciple-Making Process. The first role of a disciple of Jesus is to bring people to Jesus, and the second is to let Jesus be the rabbi as we support one another in the process. The latter is the basis for the rule that there is no teaching or preaching allowed in a discovery group.

As before, record individual needs for prayer, group discoveries, personal and corporate *"I/we will"* statements, and the names of people selected to share the passage with. Please remember that the people with whom you would share these 15 passages are believers who may be interested in starting another group, and joining you when you begin engaging those people who don't have a relationship with Jesus. For engaging people who are not-yet believers, use the "Discovering God" series in Appendix 2.

Discussion with your group — Let's get real

Take some time to evaluate how your Discovery Group is going and if there are some changes that you need to make. Is the facilitator doing a good job of asking questions to draw everyone into the sharing time? Are the members of the group following through with their *"I will"* statements? Are they consistently sharing what they have learned during the study time? Have you identified someone outside the group to reach out to? What can you change to be more effective? Good facilitation skills are essential for successful discovery groups (see Chapter 4).

Decide what changes you want to try, and then make them during the next three meetings when you will have some opportunities to see how they work.

.

Written Discovery Assignment:

The next two chapters focus on prayer, but prayer starts with our orientation to living in the presence of God. We will, therefore, start by doing a written study of **Deuteronomy 6:1–15** — Internal spiritual life

Chapter Seven
Living Fully for God — The Shemah

It was the fourth time that I was challenged to do a discovery study of Deuteronomy 6, "the Great Shemah," that the word disciple moved from something that I tried to *make* to something that I *became*. My first pass through Deuteronomy 6 was to see it as an illustration of how I could engage people in a way that would help me discover if God was at work in their lives. The expression used to explain this to me was "to be obviously spiritual without being religiously obnoxious." The second time, I saw it as a way to integrate family and outreach. The third time, I looked at ways to interpret such things as "signs on your hands" and "frontlets on your forehead" in practical application.

But the fourth time my mentor Ricardo Pineda challenged me by asking, "How will you obey each of the commands?" It was then that it moved to my heart. I realized why the Shemah is thought of as the core of Judaism, and I saw that it was the core of a disciple's life, as well. As you do the discovery study on Deuteronomy, I hope that it has a similar impact on your life.

David Watson writes in *Contagious Disciple-Making* concerning Deuteronomy 6:4–9:

The passage opens with the Hebrew word Shemah, which can be translated as "hear," "observe," or "obey." The intent of the word is for us to "hear and obey" the rest of this passage.

We must understand that there is only one God and He is our Lord. And what follows helps us understand how we connect to Him. We must love Him with all our hearts and all our souls and all our strength.

"Love the Lord your God . . . with all your heart." The word "all" means all, and that's all it means! If you have reserved stuff in your heart for other things besides God, you're not going to experience the depth in relationship you desire. . . .

We know we struggle. There are things we like to do that we know we should not. . . It's in our hearts and we struggle with it. The longer we wrestle without the intent to conquer that battle, the less we experience God's presence in our lives because we've reserved part of our hearts for something or someone else.... Anything less and we miss what God has for us.

"Love the Lord your God with . . . . all your soul" . . . So here's the picture. . . . Love the Lord with that part of you that's eternal. If you've invested in God for eternity, you'll look at life differently. He says, "I want you to love Me with that part of you that's eternal so you will know beyond a doubt that you are connected to Me." It's that forever connectedness at the soul level that gets you through disaster points in your life that you don't think you can live through. If you haven't been through any of those yet, just wait awhile and they will catch up to you. If your love for God does not connect at the soul level, then when you hit the wall of disaster in your life, you won't have anything to take you through it. Then suddenly "it's God's fault; He's doing this to me," and you start asking all kinds of questions about who God is and what His place is in your life.[15]

The intent of the discovery study on Deuteronomy 6 is that God's word will penetrate to the depths of who you are individually and in your relationships in your discovery group. As you study, memorize, obey, and share the passage in your own words, you will find that God's word becomes engraved on your heart. Your desire will be to teach your children and grandchildren. If it takes hold of you, you will find yourself speaking about God and his words in your home. When you walk along the way and meet people and talk to them, your conversations will turn to what God is doing in your heart—not with religious words, but in the expression of God's actions in your life in everyday language.

Making Discovery Studies part of your life is one very practical way of living out the Shemah. When you and the members of your household are studying a scripture passage together, the conversations often move into talking about God.

So where do you find time to do Discovery Studies, prayer times, and times to outreach? Everyone's life is filled with activities; some can obviously be discarded, but others are more difficult. I personally used to read through the Bible every year. I now have replaced this overview reading with ongoing Discovery Studies. Both my wife Cindy and I have made them a regular part of our time together with God.

That is what I have changed to implement the Shemah in my home. When I am in a store or restaurant or meeting a neighbor, I have found that asking one or two of the first three discovery introduction questions is a great way to start a conversation that can very quickly move to a spiritual dimension. "What are you thankful for today?" opens up all kinds of opportunities to talk about heartfelt thoughts. Sometimes, asking what problems they are facing can begin a conversation that leads to a sharing of their lives and maybe an opportunity to pray or to talk about their faith or need for God. Having Bible stories worked into your heart and mind and ready to share can be very useful when an occasion arises. There are many other ways to open spiritual conversations, but these all work best when they flow out of your everyday life and reflect a care for the person whom you are engaging in conversation.

One saying that I try to keep in mind is: "before you go, be prepared. When you are there, be aware." Being intentional in everything is part of following Jesus. He did not stumble through life, but lived *intentionally* every minute of the 33 or so years that he was on the earth. The place to start, as Paul said, is to "let the word of Christ dwell in you richly" (Colossians 3:16). Living the Shemah starts with your own prayer and worship life. It needs to fill your home; then it needs to affect what you do and how you prepare yourself every day.

Before you go, be prepared.
When you are there, be aware.

This chapter will prepare you to study about prayer and to find people of peace. How many times have you heard exhortations to pray, and how many times have you tried but not made much progress? Like Disciple-Making, prayer is not something that you add to your life successfully. Prayer needs to grow out of who you are and your relationship with God. Likewise, finding people of peace hinges on living as a disciple to whom Jesus can bring his workers. He has selected them to bring in the harvest, but they need to be trained by disciples who model what it means to *be* a disciple, people who can point them to the one Rabbi who is fully worthy to follow. It is a common misconception to think that successful Disciple-Making hinges on our efforts, without recognizing that we are fully in partnership with Jesus and the Holy Spirit. Jesus is not looking for good intentions; he is looking for disciples who live in obedience to his word and his Spirit. As you begin to live Deuteronomy 6, you will find that your prayer life begins to deepen and Jesus will bring people of peace into your path. Prayer and finding a person of peace are connected.

Prayer needs to grow out of who we are and our relationship with

5. Discovery Group Exercise: Deuteronomy 6:1–15

Start this session by watching "The Form" from Ed Gross' *First Century Discipleship*, video 5e (see Appendix 6). As before, record individual needs for prayer, group discoveries, personal and corporate "*I/we will*" statements, and the names of people selected to share the passage with. Please remember that the people with whom you would share these passages are believers that may be interested in starting their own discovery group and then joining you when you begin engaging those people who don't have a relationship with Jesus.

Discussion with your group
Find ways that you can obey this passage.

During the discovery study, explore at some depth what it might mean to apply each part of the passage to your life and the life of your family. I would recommend a verse-by-verse, phrase-by-phrase study and obedience applications (see Appendix 3).

What do you learn about:
Consistently Obedient Lives?
Consistency is an important part of being a disciple. As you read the stories of the lives of the Twelve who followed Jesus, you see that it is not easy. We, however, have the advantage of not only having the Holy Spirit *with* us, but also *in* us (John

14:17). Once the Holy Spirit was given at Pentecost, you can see that there was much more consistency in the lives of the disciples. Take a few minutes to discuss this as a group. Is there something practical that you can do to be more consistent in your relationship with Jesus?

What is your experience with the Holy Spirit?

How do you see the Holy Spirit manifesting himself in your life? Discuss this in your group. If anyone needs a greater infilling of the Holy Spirit, take some time and pray for one another. We have learned that he is our teacher. The work of living as a disciple and making a disciple requires the active participation of the Holy Spirit.

Conspicuous Spiritual Expressions?

Take some time to discuss how you might begin to "speak of these things as you walk along the roads" of life (Deuteronomy 6:7). Remember, these are not merely expressions that you say, they must flow out of a desire to get to know the person whom you are addressing. Your immediate purpose is to open them to responding to you as the Holy Spirit opens their heart to you. Their response may not be totally open initially, but if there seems to be a heart connection, continue to follow up with them. We will learn more about this in the chapter on finding people of peace.

Here are some questions and pointers developed by a friend who works with Muslims as a member of Pioneers:[16]

1. "Could I pray for you right now?"

2. If someone asks you: "How are you?" You might respond with: "I am better than I deserve." (This could open a door to discuss grace vs. deserved condemnation.)

3. Rephrase traditional religious phrases to inject new meaning or catch attention rather than using rote phrases which might just be ignored. Sometimes these phrases are called "Churchese." They include any phrase that is unique to your Christian life, such as "praise the Lord or glory to God," all references to being "saved," "new life," or "sin." How can you convey the same meaning in words that are not foreign to the listener's ear?

4. Learn to express gratitude beyond a simple "thank you." For example, try to make a connection with the person in the way that you thank them for a service.

5. In general conversation, commenting that something they have mentioned is a blessing from God.

6. In longer conversations, when complaints and problems are mentioned: Asking why they think bad things happen, moving toward asking if they've ever read the story in the Bible (Genesis 3) about how sin came into the world.

7. When you meet someone new say, "The kingdom of God is near."

8. "You are not smiling today, what is wrong?"

9. "You look sad today. Do you have a problem?" Of course, everyone has a problem.

10. "I believe children are a gift (or blessing) from God."

11. "God is providing everything we need."

12. "May God bless you and your family."

13. "May the peace (grace, blessing, joy, love) of the Lord Jesus be with you and your family."

14. "I'm thankful that God arranged for us to meet today."

15. "I believe that God not only loves you, but also wants to bless you and your family."

16. "I love God because He loved me first."

17. "Can I tell you an interesting Bible story that I read recently?"

18. "I am a follower of Jesus, so I often pray for people I meet. Do you have something that I can pray for you about?"

19. You sneeze and someone says, "Bless you." You respond, "Thank you, he does!"

20. When someone wrongs you or makes a mistake, reply: "If that's the worst thing that happens to me today, then it is a great day!" It's not overtly God-oriented, but people are pleasantly shocked by the positive attitude. Then the response can be more God-centered.

Engagement Ministries You may hear people refer to engagement as "access ministries." The term "access" only describes the first part of engagement—gaining access to a community Getting inside a community is the first step, but building relationships opens doors to begin finding people of peace. In the entire process of making disciples in a new culture or with a new group of people, engagement takes the greatest amount of time and effort.

Discuss how you are currently engaged with the community that you are trying to reach. What additional things can you and your group do to better engage the people you are trying to reach? Are there any organizations which have already engaged this group of people? Try to leverage existing opportunities. Look to God to direct you in this area.

Written Discovery Assignment
The next two chapters will be on prayer and then on finding a person of peace. We will start with Luke 11:1–13 — Focusing and persisting in prayer

Implementation Assignment:
Discuss with your family or those who live with you how you can begin to incorporate the Discovery Process in your life together. Try engaging people you meet by asking them what they are thankful for or some other question to engage them at a deeper interpersonal level.

Supplemental Reading
Contagious Disciple-Making, David L. and Paul D. Watson, Ch. 11 — "Be a Disciple Who Makes Disciples"

Are you a Christian or a Disciple?, Ed Gross, Ch. 13 — "Following Jesus' Teaching Concerning the Old Testament"

Chapter Eight

Engaging God in Prayer

In the last chapter, we tried to establish the foundation of effective prayer: a life lived fully for God. Prayer for a disciple involves making yourself available for God to use to fulfill your prayer. Like everything about Disciple-Making, it is active and not passive.

> *For a disciple, prayer is active. It means asking for God's will to be done and making yourself available to accomplish it.*

Jerry Trousdale writes

> *A dramatic revival is taking place worldwide, as thousands upon thousands of Muslims are moving from the enslavement of hopeless legalism to embrace the only means of salvation and eternal life, available as a free gift through the sacrifice of Jesus Christ. The question that many ask is why is this happening now? Why and how are entire mosques of Muslims becoming followers of Christ? The final answer, of course, is this: God has chosen to do so at this time. But on a human level, there is one constant theme that keeps coming up in the interviews we have conducted with Christ followers from a Muslim background: abundant prayer.*

> *Prayer is the greatest weapon that any Disciple Maker can wield, and God's people are using it effectively around the world at this very minute. Prayer takes the spiritual battle out of the human realm and puts it fully into God's hands, and not even the powers of hell itself can stand against His mighty Spirit. It is prayer that has opened the doors of mosques, torn down the walls of bigotry, and broken the weapons of hatred. When God's people kneel in prayer, God's will is done on earth as it is in heaven (Matthew 6:10).*[17]

Earlier, we read about successful Disciple Makers in India praying regularly and for long periods of time. Here are some of the characteristics that Jerry Trousdale describes of African Disciple Makers:

- Weekly fasts
- Regular six-hour to all-night prayer vigils
- Midday prayers by church members and ministry teams
- Personal early morning prayer for one to three hours

- Family devotions based on Discovery Bible Studies and prayer

- Early and ongoing training in prayer both for those in the process of discovering God and for new believers

Jerry continues:

When Muslims discover that God welcomes the prayers of our hearts and answers them, their spirits begin to rejoice. The former disciplines of forced Islamic fasting and rote repetitions of the same prayer seventeen times a day are willingly left behind as people discover the freedom to pray as God leads them. This happens even before they fully understand Jesus; in part because they see their mentors in the gospel living lives of much prayer themselves.[18]

Our personal prayer is only a part of the prayer that is needed to launch and sustain.

David Watson writes:

As we started looking at Disciple-Making Movements worldwide, we made a critical observation: A prayer movement precedes every Disciple-Making Movement. There are two sides to catalyzing a prayer movement. First, we must become people of prayer. Second, we need to mobilize people to pray.[19]

In Chapter 12 of *Contagious Disciple-Making*, the Watsons provide a comprehensive strategy to develop a broad prayer network to support the Disciple-Making movement that you are working to initiate. Developing a prayer network is one of the areas that I am pursuing. In the following paragraphs, I will lay out a framework that I am seeking to implement which other movements have identified as critical.

PERSONAL PRAYER LIFE

Living and modeling a deep and broad personal prayer life

My prayer life has increased from about half an hour of prayer a day to about an hour and a half. You will notice that is still a fraction of the prayer lives of people who have seen great movements start and grow. I am confident that, as I devote more time to prayer in my personal life and the amount of corporate prayer increases, we will begin to see great breakthroughs in North America.

- I currently intercede for about an hour every day for the communities for which I have accepted responsibility. (We will talk more about communities a little later.) I try to maintain regular communications with individuals in each of these communities.

- I spend a few minutes daily talking to God.

- I also work on my Discovery Studies and discuss them regularly with my wife. This is a core part of my time with God.

- Another characteristic that has become part of my life is that I pray immediately whenever I learn of a need. I discovered years ago that, when I am talking with someone and the Holy Spirit has opened that person's heart to share, if I will pray right then, I have clear access to the Holy Spirit to guide my prayers, so I pray with power and understanding. Then, when I am home, the prayer request has become part of me and I continue to pray.

- My newest undertaking, which I learned from *Contagious Disciple Making*, is to ask one person a day what his or her needs are and pray for him.

My own experience matches that of David Watson:

> *Here is something I've learned: knowledge transfer is not intimacy. It's part of intimacy, but if all communication comes in the forms of texts and lists, intimacy soon disappears.*

> *We've been trained to talk to God by reading Him our lists rather than having conversation. We mutter hasty sentence prayers as we race through our day without stopping and listening to what God has to say.*[20]

In my daily prayer life, I try to take a few minutes every morning to write down what God says to me and my responses, as well as the questions that I would like him to answer. I have been doing this for many years. These conversations have grown in depth over the years.

You can start by writing down a question that you have and ask God for an answer. Don't come with expectations, but be ready to write down whatever comes to mind. It may be scripture, or it may be a sentence or a phrase. If you feel like writing about your love for God or some struggle that you are enduring, pour out your heart.

If you don't like to write, then take some time to talk to God verbally. You need to recharge your relationship with God daily. God has reminded me that the person who is successful in prayer is not the one who intercedes for long periods of time, but the one who spends long periods of time with God listening and conversing with him. Quiet times of listening and prayer, like obedience, grow as our love for Jesus grows. And in this virtuous cycle, love for Jesus grows as we obey and spend time with him in prayer.

Where will you find the time? I remember facing that question as a young man. I had a young family, a full-time job, and a life of ministry that easily added another 20 hours a week to my schedule. My personal time with God had dwindled to almost nothing.

I had been given the job of reaching out to a Christian leader, a farmer, who lived in the country a few hours away. I was supposed to guide and support him. My wife Cindy and I were visiting in his home with our two little children. After breakfast, the son of our host offered to take me flying. I had just recently gotten out of the Air Force and had worked as a flight instructor for a few months before moving to our new city.

When we took off from the first touch-and-go landing, the engine quit. As I was sitting in a suddenly totally quiet plane with a full load of fuel and about to crash, I was thinking to myself that we would both be killed. I remember asking myself, "Will this hurt?" and answering, "Guess I will find out." Next, I called out God. There was no answer. So, there I was, at the point of probable death and I was not in God's presence. I had gotten so busy doing things for God that I had let my relationship with him slip away. It was not the place I wanted to be when I died, wondering if my profession of faith would get me into heaven. It was not a good feeling.

After I recovered from the crash, both physically (I only had minor injuries) and psychologically, I did some deep soul searching. What would it mean to have done "great things" for God and have forfeited my loving relationship with him? God can get by without my work for him, but I cannot get by without daily telling him how much I love him.

So finding time to spend with God became my top priority. I hope that it becomes yours, as well. Once it does, you will find ways to carve out time in the morning, at home, at work, or when you are traveling You will quit doing some of the good things to make time for the most important thing you can do, regularly spending time listening and talking to the God you love.

COMMUNITY ACTION AND PRAYER PLAN[21]

The second part of the framework of personal prayer is to develop a **Community Action and Prayer Plan.** (See the outline in Appendix 4.) The reason to develop this plan is to direct your engagement both in prayer and physically with the group of people whom God has given you to reach. When we began this journey, you were asked to select a few potential groups to reach, and to identify people who can help you reach those groups of people. Your list should have included both those outside the community interested in outreach, and those inside who may provide access to the community.

There are eight parts of the community prayer plan which require you to evaluate the group you will reach (see appendix 4).

1. **What community are you praying for?** Defining a community may be simple or complex, but it must be concise. Communities can be those which you are or are not part of. Some of mine include: the people in Andhra Pradesh, India; my unsaved siblings; the neighbors around my church; the people just north of Jinja, Uganda; and the community of coworkers in my city. These are communities to which I have access and for which I pray. I

can pray for more communities than I can engage at the same time.

2. **What is God doing with them?** You need to know the community that you are seeking to reach and pray for. What are their physical, emotional, and spiritual needs? Find out by prayer walking (praying as you physically survey an area), researching their history, and talking to the people who have contact with them such as social workers, teachers, neighbors, store owners, family, coworkers, and so forth. Get to know people in the community and ask them questions. This will give you new insights into praying for them

As you become familiar with the community and understand what God is already doing, write down your observations in a community prayer plan. This will allow you to focus your prayers and begin to plan specific ways to engage the community.

3. **Who will join you as partners in reaching them?** — Some of the names of people you wrote earlier will go in here (see figure 2.1). This can also include ministries and social services that are

connected to the people you want to reach and who are willing to partner with you in reaching them. You can write down some information about each of them to help you pray for them and to understand how you can build partnerships.

4. God's guidance to reach this community of people (Vision) — This can include direct words from God or scripture passages. It can be advice from other people. Whatever you receive, try to put it into sentences that are clear and give enough vision to help establish a strategy.

5. Who do you know in the community? This should be a growing list of names, biographical and location information. What are their needs? What do they do? Who are they connected to?

6. Who are the potential persons of peace? Out of the list of people you get to know, who seems to respond positively to you? Who are their contacts? What influence do they have?

7. What barriers are there? What are the political, economic, relational, and spiritual barriers of the community? These are both opportunities and hindrances. Identifying them should also help you develop an engagement strategy.

8. What other communities can this group contact? It is important to keep looking ahead. What other communities are the people who we are trying to reach connected to? How might the good news move to them?

Take some time to write out community prayer guides for each of the target communities. These guides should allow space for adding people and information. Once you have assembled guides for each community, you can begin to pray addressing each of the areas. It will allow you to pray with greater understanding and focus.

These prayer guides can also be useful to develop plans to reach the community. Engagement ministries are usually focused on the physical needs which you should have identified. If there are ministries meeting those needs, then you can work to build relationships with them, or join their work.

Personal Prayer structure ACTSS:

This acrostic has been used by many ministries. It is intended to give structure to personal prayer.

Adoration of God and for what he is doing

Confession and alignment with God's purposes

Thanksgiving for partners and successes

Supplication and **S**piritual Warfare for needs and resources, spiritual strongholds, and protection

Praying for a Saul of Tarsus and for faithful people like Timothy and Titus

As we discussed in the section on counter-intuitives in Chapter 6, we want to invest our time in people who are both faithful and empowered with the Holy Spirit to do greater things than we can. Regularly take time to ask God to prepare you and to bring you to those individuals who will have the greatest impact for the kingdom of God.

Praying Scripture

One way that we can align ourselves with God's purposes and plans is to pray the scriptures. Praying through Matthew 28:16–20 and Luke 10:1–11 can connect you both individually and as a group with the heart and spirit of Jesus' Great Commission. Appendix 4 includes directed prayer through these two passages. Additionally, there are many parts of scripture that include wonderful Spirit-filled prayer, the Psalms in particular and several of Paul's Epistles. To utilize these passages in your prayer, change the third person "he" to "you" and insert the name of the people for whom you are praying in place of "they" or "you." There are a few examples in Appendix 4 of praying the Epistles in addition to the Community Prayer Guide and the directed prayer through Matthew 28:16–20 and Luke 10:1–11.

The Lord's Prayer

As you look at the Lord's Prayer in Luke 11, be aware that this is more than a prayer that Jesus gave us. It also provides a format for private and corporate worship.

Father, hallowed be your name.

- Worship and adoration

Your kingdom come.

- Invitation and intercession (community prayer plans)

Give us each day our daily bread,

- Supplication (personal finances, health, co-laborers, understanding)

and forgive us our sins, for we ourselves forgive everyone who is indebted to us.

- Repentance and forgiveness

And lead us not into temptation.

- Deliverance and guidance

Corporate Prayer

It is a Christian platitude in the Western Church to say that prayer is important, or even critical. But to actually do it is a different matter. There is no disciple-making or church-planting movement where there has not been a corresponding prayer movement. In our Western culture, it is relatively easy to get people to do things for God. The block to widespread movements in North America and Europe has been the lack of individual and corporate prayer.

As you begin living as a disciple of Jesus with a small group of others, look to this group as the first level of corporate prayer. You are already praying for each other's needs. Simply add intercessory prayer for God's kingdom to come and the fulfillment of the Great Commission which involves Disciple-Making Movements. Consider actually praying Matthew 28:16–20 and Luke 10:1–11.

The next level of corporate prayer could be your ministry partners. Introducing your prayer plan to them and getting their input can provide deeper substance to your prayer together. If they in turn will share the vision for praying for this community of people with their spiritual network, you will begin forming a larger network.

The third level of corporate prayer would be to inform and engage prayer groups in churches and existing intercessor ministries. There is a growing movement of "houses of prayer" and intercession ministries around the United States. If these will embrace the vision of Disciple-Making Movements and fulfilling the Great Commission, they could provide another level of prayer and intercession. I have been praying for this and believe that God is beginning to open a few doors.

Aviation Analogy of Prayer

One focus of prayer should be to see a prayer movement of thousands of people who will pray and intercede for the start and growth of Disciple-Making Movements. How can we get that to happen? In *Contagious Disciple-Making*, Paul Watson outlines a very comprehensive strategy of prayer.

Here is an analogy that may prove useful. As a young man, I was a pilot in the Air Force and flew the military version of the Boeing 707. This was one of the largest aircraft of its day and, to change the direction of the airplane, they devised a unique system of moving the ailerons (the back edges of the wing that go up and down). The large airplanes of today have direct electric/hydraulic motors to do this, but the airplanes that I flew relied on me, the pilot, to manually turn the control wheel to pull a cable that led out to the wing. This action did not directly move the ailerons, but rather moved a trim-tab in the opposite direction. So I turned the controls, which pulled the cable. The cable moved the small trim-tab, which applied pressure and moved the aileron and slowly began to turn the airplane. Compared to hydraulic driven ailerons, there was a very large delay between moving the control column and actually making the airplane change direction.

Here is the application to prayer: If I ask you and you ask a few other people to pray for the fulfillment of the Great Commission, it is equivalent to the physical input of pulling the cable on the airplane. If they, in turn, will join you in prayer and ask God for a prayer movement to intercede for Disciple-Making Movements and the Great Commission, it can begin changing the course of events. Over time, then, we will see movements of men, women, and children who are living as disciples of Jesus, empowered and making more disciples.

Every major Disciple-Making Movement has been preceded and accompanied by large movements of prayer. Remember, there is a lag time between the input and the desired result. Stay patient in prayer and see what happens.

I have participated in a group of intercessors for the "10/40 window" for a few years now. (The 10/40 window is the region on either side of the equator in which live the majority of people who have not been effectively reached with the gospel.) Large-scale intercessory prayer for this area has been going on for decades. As we look at all of the church-planting and disciple-making movements occurring in this area, the connection with ongoing intercessory prayer is hard to miss. What would happen if we begin this level of intercession for North America and Europe?

**6. Discovery Group Exercise: Luke 11:5–10

Watch video 9, "Prayer," by Jerry Trousdale (Appendix 6).

With your Discovery Group, complete the group process. For the scripture study, do an oral study of Luke 11:5–10 (See Chapter 3).

Change facilitators in your training group so that each person has an opportunity to facilitate. At the conclusion of your time together, evaluate how the facilitator did in maintaining order, involving everyone in the sharing time, and drawing out the important discovery points in the passage.

In addition to the standard discovery questions about God and man, what do you discover about prayer and the work of the Holy Spirit in this passage?

Questions

- What are some successes resulting from your own prayers?

- Where can you find more time to pray? (What can you give up to find the time?)

- What can you do to better focus your prayers?

- Who can you invite to pray for Disciple-Making Movements and fulfilling the Great Commission where you are?

Implementation Assignment

With your Discovery Group, discuss one of your community prayer plans and lead them in praying through each of the eight parts (see Appendix.4)..

Written Discovery Assignment: Matthew 9:35–10:16 and Acts 16:25–34

The next chapter will be about finding a person of peace. Do written studies on **Matthew 9:35–10:16** and **Acts 16:25–34**. The Matthew 9 and 10 passage describes the mission of the Twelve to reach others to make disciples. There are a few distinctions between their assignment and that of the other Seventy-two which are worthwhile noting.

The second passage is to help you identify the characteristics of people of peace. There are many examples of people of peace in the Bible: Lydia, the Samaritan woman at the well, Cornelius, Zacchaeus, even Andrew and Philip, and the thief on the cross all demonstrate traits of a person of peace. There are also stories in the Old Testament, Rahab, who hid the Israeli spies, and the widow from Zarephath near Sidon are examples. Almost everyone who has responded to a call of God demonstrates some characteristics of a person of peace. From these we can begin to identify characteristics of a person of peace as well as the role that we are to play as a Disciple Maker.

Discuss one of your community prayer plans and as a group, pray for each of the eight parts for that community.

Reading Assignment: Matthew 9:35–10:16

We will be looking at this passage in parallel with Luke 10:1–11 to discover some of the responsibilities of the Disciple Maker.

Supplemental Reading:

"Miraculous Movements," Jerry Trousdale, Ch. 3 — "Pray the Lord of the Harvest"

"Contagious Disciple-Making," David L. and Paul D. Watson, Ch. 12 — "Prayer"

Chapter Nine

Finding a Person of Peace

Question: What is a Person of Peace?

In this chapter, we will discover some of the characteristics of a person of peace in Acts 16:13–21. We will also look at what a Disciple Maker does in finding him, so that you will understand your role and responsibility in the Discovery Process.

If there is no person of peace there is no disciple-making.

Finding people of peace is the first job of a disciple-maker. If there is no person of peace, there is no disciple-making.

God is serious about preparing people to receive the invitation to become disciples of Jesus. In *Perspectives on the World Christian Movement*: *A Movement of God Among the Bhojpuri of North India*, David Watson tells the following story:

An old man sat on the edge of the road approaching the village. When he saw me (David), he started. He slowly stood up and came to meet me.

"Finally!" He exclaimed. "You are finally here." Before I could say anything he took my arm and pulled me into the village.

"Here is the man I told you about," he told people as he pulled me along. "Here is the man I dreamed about every night for the last twenty years. My dreams told me that we must listen to everything this man tells us."[22]

My own stories are not so dramatic, but one which illustrates the same point. I had one young man walk up to me in Uganda and another a month later in the United States, both of whom God had prepared to hear the good news. In the latter case, the young man was a waiter in a restaurant who overheard me talking about making disciples to some friends and moved closer and closer.

When I talked with him, he said:

"I had a dream a few weeks ago where God told me that my house was going to be raided by the police. I told my buddies, but they convinced me that it was just a dream. However, my cousin got me to leave the house that night and sure enough, the police raided it and they all wound up in jail on drug possession charges. I knew that I needed to change what I was doing, but I didn't know how. Then this morning a voice told me that I was going to meet someone who had the words I needed to hear."

These stories are not the norm, but are not unusual, either. So what are the characteristics of a person of peace? Both of these stories illustrate that God is at work in some people's lives before we arrive on the scene. The old man in the village had waited for 20 years, and my friend had waited for several weeks, until God could use us in their lives.

Characteristics of a Person of Peace and Role of the Disciple-Maker

Matthew 10:1–16	Luke 10:1–9
And he called to him his twelve disciples and gave them authority over unclean spirits, to cast them out, and to heal every disease and every affliction. [2] The names of the Twelve apostles are these: first, Simon, who is called Peter, and Andrew his brother; James the son of Zebedee, and John his brother; [3] Philip and Bartholomew; Thomas and Matthew the tax collector; James the son of Alphaeus, and Thaddaeus; [4] Simon the Zealot, and Judas Iscariot, who betrayed him. [5]These twelve Jesus sent out, instructing them, "Go nowhere among the Gentiles and enter no town of the Samaritans, [6] but go rather to the lost sheep of the house of Israel. [7] And proclaim as you go, saying, 'The kingdom of heaven is at hand.' [8] Heal the sick, raise the dead, cleanse lepers, cast out demons. You received without paying; give without pay. [9] Acquire no gold or silver or copper for your belts, [10] no bag for your journey, or two tunics or sandals or a staff, for the laborer deserves his food. [11] And whatever town or village you enter, find out who is worthy in it and stay there until you depart. [12] As you enter the house, greet it. [13] And if the house is worthy, let your peace come upon it, but if it is not worthy, let your peace return to you. [14] And if anyone will not receive you or listen to your words, shake off the dust from your feet when you leave that house or town. [15] Truly, I say to you, it will be more bearable on the day of judgment for the land of Sodom and Gomorrah than for that town. [16] "Behold, I am sending you out as sheep in the midst of wolves, so be wise as serpents and innocent as doves.	After this the Lord appointed Seventy-two others and sent them on ahead of him, two by two, into every town and place where he himself was about to go. [2] And he said to them, "The harvest is plentiful, but the laborers are few. Therefore pray earnestly to the Lord of the harvest to send out laborers into his harvest. [3] Go your way; behold, I am sending you out as lambs in the midst of wolves. [4] Carry no moneybag, no knapsack, no sandals, and greet no one on the road. [5] Whatever house you enter, first say, 'Peace be to this house!' [6] And if a son of peace is there, your peace will rest upon him. But if not, it will return to you. [7] And remain in the same house, eating and drinking what they provide, for the laborer deserves his wages. Do not go from house to house. [8] Whenever you enter a town and they receive you, eat what is set before you. [9] Heal the sick in it and say to them, 'The kingdom of God has come near to you.'

We live in a spiritual world which we, for the most part, cannot see. Experiences like these are exciting, and we know that they are from God because they extend the kingdom of God, and because they conform to stories in the Bible.

I like to encourage believers to be spiritual risk-takers, but to hang on tightly to the safety line of the Bible. The words of the Bible are tested. With the empowerment of the Holy Spirit, both the Spirit and the Bible provide life and protection.

7. Discovery Group Exercise Matthew 9:35–10:16

Complete the five-part Discovery Process with your group. In addition to the standard questions, take some time to compare the differences between the mission of the Twelve and the Seventy-two in Luke 10:1–11 that you studied earlier.

Discussion Questions:

• Where were each of the two groups to go? What are some clues to the destination of the Seventy-two?

• What are the common instructions of the two groups?

• Where might the Seventy-two come from?

Discuss one of your community prayer plans and, as a group, pray for each of the eight parts for that community. Both the Twelve who were sent out first and the Seventy-two that were sent out later had similar missions, but the target group of each was different. The Twelve were sent to the observant Jews—kosher Jews whose food was clean. The Seventy-two went to a more diverse group of people. Jesus would have had a reason to tell them twice to eat what was set before them if they were going to people whose food the Seventy-two might normally not eat. Some of these people could have been Jews not keeping kosher kitchens. Others would have been Gentiles or Samaritans. He also had reason to warn them about being sheep among wolves. Because of the hostility of the Pharisees and Sadducees, Jesus could not explicitly tell his disciples to reach non-Jews, nor should they talk about where they were going.

The fruit of the mission of the Twelve may well have been the additional Seventy-two disciples who, in turn, could be sent out to reach more people. Multiplication has been and is, the goal of every step of the Disciple-Making Process.

Mission of the Twelve

One of the key things that we can do is to keep in mind the mission of the Twelve. For those who are set on reaching the lost as soon as possible, this may seem to be a delay. But if we initially engage more believers and invite them to "come and see" what it means to live as a disciple of Jesus, we can rapidly multiply the number of Disciple Makers. This is what Jesus did.

Jesus was not only looking toward a multiplication of disciples and Disciple Makers; he had a genuine interest in seeing these "lost sheep" fully enter the kingdom of God. Likewise, reaching people within the church is important in itself. The church is experiencing attacks from without and within. Without experience, all truth lies in the realm of doubt and therefore is only as secure as the most appealing argument. Disciple-Making moves the truths of the Bible into the realm of experience for those who practice it.

Without experience, all truth lies in the realm of doubt and therefore eludes us.

A church full of people like the Bereans— people who search the scriptures, apply it to their lives, and are not afraid to ask preacher or pastor, "Where does it say that in the Bible?"—such a church will not be easily subverted. Neither will they be easily moved by attacks and deceptions outside the church.

So Biblically oriented, obedience-based, and experiential Disciple-Making is both the best defensive weapon and the most effective offensive weapon by which the church can withstand attack and overcome even the gates of Hell.

Application of the Mission of the Seventy-two (Seventy)

Like the Seventy-two, once we engage the lost, we must be prepared to handle cultural differences with the people whom we are sent to reach, even when those differences are unacceptable to our religious training. We will talk more about this in the chapter on crossing cultural frontiers. Review the characteristics of people of peace in the following chart.

A BRIEF OVERVIEW OF FINDING THE PERSON OF PEACE Read LUKE 10:1–11 AND MATTHEW 10:5–14	
LUKE 10: MATTHEW 10	CHARACTERISTICS OF THE PERSON OF PEACE
Luke 10:5	• Opens his/her door to you • Receives your blessing and shows interest
Luke 10:6	• Opens his/her house to you; is hospitable
Luke 10:7	• Offers to sustain you in some way • He/she is worthy
Matthew 10:13	• Has influence in his home or community • Receives you
Matthew 10:14	• Hears your words

Table 9.1 Characteristics of People of Peace

Though the target groups were different, the process was the same that was used by both the Twelve and the Seventy-two. Both teams were to find worthy people of

peace. In these two passages, we see some common characteristics of people of peace. They are open, hospitable, and generous. They are established in their social network. Most important, God has been at work in their lives so that they want to hear what you have to say to them.

There are many examples of people of peace in the Bible. Each of the disciples that Jesus called was a person of peace. Some other worthwhile examples are the Samaritan woman at the well in John 4, Cornelius in Acts 10, and Lydia in Acts 16:13–15. The calling of the disciples that you studied in John 1:35–5, even Rahab, Ruth, Moses, and Abram in the Old Testament, are other examples of people of peace. In your next discovery study, you will look at the Ephesian jailer. In all of these stories, you will see different characteristics. There are many that are unique to the particular individual and a few that are common to all. The key factor is that the Holy Spirit has been working in that person's life so each has a positive response to the message and a willingness and ability to share it with at least a few other people.

If they are unwilling or unable to share what they learn, they are not people of peace. However, as you get to know them, they may introduce you to someone else in the community who will fill the role of the facilitator. Nevertheless, once it is clear that there is nothing they will do to reach out, it is time to look for other people of peace.

It can be difficult to move on from a friendship that you have formed. While it is possible to keep some ongoing relationship, you know that you only have so much time to invest. To fulfill the call to make disciples, you need to act decisively to move on and ask God to direct you to another person. This decision is easier to make earlier than later.

I know a couple who have invested several years into a relationship with a Muslim family. They have become like extended family, but this Muslim family is not open to pursuing the God of the Bible. The years have moved on, but they have not been successful in making any disciples.

David Watson has quoted a friend on page 135 of *Contagious Disciples Making* who says that the primary characteristics of people of peace are that they are open, hungry, and willing to share with others. He uses the abbreviation OHS to remember the list: Open, Hungry, and Sharing.

Recall that, before Jesus sent out the Twelve disciples (Matthew 9:35–38) and the Seventy-two (Luke 10:2), he instructed them to pray the Lord of the harvest to send workers. Regardless of who prayed, the person of peace whom you find is the person that the Lord has sent to bring in the harvest, which is their social network. Your job is to coach and mentor them.

The scarcity is not people of peace, but in those who ask the Lord of the harvest to send laborers and are themselves capable Disciple Makers.

Role of the Disciple Maker

Let us look again at the passages in Matthew 10 and Luke 10 which we used to identify characteristics of people of peace. When we examine the characteristics of a Disciple Maker in them, we will find a much longer list.

When evangelists or believers discover the concept of the person of peace, they frequently start looking for them. However, they usually don't find any and often become very frustrated. They have overlooked two things. First, that Disciple-Making is a partnership between Jesus and his disciples. If you are not living as a disciple, you cannot be partnered with Jesus. You are not usable. Second, finding people of peace requires obedience to pray and ask the Lord of the harvest for laborers. The following two tables identify what Jesus ordered the Twelve and the Seventy-two to do. The last table gives a summary.

Look over the different commands that Jesus gave in these two passages and affirm that you are prepared, using the checklist in Table 9.5

Role of the Disciple Maker	
Matthew 10	WHAT THE DISCIPLE MAKER DOES
Matthew 10:1	Is a disciple Has authority from Jesus
Matthew 10:2—4	Is part of a team
Matthew 10:5	Goes where Jesus sends
Matthew 10:6	Goes to people of Israel (the Church)
Matthew 10:7	Proclaims that the Kingdom of God is at hand
Matthew 10:8	Heals the sick, raises the dead, cleanses lepers, casts out demons Does all of this for free
Matthew 10:9	Does not make money from his service
Matthew 10:10	Relies on generosity of people for support
Matthew 10:11	Inquires/searches/identifies Spends time with a candidate
Matthew 10:13	Gives blessing
Matthew 10:14	Proclaims words of the Kingdom Leaves when not received
Matthew 10:16	Remains prepared for difficulties

Table 9.2 from Matthew — the Role of the Disciple Maker

Role of the Disciple Maker	
Luke 10	WHAT THE DISCIPLE MAKER DOES
Luke 10:1	• Goes out with a partner • Goes where Jesus is going
Luke 10:2	• Prays for laborers
Luke 10:3	• Goes with danger all around
Luke 10:4	• Leaves behind baggage (trusts God for provision) • Does not waste time
Luke 10:5	• Accepts invitations
Luke 10:6	• Says "Peace be to this house"
Luke 10:7	• If favourable response fellowships with them • Stays in one house. Works through the people there • Accepts hospitality of non-kosher Jews, Samaritans and Gentiles
Luke 10:9	• Heals the sick • Tells them the words of the Kingdom of God

Table 9.3 from Luke — the Role of the Disciple Maker

Summary of What a Disciple Maker Does
• Prays for laborers, provision, safety, blessings, healings, deliverance • Goes where God sends • Relies totally on God • Goes in the face of danger • Enters a place or area proclaiming the Kingdom • Does **not** waste time • Inquires with discernment • Visits the person of peace candidate, engages him and family if possible • Gives greetings; asks spiritual interest questions • If favourable response, gives blessing and asks evangelistic questions • Heals the sick • Spends time with person of peace and their family • Fellowships with them, discerns • Ministers to them • Proclaims Kingdom words (Deuteronomy 6) • Always is bold and truthful

Table 9.4 — Summary of the Role of a Disciple Maker

Disciple Maker Check List

Disciple Maker Checklist	Yes
I am a disciple	
I have authority from Jesus	
I am part of a larger team	
I have a partner	
I know where Jesus is sending me	
I have prayed and am praying for the laborers (people of peace)	
I have prayed and am praying for protection and provision	
I understand and am prepared for the difficulties I may face	
I can clearly proclaim that the Kingdom of God is near (figure 1.1)	
I am willing to work in the "supernatural" (healings, etc.)	
I will not become distracted from the mission	
I have investigated the people of the place I am going	
I am willing to accept other cultures without changing them	
I am prepared to say and give "peace unto this house"	
I will work only with one household at a time	
I am prepared to leave if I am not received	

Table 9. 5 Checklist for a Disciple Maker

When Christians begin to understand the power that lies in the process of Disciple-Making Movements, they begin to focus on finding a person of peace who will initiate a movement. However, you will notice in the Luke 10 and Matthew 10 passages that there are many more things to observe about the requirements for a Disciple Maker than there are for a person of peace. Preparation is the key to success.

Jesus probably spent more than a full year training the Twelve disciples before he sent them out. This checklist is intended to be something of a reality check.

I am a disciple: You are a disciple as soon as you accept the call to follow Jesus and begin applying the five disciplines of a disciple discussed in chapter 2. As we saw in the study of John 1:35–46, a disciple can begin to call others immediately. The fifth discipline of a disciple was to be a Disciple Maker.

I have authority from Jesus: Begin by asking Jesus to give you the authority that you will need for your work. You will only be effective to the extent that Jesus gives you authority.

I am part of a larger team: Whether it is a team of intercessors or other Disciple Makers, you need to be connected with other people in the work of Disciple-Making. Who are some of your other team members?

I have a partner: If you are married, ideally your partner will be your spouse. Genesis 2 places man and woman as companions to support each other in the work that God gives them. You are encouraged to make an effort to establish that unity as the starting point of your work as a Disciple Maker. Working as a married couple increases the variety of people whom you can effectively engage. There will be, however, many times when this is not possible. You may be single, or your spouse may have other responsibilities. In this case, identify who your partner will be. Your partner does not have to be with you every time you connect with the person of peace, but your partner should know him or her and be actively supporting you by being with you in prayer, if not also physically. Keep your partner informed of each meeting.

I know where Jesus is sending me: You need to know whom Jesus wants to reach. Having confidence that Jesus desires to reach specific people will give you direction as you engage them. This does not always mean a supernatural revelation. There are practical things to consider, as well. In the end, you should be confident that you are in alignment with the Holy Spirit.

I have prayed and am praying for workers: Praying for laborers is an assignment that you can get help with, but it is not something that you can delegate. Remember, you are asking for the worker with whom you will be working. He is the one who will be doing the harvesting.

I have prayed and am praying for protection and provision: Like praying for workers, praying for protection and provision is something that you should look for assistance with, but cannot delegate away. Of all the disciples of Jesus, we have more examples of Paul's work than any other. Look at the examples of Paul having people pray for him before they sent him off, and his own seeking God as to where he should go. You will also see that he took pride in never taking financial support from the people he was trying to reach, but worked as a tent maker when needed. However, when other team members joined him or churches sent support, he received the support and stopped working (Acts 18).

I understand and am prepared for the difficulties that I may face: These are not always physical, but can include financial, emotional, and relational challenges, as well. If you are facing a work that is too difficult for you, consider something less challenging. God can use you without pushing you beyond your limits. As a matter of fact, the experience which you have built in easier environments can prepare you for more challenging things in the future.

I can clearly proclaim that the Kingdom of God is near: Personally grappling with making disciples has forced me to reexamine my understanding of the gospel. Frankly, formerly it had not been much deeper than to have a person repent from their sins and be saved. I had expected that the experience of repenting and receiving forgiveness of his sins would give him the desire to live for Jesus. I was focused on making life better for the hearer, not on having him glorify God, develop a relationship with Jesus, or live in the Kingdom of God.

Many people who are hostile to Christianity as a religion are nevertheless intrigued by the announcement that Jesus came proclaiming the Kingdom of God which brings all languages and cultures into it, not into a religion (Revelation 5:9 and 7:9). (Review the "Kingdom Circles" in Figure 1.1.)

I am willing to work in the supernatural: There are many natural ways that we can heal the sick and cleanse lepers, and Jesus commands us to do it, but he doesn't specify how. He just says to get the job done. In other words, medical missions and outreaches are certainly valid. However, raising the dead and casting out demons definitely require an exercise of the supernatural power of God, as well as miraculous healings of the sick. Remember that doing this is predicated on the authority that Jesus has given you.

I will not become distracted from the mission: It is easy to become distracted when legal, financial, and physical obstacles present themselves, or when personality conflicts occur with the people you are reaching or with coworkers. In addition to the negative distractions, there are also the pleasant ones, such as friendships, successes, and pride.

I have investigated the people of the place I am going: Finding and working with worthy people can take some time. It is important to learn about their culture: their customs, beliefs, and method of communicating. Tim Miller, in his book *Poised for the Harvest, Braced for the Backlash,* recommends learning the proverbs and sayings that people of a culture commonly use. Learn to express the gospel using those proverbs and sayings, directly or as transitions.

I am willing to accept other cultures without changing them: When Jesus sent out the other Seventy-two, he gave them a few instructions that he did not give to the Twelve who were sent to the "lost sheep of the house of Israel." The subject of working in other cultures is covered in Chapter 11.

I am prepared to say and give "peace unto this house": Verbally saying "peace unto this house" is one of the easiest things to do, but it is easily overlooked. Though it is a simple act of obedience, it takes practice. Being a person who brings peace is another matter. This peace is the fruit of being a disciple of Jesus, which Paul describes in Galatians 5:22–23:

"But the fruit of the Spirit is love, joy, peace, patience, kindness, goodness, faithfulness, gentleness, self-control; against such things there is no law.

I will work only with one household at a time: This is one of the major shifts from traditional Western-style evangelism. It requires a significant change in our orientation from the excitement of praying with as many people as possible to receive Jesus. Forming long-term relationships with a few people is dramatically different. It means taking personal responsibility for developing them as laborers who will reach deeply into their social structure and may even birth a Disciple-Making movement.

I am prepared to leave if I am not received: Remember that we are only committed to work when and where Jesus and his Holy Spirit are at work. It can be difficult to disengage from people once you have formed a relationship. Discerning when you need to leave can be easy, or it can be difficult and take much prayer. Remember that our mission is to make disciples who will make disciples, and to assist Jesus in building churches that will plant other churches. Sometimes this may mean going to a different place where you can be more fruitful.

Nine Characteristics of a Disciple Maker

These are not requirements for you to begin making disciples, but they do give some indication of how successful you will be. Remember that developing as a disciple and Disciple Maker is a process. Set your sights on letting the Holy Spirit increase your capacity in all these areas.

• He will **love the Lord** with all his heart, mind, soul, and strength. In other words, successful Disciple Makers are living out the Shemah of Deuteronomy 6.

• A successful Disciple Maker **loves people** as much as himself. It takes work and there is a cost to becoming a Disciple Maker. If the people for whom you will be giving your life are precious to you, then instead of tiring, you will be invigorated. This is the essence of loving your neighbour as yourself (Leviticus 19:18 and Matthew 19:19).

• He has a **life of deep and growing prayer.** As discussed in the previous chapter, prayer precedes and undergirds everything.

• A Disciple Maker's life is one of **obedience and learning**. Not only is he a disciple who learns from the Bible on a regular basis, but he is aware of what God is doing around him. Every encounter with a person is an opportunity to learn.

• Disciple Makers are characterized by lives of **deep humility**. Many people mistakenly think that humility implies being self-demeaning and of a lowly attitude. Jesus is frequently referred to as being humble, but he certainly was neither of these things. When you study the life of Jesus, you see that humility does not mean thinking less of yourself, but thinking of yourself less and of others more. Jesus surrendered all that he had because he loved us enough to do that. He was powerful in addressing hypocrisy and was merciful to the lowly. He thought only of his Father in heaven and the people he came to rescue.

Great Commission Disciple Making

A Disciple Maker's life is one of **faith and patience**. They go hand in hand. Faith is one of the few key words with a Biblical definition. It is "the assurance of things hoped for, the conviction of things not seen" (Hebrews 11:1). It is the reality that Jesus has restored our relationship with our heavenly Father and the hope of Jesus' return that warrants our faith. Faith in faith is an illusion. Faith in Jesus and his kingdom has substance. Once a person has *that* kind of faith, it is easy to have patience.

We are working for an eternal king in an eternal kingdom. His purposes will be accomplished and his timing is perfect. He was working in the world before we were born or born again. He has given us a small but essential part in space and time of what needs to be done to fulfill the Great Commission.

• You will find that a Disciple Maker lives a **life of sacrifice**. By this, I mean a willingness to pay whatever price is necessary to accomplish what God has given him to do. Disciples look for opportunities to obey and do what Jesus wants them to do. It is not sacrifice, but obedience that Jesus calls us to (1 Samuel 15:22). Having a loving relationship with Jesus makes the cost to be paid worthwhile.

> It is not sacrifice, but obedience that Jesus calls us to.

Being a Disciple Maker will likely lead you into spiritual and natural conflicts. Be gentle with your opponents. Recall that Saul of Tarsus began his journey that eventually led to *building* the church by *persecuting* that very church. It was not by persuasive words of men, but by an encounter with Jesus (and possibly the testimony of Stephen in Acts 7) that redirected the course of Paul's life. "Pray the Lord of the harvest to send more workers."

• The successful Disciple Maker will be **willing to work** with the person of peace to disciple the lost, develop a local church, train local leadership, and then move on as soon as possible. Our role is to introduce people to Jesus and to work in partnership with the Holy Spirit. It is Jesus who makes the disciples. The role of a Disciple Maker is a small part of the process, but it is absolutely critical and it is needed in many places. The Great Commission is not a call to build a place of residence, but a call to make disciples wherever we go. Paul's story is a good example. Once a church was planted, he moved on, but he maintained a relationship with the people in each of the places where he started a work.

• The last characteristic in our list is that a Disciple Maker has great joy in **giving all the glory to God**. If you want the recognition and praise of people more than you want to glorify God, you will not last long as a Disciple Maker. Personally, there is nothing more that I want than that Jesus and our Father are glorified and that his kingdom will increase. My greatest joy is the knowledge that I have a part in fulfilling the Great Commission, that what I do will produce eternal fruit.

Personal Testimony

When I think of giving all glory to God, I often think of my relationship with my father. He was a child of the depression who grew up in the Appalachian coal country of West Virginia. He was a hardworking, hard driving, no-nonsense man. Yet I loved him and respected him, because I was his son and because other men respected him.

From the time when I was five years old, my father would take me with him to his work, which meant that I spent many Saturdays on highway construction projects, mine excavation projects, and dam construction projects. These were the days before government enforced work safety rules. The rule of thumb for this type of construction was that, for every million dollars of work, one man would lose his life. As a boy, I knew a few of these men who died in construction related accidents. The attitude of all of them was, "that is why we earn the big-bucks."

The summer that I turned 16, my father put me to work as a rodman on a four-man survey crew. When I turned 18, I had a summer job as a miner on a ballistic missile shafting crew; the following summer, I went to Alaska to rebuild a highway after the Good Friday earthquake. I spent my 21st birthday working on construction projects in Vietnam, and my 22nd on a pipeline crew in the Netherlands.

My father was testing and developing me to follow in his footsteps. I was honoured that he entrusted me with these opportunities and responsibilities. I was also aware that my performance reflected on him. Approval from my father did not come with words of praise, but with opportunities to take on more difficult tasks.

During my last year in college, when I was visiting him on one of my vacations, my father took me down to his office and in-troduced me to all of his colleagues. By this time he was an executive vice president of one of the four largest construction companies in the world. To each of the people we met in the office he would say, "I want to introduce my son Jim." There could be no greater words of praise and appreciation that I could receive than to have my father demonstrate that he was proud of me, as if I were an equal of any of his colleagues.

So for me, giving all glory to God is similar to my attitude toward working for my father and his company. Every action that I take, every success and failure, reflects on my heavenly father and upon Jesus my Lord. My natural father had his share of personal faults and failures, but our heavenly father is perfect.

I was not working for the acknowledgement. It was sufficient for me that the men I worked with could look at me and say, "This young man is a credit to his father, and I can respect his father because I respect his son." I was honoured to be my father's son and to be entrusted with part of his lifetime's work. Now to have the greater opportunity to be a disciple of Jesus and to offer this opportunity to others is one of the greatest pleasures of my life.

Integrating the Nine Characteristics

Looking at the list of nine characteristics of a Disciple Maker can appear overwhelming. If you are thinking, "How will I do this?" or "My character is not that strong in all of these areas," take comfort. The beauty and power of being a disciple of Jesus is that, once you are his disciple, your nature begins to change. Over time, all of these things take place. Daily obedience to the words of God allows the Holy Spirit to transform you by renewing your mind (Romans 12:1–2).

Grace *is the presence and power of God working in and through us to accomplish his purposes, for his*

Start reading, discovering, and allowing the Holy Spirit to engage you with God's word. Begin responding to what the Holy Spirit shows you by taking small practical steps and sharing what you learn with others. Changes will take place in your life. Your priorities and desires will change. These nine characteristics are not something you strive to attain. They are characteristics of someone living as a disciple of Jesus. Make that your aim. It is the grace of God working in you and through you to accomplish his purposes that will develop these characteristics (John 14:16–17, 23).

What is our role as the Disciple Maker? We have looked at some of the scripture references and at nine characteristics of a Disciple Maker. Let's not lose sight of the forest for the trees. We have come to make disciples in order to complete the work which Jesus came to do, to reconcile the peoples of the world to his Father.

• As disciples, we need to fully live the Shemah in every part of our lives. Shemah means to hear and obey the word of God. It is learning to hear and obey God that gives power to our prayer and enables us to be effective Disciple Makers.

• Keep in mind that it is Jesus working through the words of the Bible and the action of the Holy Spirit who do the discipling.

• You invite people of peace to become disciples. This is not our project. It is the Holy Spirit's work. We are to work with the people He selects. We do, however, have the privilege of asking the Father to send workers.

• The person of peace is the worker in the field. Therefore, you need to determine what that person's field (*Oikos*) or social network is. This is part of building a relationship with him.

• Your role is to train, coach, and mentor the person of peace to facilitate Discovery Groups in his or her social network. As he grows and shows ability, your job is to train him as leader-disciple.

• Jesus disciples them. You hold them accountable. The accountability is part of the relationship which grows into mutual accountability as they mature. Over time, as you work with and encourage them, they transition from being disciples-in-training to being coworkers and finally long-term colleagues and friends.

General Biblical Approach

The discovery series used to disciple people to Jesus follows the general format of the Bible. Look at how Jesus developed his disciples and try to duplicate that.

• First — Build upon the foundation that Jesus used: the **Old Testament.** It is not an accident of history that the Bible is laid out the way it is. The disciples whom Jesus trained were well-grounded in all of the Torah and prophets. We should lay in enough of this background from the Old Testament that the discovery group will have an understanding of the promises and the processes that God used to prepare the Jews for the arrival of their messiah Jesus.

- *Second* — Do what Jesus did, the way he did it. Use the **Gospels.** These four accounts give us sufficient amounts of Jesus' teaching to become his disciples. Most of the studies in this book are from the gospels. Remember, our Rabbi is Jesus, and he left us his written words and the Holy Spirit to complete the task.

- Third — Once group members have all become baptized believers, it is normal for them to begin to take on characteristics of a simple church using **Acts and Epistles** as guidance. Just as the Disciple Maker assists Jesus and the Holy Spirit, allowing God to make disciples rather than making them himself, so also we see in Matthew 16:18 that it is Jesus who builds the church, not the disciples. Our role is to assist this process, not to direct it. As with the Disciple-Making Process, our role is to guide the new believers to scripture passages where the Holy Spirit can guide the new group of believers to discover the basics of becoming a church.

- Fourth — **Do everything in proper order.** Expect the Holy Spirit and the Bible to do the teaching. Truths from the Bible revealed by the Holy Spirit become part of the people who discover them.

Personal Assignment 6:
The Disciple Maker

As disciples, we should desire to make disciples, but since Disciple-Making is about relationships, our initial success will depend on our current set of relationships. The following short exercise will help you evaluate what type of relationships you are working with.

Begin by listing in a notebook or a piece of paper the top 20 closest current relationships in your life. Then mark:

+ Beside those who are Christian

– Beside those who are lost

? Beside those whose spiritual condition you are unsure of

Evaluation

The next step is a simple evaluation. Count the number of each of the three categories marked +, –, and **?.**

- High number of "+": You live in a Christian world. You can begin inviting believers to become disciples of Jesus. This was the first assignment of the Twelve. However, as you build a base of disciples, your eventual goal should be to reach beyond believers to engage the lost people all around you.

- High number of "-": You have access to the lost. You are positioned to immediately begin engaging lost people. Remember to make sure that you have a supportive team. Jesus sent the disciples out two-by-two. This is not meant to be a project for lone-ranger disciples.

- High number of "?": Start sharing some of the passages you have been learning with people and ask what they think about them. You will quickly find out what these people's relationships are with God. There answers may lead you to people of peace.

- You should discuss this exercise with your Discovery Group in Exercise 10: Cultural Adaptation Meeting.

**8. Discovery Group Exercise: Acts 16:25–34

The Philippian Jailer

Watch video 10, "People of Peace," by Dave Hunt (Appendix 6). Then complete the Discovery Group Process. In addition to the basic three questions, make a list of the characteristics of the person of peace and the characteristics of Disciple Makers.

Characteristics of a Person of Peace:

Characteristics of a Disciple Maker:

How would you apply these to your own life?

Implementation Assignment:

With your discovery group, begin to discuss potential people of peace whom you have identified. Now that you have a bet-ter understanding of the characteristics of people of peace, review and update your community prayer guide. For non-believers, the "Discovering God" series starting with Genesis provides the best passages to learn and share.

Next, lead your Discovery Group in pray-ing for workers. Write out a general de-scription of the person of peace that God gives in prayer. Then ask God to lead each of you to the person of peace the following week. Before you go, be prepared; when you are, there be aware and available to follow-up.

Treasure Hunting

Some of the evangelism teams at Bethel Church in Reading, California have devel-oped a group exercise which they call "Treasure Hunting." It is used by many other churches and organizations in their evangelism training. It consists of having small groups pray together, asking God to give them clues as to people whom God wants them to find. They share what clues or senses they believe God has given them. Once they have discussed these, they go out to find the person or people who fit the description based on the clues they have gathered. If you are familiar with this, then with a little modification you could use it in your group for this ex-ercise.

Whatever your approach, the focus should be to find a person of peace with whom you could work to help them lead their family or social group in a Discovery Study.

Written Discovery Assignments

In the next chapter, we will look at two different passages that give a basic outline of the two goals of a Disciple Maker, to make disciples and plant churches.

- **Matthew 28:16–20** — Our commission as disciples
- **Matthew 16:13–21** — Instructions for planting churches

Supplemental Reading:

"Miraculous Movements," Jerry Trousdale, Ch. 5 — "Engaging Lostness"

- *"Contagious Disciple-Making,"* David and Paul D. Watson, Ch. 13 — "Engage Lost People"; Ch. 14 — "Finding a Person of Peace"

Chapter Ten
Starting a Discovery Group

Question: How do you start a discovery study with a person of peace?

Discovery Groups are both Disciple-Making groups and foundational to starting churches. Later in this chapter, you will be doing a group discovery on Matthew 28:16–20, the Great Commission, and Matthew 16:13–21. In the Matthew 16 passage, Jesus shows us that the church will be founded upon the "bedrock" that consists of disciples. In context with what you have already learned, you and your Discovery Group should be able to develop your strategy and the tactics to reach the group you have selected.

Your goal should be either to see a strong and growing home fellowship develop or to see a simple church birthed. Regardless of whether the groups continue as home fellowships or grow into churches, each should regularly reproduce itself consistent with the Disciple-Making model which you have been learning.

Starting a discovery group depends upon you developing a coaching relationship with the person of peace.

Working with your person of peace to start a discovery group

One of the differences that a Disciple Maker has in building relationships with a person of peace, compared to an evangelist working with a prospective convert, is the focus and scope of the relationship. For most westerners, relationships are with individuals. We ask questions and tell personal stories that focus around the activities of individuals that we are reaching out to. "What do you do (work or school)? What sports, movies, television programs, or music do you like?"

As a Disciple Maker, one of the first things is to become familiar with the social network of the person of peace and his or her position in it. If he is not a leader, can he influence the leader? To do this will mean that you learn the details of the personal life of your person of peace.

Personally, I have found that, as soon as I begin asking about a person's family and friends, the depth of our conversations increases. I find out about how he grew up, who he is living with, and who his friends are. I learn about who cares for whom. In learning about his life, our friendship deepens.

I find it helpful to write down the names of the friends and family members, what their needs are, and begin praying for them. Each time we meet, I ask more questions and discover more about my person of peace. Many of my questions seek out how willing the person is to start a Discovery Group with his social network, and how open they are to being part of it. As long as there is progress in our conversations, I continue with the relationship.

With one of my first people of peace, when I mentioned starting a Discovery Group with his social network, it became apparent that his friends were not the best place for him to start a Discovery Group. In his own words, they were trying to "evangelize" him back into selling drugs. I then began to focus on his family and to identify their needs and openness. Working with the person of peace can be a process with twists and turns. Keep moving forward as long as there is progress, even with occasional setbacks, but once it is evident that the other person is not moving forward, then it is time to back off, at least for a time.

A Muslim refugee family with whom we were beginning a discovery study seemed interested in learning about God in the Bible. The wife had been a refugee in Jordan and had been helped by some Roman Catholic doctors. As we discussed their social network, we found that they had very few family ties in this country. She was a Shia and he was a Sunni. The other people they knew from their country were from different tribes, and they didn't trust or interact with them. Whatever their interest in studying the Bible, they were not good candidates at that time to be laborers, for they had no field to harvest.

Remember that the person of peace is the one whom God has sent you to in order that he or she can be equipped to bring in the harvest. You are working with the Holy Spirit. Your part is to bring the person of peace to the Bible and hold him accountable to what the Holy Spirit and the Bible tell him to change.

His life may be disordered; however, it is *not* your job to straighten out the mess. In time, the Holy Spirit will address each area of his life. If he brings up a personal or group problem, find a scripture passage or series of passages that addresses it. Let him and his group discover what God has to say about the subject, and take concrete steps as he is led by the Holy Spirit. Once it has been addressed, return to your original study. Remember: it is essential that a solid scriptural foundation is developed.

I had an interesting experience as I was introducing my waiter friend to Discovery Studies and determining his interest in starting a study. He told me that he had recently changed jobs. When I called him to confirm our meeting, he said that he had a real problem which he needed help with. When we met, he told me the following story. "I have always been an easy-going guy. I never got mad at anyone; but in this new job, I have yelled at a coworker once and my supervisor another time. It is like something has come over me and I am doing things that I don't want to do. I don't understand it!"

It occurred to me that he was describing the same situation that Paul addressed in Romans. I asked a few more questions to make sure that I understood it clearly, and then told him that we would change our study for our next meeting. We did a study on Romans 7:13–25. He was able to draw a direct connection between the Bible and his world. Once he had developed his awareness, he was able to address the situation with a couple of "*I will*" statements. The following week, we returned to the Discovering God series and our study of Genesis.

If someone in the Discovery Group is sick, you may want to direct the facilitator to study one of Jesus' many miraculous healings, or the accounts of Peter healing the lame man (Acts 3:6) or raising Dorcas (Acts 9:40), or Paul praying over the young man killed from a fall (Acts 20:10).

Starting the Discovery Study

There are two basic approaches to starting a Discovery Group with your person of peace. Which one you choose will depend on the relationship that you develop and the confidence that your person of peace has to start a study. In general, the less direct involvement you have in starting the group, the better it will be in the long-term development of the group. Your goal in making disciples is to establish a supportive Discovery Group that will function on its own and will continue replicating itself by starting other groups of disciples.

The least intrusive method is for you to train the person of peace to facilitate a study by doing several studies with him or her. In these one-on-one studies, you facilitate the first few meetings, then have him facilitate while you coach.

After a few times of coaching, you can have him start his own Discovery Group with his family or social group. Before each of his meetings, you should complete or review the same study together. Make sure that he understands the text and the key discoveries of the passage. You should also review what happened during the preceding meeting of his group.

If you are coaching a group of facilitators, you can have them take turns facilitating this training group so that they can learn facilitation skills from one another. This type of coaching group can occur if there is rapid multiplication before the members of the initial group are ready to coach on their own, or if the initial group is too large and has to be divided. (See figure 11.1.)

In using this approach, you will never go to the facilitator's Discovery meeting unless you need to evaluate how things are going. If you go into a group, let the facilitator introduce you as someone interested in how the group operates. Do not let yourself be set up as an expert! Simply observe and, if necessary, ask a few questions, but never make corrections or offer opinions in the group. Give your evaluation in your next one-on-one meeting.

The second approach is to go with the person of peace to his group and demonstrate the process the first time. After this first Discovery Group meeting, meet with the facilitator apart from the group. Ask some general questions. What did he learn? What was happening with the other people in the group? How would he facilitate the group? In this same meeting, explain that the next time he will lead the meeting, but you will be there to answer any questions as the meeting goes along. The third time, you should just observe and make your coaching comments at the follow-up coaching meeting. From that point on, you will simply coach the facilitator in your time together in the outside coaching session. The goal is that the group will develop its identity and leadership apart from you.

Catalyze – to assist a process without being consumed by it or integrated into it.

Regardless of which of the two approaches you use to catalyze the start of a group, your follow-up meetings with the facilitator are critical, to review both what *has* happened and what *should* happen in the next meeting. It is important from the beginning that the facilitator makes sure that everyone in the Discovery Group is participating. This includes making their "*I will*" statements, fulfilling those statements, and telling the passage and what they have learned to someone outside the group. Even if there are lapses in completing everything, it is important to keep this standard from the beginning.

The facilitator should expect the participants to be uncertain the first few meetings. In general, the format of the group is set in the first three or four meetings and is difficult or impossible to change afterwards. So the facilitator should set and

hold to expectations of memorization, application, and telling in all of the meetings. Also, becoming familiar with the process is one reason why, after the first couple of meetings, the group should normally not add new members. If others want to join the group, they should be encouraged to start their own group. You can add this person to your facilitator training meeting with your current person of peace, as we mentioned earlier. If your primary person of peace is capable and willing, he can start a separate mentoring meeting with this new person apart from your meetings with him. If this happens, your one-on-one meeting will need to include reporting and discussing how the second group is doing. (This will be explained more fully in Chapter 11).

So what is an optimum size for a group? In general, six to eight people provide the greatest amount of interaction. However, the key is the social group of the facilitator. If his social group is small, then that is the best size of the group. If it is an extended family or social group, then that is the best size of the group. When a group is greater than a dozen, split it into separate groups for the actual study, and then come together for a "join time" to share what each group has learned.

When Cityteam started their first Discovery Group in San Jose, Carmen (the woman who invited them to start a study group in her home) had invited more than 60 people. After the first meeting, they split into three separate study groups of about 20 people to address both the limited space and the group dynamics. So the lesson here is to be flexible and adaptable.

The other area to concentrate on when starting a group is to train the facilitator in the mechanics of facilitating the meeting. Is he or she able to draw people out by asking questions? Does he make sure that everyone contributes regularly? Does he consistently ensure that key discoveries are being made from the passage? Does he maintain the "no teaching or preaching" rule? Does he keep the group's time on track and not allow the session to degenerate into counseling or gossip?

Ongoing Coaching and Mentoring

When coaching, it is important to keep in mind that the Disciple-Making Process is one of low control but high accountability. Expect that the Holy Spirit and the scriptures will provide the direction to your person of peace as he matures, but you are the one who must hold him accountable for fulfilling his commitments.

David Watson's approach for a mature facilitator is, "If they fail to follow through once, I ask why. If they fail twice, I tell them they have to fulfill their commitments. If they fail three times, I put the relationship on hold, until they can demonstrate that they are willing and able to fulfill their commitments." David was putting into practice Luke 10:10–11: "Whenever . . . they do not receive you . . . even the dust of our feet we shake off in protest."

With a person of peace who has not yet come to a place of making a commitment to Jesus, you will have to be forbearing, but the same standard remains;: obedience to God means accountability to you the disciple-maker, and the group members to the facilitator and to one-another. This is not a matter of controlling the person; rather, it is simple accountability for the commitment that each person makes to God based on what they have learned from the Holy Spirit. If a person habitually fails to keep commitments to you, be assured that he will not keep his commitments to God, either.

Disciple-Making is a low control, but high accountability process.

As much as you may like a person, remember that you are on an assignment from Jesus, just as the Seventy-two were. Your job is to find and prepare the person of peace to bring in the harvest in his family and social network, and to prepare him to do the same (Luke 10:4).

You need to be constantly observing your facilitator and evaluating his abilities, personal discipline, dependability, commitment, and personal initiative—that is, "What is the facilitator's character and ability to make other disciples?"

As you work with a person, you should ask God how he wants to use this person. Shodankeh Johnson, a church planting leader in Sierra Leone, has a saying that I particularly like: "It is not a person's background that counts. It is his in-ground and his end-ground." In other words, don't let a person of peace's history or background set your expectations for that person. Rather, ask what his character is, and ask God to show you what he himself can accomplish with this person in the future.

Shodankeh has told the stories of common house thieves and prostitutes who became significant church planters after they become disciples of Jesus. However, it required a disciple-maker who could discern the character of the person (his "in-ground"); a disciple-maker would ask God what he wanted to do with the person (his "end-ground"). And, of equal importance, a disciple-maker who would take the time to train and challenge the person of peace to fulfill that calling himself.

> *It is not a person's background that counts. It is his in-ground and his end-ground."* Shodankeh Johnson

As the Discovery Group matures and the facilitator grows more capable, he or she should look for other people to train as facilitators to start other groups. For some people, leading a single Discovery Group will be their limit; other people may have the ability and calling to mentor and train many others. Helping people reach their potential as disciples is one of the challenges that you as the disciple-maker have to face.

As your relationship matures with the facilitator, it transitions from that of trainer to coach, then to mentor, and finally to colleague. I have become close friends with some of the men whom I have been privileged to coach. We are co-laborers in this work.

Assuring True Replication

As your network expands and deepens, one of the most important jobs you have is to assure that each group reproduces and remains faithful to the primary standards of discovery-based Disciple-Making. Each group should be faithful to study, commit to memory, apply, and share passages of the Bible. If a group fails in any of these areas, it will fall short of fulfilling the commission that Jesus gave us.

A mature disciple should be accountable for his own group and also for the groups of the people whom he is mentoring. Be sure that he is holding everyone to the same standards. David Watson's goal is that there should be three levels of accountability up and three levels down. This has been demonstrated to maintain fidelity to the standards of DMM.

Mission, Strategy, and Tactics

Chapter 10 of *Contagious Disciple-Making* gives a thorough description of mission, strategy, and tactics. Here is a short summary. **Mission** is what you are trying to accomplish. Jesus' mission was to reconcile the world to his father. **Strategy** comprises the essential things that have to be accomplished to fulfill the mission. Jesus' strategy was to seek and save the lost, and to usher in the kingdom of God. **Tactics** are the different things that can be done to accomplish the strategy. Jesus' tactics included: healing the sick, expelling demons, confronting religious leaders, announcing the kingdom of God, breaking the bonds of sin, ransoming us from eternal punishment by his death on the cross, and making disciples who could make disciples.

**9. Discovery Group Exercise
Jesus' objective for his disciples:

The mission of reconciling the world to God can only be fulfilled by accepting the Great Commission, as laid out in **Matthew 28:16–20**. Having moved along in your own process of disciple-making, now is a good time to do your own discovery study on this passage. In your own notebook, complete a three- or four-column written study, and then discuss the passage with your Discovery Group and write your own discoveries and "*I will*" statements.

The goal of this study is to understand the role that disciple-making plays in establishing churches. In Chapter 1, the chart "From Evangelism Toward Discovery-Based Disciple-Making" presents the focus of the Great Commission as being to go and start churches. Looking at these two passages together should allow you to discover the importance which making disciples has in accomplishing this goal. The role of the disciple-maker is to be a catalyst in the process. He should not be identified with or allow himself to become part of the work of the worker who facilitates any of the groups that start.

Watch video 12b, "Preparing a Person of Peace for leadership," by Jim Yost (Video Training Resources).

9a. Study Matthew 28:1–10, 16–20

You do not need to do a full study on the first ten verses, but read them to give context and understanding of why the disciples went to Galilee. However, do complete the full discovery study of verses 16–20.

The first ten verses of Chapter 28 provide the context and the method that Jesus used to direct the eleven disciples to go to Galilee. The last five verses give Jesus' final command.

After completing the discovery study of these verses, consider what supporting structures you will need to be fully successful in your mission, as well as your own individual and group responsibilities as disciple-makers. Develop a plan to provide the structural support that you will need to reach people in fulfilling the Great Commission.

Jesus' Plan for Building the Church

As key as it is to fully understand and embrace the command of Jesus to make disciples, it is equally important to realize what purpose Jesus has in filling the world with disciples. We will learn in our study of Matthew 16:13–21 that Jesus' mission includes doing something through these men. Creating a foundation of disciples is Jesus' prerequisite for his work of building his church (Matthew 7:24–25; Psalm 127:1). It is Jesus who makes disciples, and it is Jesus who builds the church. Both are part of the same work.

Jesus spent the greatest part of his years of public ministry training and forming his disciples. In the gospel accounts, Jesus does not provide the clear answers to our questions that the epistles do. The epistles identify problems and issues that need to be addressed. They then give specific instructions on what is to be done. Jesus, I am told was asked 183 questions in the gospel accounts, but he only answered three. For years, this frustrated me. It was not until I began to dig into the passage which you will study next that I realized: everything that Jesus did was meant to bring his disciples to the point which Simon Peter reached in Matthew 16:16. A very important question to ask as you study this passage is this: After praising Simon Peter, Jesus immediately begins speaking about going up to Jerusalem and all of the things that would occur there. What was so critical to Jesus' mission about Simon Peter's profession of faith Jesus would make a complete shift in the direction of his ministry?

It is Jesus who makes disciples and it is Jesus who builds the church. Both are part of the same work

As you study this passage, there are a few things about Jesus' remarks in verse 18 that give it a lot of color and deeper meaning. First, the name Simon means "one who hears." Second, Peter's father's name is John, according to John 1:42. Jonah is the prophet. Third, the Hebrew word "bar" means "son of." Fourth, the Greek word for Peter means "little rock" and the Greek word for "rock" that the Bible uses in the phrase "upon this rock" means "bed-rock." As you read Mathew 16:13-21 keep these in mind as they will help give you insight into what Jesus was saying.

In addition to the standard questions "What do you learn about God?" and "What do you learn about man?", dig into what Jesus is saying about planting churches. What was Simon's background? How does it differ from yours? What was the result of Simon Peter being discipled by Jesus? How does it apply to us and to our mission of becoming and making disciples? What is the key to Jesus building his church?

As you and your group meet, there are some important *"we will"* statements that should be developed. Spend time probing this passage— enough that it will set the direction in which you will move in the future, both as individuals and as a group. Address it in both general terms which may lead to a mission statement, and specific terms that may lead to a strategy for your discovery group to reach those who do not yet know or follow Jesus.

**9b. Discovery Group Exercise: Matthew 16:13–21 —"Instructions for planting churches"
Watch video 12b, "Preparing a Person of Peace for leadership," by Jim Yost (Appendix 6).

When your Discovery Group has completed this study, take some time to synthesize what you have learned about your role in the Disciple-Making Process in Matthew 23:8–11 and John 14:24–27, and your role in planting churches.

• Who makes disciples? (See also Personal Assignment 4.)

• Who builds the church?

• What is your role in making disciples?

- What is your role in building the church?

- What resources does God give you to complete your part of making disciples?

- What resources does God give you for your role in planting churches?

It is important to understand that our partnership with Jesus and the Holy Spirit does not change as we move from making disciples to planting churches. The resources and our role remain the same and are adequate for both tasks.

Implementation Assignment:

- Develop a "mission statement" for your Discovery Group, and develop a short strategy plan for achieving your mission.

- Continue to pray for more workers and the specific needs of the people of peace with whom you are working, as well as the needs of their own discovery group.

Supplemental Reading:

Are you a Christian or a Disciple? by Edward N. Gross, Ch. 15 — "Following Jesus in Making Disciples"

"*Contagious Disciple-Making* by David and Paul Watson —

- Ch. 10 — "Thinking Strategically and Tactically About Disciple-Making"
- Ch. 17 — "Leadership"
- Ch. 18 — "Mentoring"

Chapter Eleven
The Disciple Maker in New Cultures

Among the responsibilities of the Disciple Maker is to de-culture the gospel. Part of the task of the new believers is to contextualize the gospel into their own culture. By contextualize we mean to bring the truths this group discovers in the Bible and put it into the context of their local culture. This includes things like: the style of worship, music, teaching, communion, baptism, the arrangement of men, women, and children when they are together, how to posture themselves for group prayer, etc. The Discovery Process enables both deculturing and contextualizing to happen as part of its design.

Every person who grows up in a culture assumes a basic understanding of the world and relational practices that conform to that society. We do this without thinking about there being a choice. It is just the way it is.

Nothing comes as a greater shock to people as they start reaching out to others outside their normal social circles than the different world views that people have. My wife Cindy and I joke about her perceptions that she did not have an accent, which she maintained until we were in a restaurant in Johannesburg, South Africa. We were with friends and she tried to order a pitcher of water. After the third try, the head-waiter came over and said that none of the three waiters could understand what she had ordered. When she spelled out "w-a-t-e-r," he said, "oh, you have such a heavy accent no one could understand you."

Our lack of our cultural awareness is usually deeper than merely our failure to realize that every region of the English speaking world has its own accent and when in their world, it is us and not them who have an accent. We assume that people want the same things that we want, understand the use of money like we do, and have the same freedom to make decisions that we do, but this is not true in many other cultures.

One of the best books on understanding other cultures is the short book, *Foreign to Familiar, A Guide to Understanding Hot and Cold Climate Cultures,* by Sarah A. Lanier, McDougal Publishing. I recommend you familiarize yourself with this and other studies on the deep differences in culture. If you find yourself offended by the behavior or attitude of more than one individual in certain groups, it is because their culture does not conform to your basic assumptions of life. Be assured that there are things in your culture that will offend others as well.

I was doing door-to-door evangelism around our church a few years ago. I struck up a conversation with a Hmong man who had a young family. As we discussed scriptures, he was obvious very interested in becoming a Christian. He said, "I want very much to become a Christian, but my father who is the head of our clan will not permit it. I cannot dishonor my father. He is very old and when he dies, I will become the leader and our family and our entire clan will accept Jesus."

The religious underpinning of societies controls much of the social interactions of those societies. Christians who live in Muslim societies have social interactions that more closely resemble their Muslim neighbors than they do those of Christians in western nations. An atheist in America will have a world-view deeply shaped by the Christian society he grew up in. An atheist in a Muslim country will have his world-view shaped by Islam. The two people will hold intrinsically different views of life even though they profess to be atheists.

The traditional European and American cultures are individualistic. In Africa, the Middle-East, Asia, and Latin America the cultures are family-based. In family structured communities, there is clear hierarchical leadership. If you ask thirty people in a family structured society, who their leader is, most or all of them will give the same answers.

In 2013 we were in Makeni, Sierra Leone, a city of a few hundred thousand people located in a very heavily Muslim area. We were visiting some friends who were translating the Old Testament into the Themne language. We asked several people on the street of their neighborhood who their leader was. We received the name of the same chief and the name of the same imam. Even though it was a city, its social structure was that of a village.

Family vs. Individual Based Societies

These extended family-based societies embrace discovery-based Disciple-Making readily and multiply along the lines of family authority and relationships. It is interesting to note that homeless people and college students, who are without any family at all, often embrace the Discovery Group process and multiply rapidly, not through hierarchical leadership, but because they look for anyone who offers any leadership. Their hunger for family and identity make them very receptive to the community part of the Discovery Process and their transient status means that they frequently form new relationships starting new discovery groups with these new people.

Our Western individualistic societies are characterized by fragmented families and a lack of leadership. Social groups are often more important than families. Roy Moran's church has seen some success among the social groups of stay-at-home moms. Social groups can be: work teams, bridge clubs, bowling leagues, bike clubs, skateboard groups, athletic groups; any group that gives its members an identity. Multiplying Discovery Groups is often more fruitful within these groups than families of the people of peace with whom we are working. One of the important priorities of working with a person of peace in this type of fractured society is to train them as leaders.

The Disciple Maker in New Cultures

In America, Canada, and Europe, one potential avenue of implementing discovery groups is with nuclear families within the existing churches. Raising children as disciples of Jesus rather than trying to teach them about Christianity has appeal. The increasing hostility of western societies to Christianity puts great pressure on Christians who want their children to grow up with a personal relationship with Jesus.

As of 2010 only 30-percent of children raised in American Evangelical homes profess Jesus by the time they are 30 years old. Children increasingly report harassment by classmates and teachers in school. The entertainment media is overtly hostile to Christian values and thought. How can parents "train their children **in** the way" so that they can be confident that "when they are old they will not depart from it?" (Proverbs 22:6). Using the Discovery Process offers the ability to strengthen the children and family against these spiritual pressures. It also gives a way to begin changing society around the family.

Culture in Large Metro-Areas

Regardless of the country, large rapidly growing mega-cities have similar demographic structures. They are largely made up of individuals whose current social groupings probably revolve more around their work and social activities than family. Within immigrant communities their religious institutions often provide an identity for them; especially when they are minority cultures.

When there are only a few individuals of a particular cultural group in a city, they can be easily reached as individuals. This is a great opportunity to invite them to know Jesus. But when there is a large number and they feel they are in a hostile culture, they can close ranks and form protective societies. This was the case for the Irish in the 19th century, the Italians in the early 20th century, and now the Somalis, Hmong, Vietnamese, Middle-Eastern, and other recent immigrant groups. Where a particular religion defines its identity, an ethnic group can become very resistant to both the gospel and people who bring it. In this case, entrance by an outsider can take strategy, time, and effort. Even an inside-believer can face great hostility.

What we do and how we approach a culture requires both prayer and research. As you learned in the chapter on prayer, we need to be deeply knowledgeable about the people that Jesus has sent us to reach and we need to be diligent and disciplined in prayer.

Let us look at four key questions that address some of the important aspects of cultural sensitivity. These are good questions to ask yourselves as you move to engage a group of people:

- **How do I engage my target community without creating unnecessary barriers to the gospel?** Even within our extended natural family there may be barriers. Aunts and uncles, cousins, nephews, nieces, children and parents, each may have different value systems. People in the same church can approach God and relationships in vastly different ways. What are some of the barriers that you have already experienced? What can you do to bridge the gaps?

As soon as you know individuals in the people group you want to reach, you can begin asking questions that will help you come to a deeper understanding of their lives. Questions about how they see and relate to their parents and other family members are always good ways to grow in understanding both the culture and the individuals' positions in it. What are their desires and goals for their lives, if they have any? What is their idea of fun and entertainment? How does their family relate to the same things your person of peace likes or dislikes? What do they do for holidays?

Compare these things with your own values. What do you like to do that might enhance your engagement with the people you want to reach? What things should you be careful not to do or say? How will you make sure that you don't offend? Is there something that you can do to build a deeper relationship?

- **How do I ensure that I am in sync with what God is doing?** Do you have any idea of what God is already doing with the people that you are trying to reach? Has anyone shared any experiences that they have had with God? This is another good avenue of inquiry and can deepen your relationship.

Learning how to be open to listen nonjudgmentally and to ask questions are important. For instance, asking people what they are thankful for is a wonderful way to start a conversation. I have never had someone that did not respond. Then it is easy to ask them why they are thankful for it. Question like these can lead to many discoveries about relationships, values and even their relationship with God.

Another avenue of building a relationship with people who don't know Jesus is to share your own spiritual experiences. Sharing stories about the things that began to open your life to the work of the Holy Spirit can be good bridge builders. Being open with people and sharing about some of the struggles you had prior to making a serious commitment to Jesus can be very helpful.

Normally we are trained to share our testimony of how we became a Christian. While these have a place, they can discourage people who are searching for God. The stories you tell must be ones that the person you are talking to can relate to in their current relationship with God. It is often pre-conversion stories that connect with people who are being drawn to God. Share one of these stories and then ask if your prospective person of peace has any similar or different experiences. The point is to help the other person begin to recognize what God is already doing in his or her life.

Encourage the person to share about his own current journey of faith. Is he an atheist, New Age, a Muslim, Jew, Hindu, or something else? Was this because of the family he grew up in? If it is a decision, can he tell you about how he made that decision? What was the series of events that led up to this point in his life? All the while you are listening, ask God to show you what He is doing in this person's life.

- **What commands of Jesus am I not consistently obeying?** It is easy to become caught up in the relational and logistical activities and forget our own calling to be disciples of Jesus. Committing to memory all of the commands of Jesus and obeying them are two of the foundational disciplines of a disciple. Our ability to mentor and coach others can only increase if we continue growing as disciples ourselves. So, along with deepening prayer, being diligent in our own relationship with Jesus is essential.

We work in a partnership with Jesus. He wants to deepen our relationship with him even as he leads the person of peace into a relationship. As Disciple Makers, we are to hold the people we are mentoring accountable to fulfilling their commitments to Jesus. Likewise, we must also be accountable.

The positive side of obedience is the deepening love relationship that we develop with God as we continue faithfully as Disciple-Makers. Paul's phrases often reflect this relationship. For example, "to die is gain, to live is Christ" (Philippians 1:21). Our ultimate goal as disciples is to be fully united with Christ to God the Father.

• **How do I encourage multiplication?**
As your person of peace learns to facilitate a group, it is important to set and hold the standard of making "I will" and "we will" statements. It is also important that people plan and share the passage they have learned with someone else. Teach the facilitator how to recognize people of peace and to pass that information on to his discovery group.

There are two options for training the facilitator of a new group. (See figure 11.1) If the primary relationship is with one of the Discovery Group members and the person you are mentoring is capable and willing, then encourage replication of the same mentoring relationship that you and he have (This is option 1).

$$\text{Option 1: DM} \longrightarrow F_O \longrightarrow F_N \longrightarrow G_N$$

$$\text{Option 2: DM} \begin{cases} F_O \longrightarrow G_O \\ F_N \longrightarrow G_N \end{cases}$$

DM – Disciple Maker
F – Facilitator, $_O$ original, $_N$ new
G – Discovery Group, $_O$ original, $_N$ new

Figure 11.1 — *Second Generation mentoring options*

Option 2: If a new group starts early in the first discovery group's development and the facilitator is unable or unwilling to mentor the second facilitator, invite the new facilitator to join your mentoring group, at least for a time. To assure ongoing multiplication, the core elements, which are the DNA of the Discovery Process, must be replicated in the new group. All the facilitators of each generation must maintain the same standards.

• **What is your cultural orientation?**
We talked earlier about the fact that all of us have inherited and been integrated into a specific culture that is different than other cultures. For example, there are foods that we considered good and others that we don't. There are greetings that we expect, ways that we relate to people of

the opposite gender, and ways that we show respect. It is good to start by telling ourselves that there is no one right way to do things. This is a reality that can be difficult to adjust to.

Crossing your legs in some cultures is very offensive, especially if the bottom of the shoe points to someone. In Mexico, you shouldn't look at a baby unless you also touch it. In most Muslim cultures a man should never touch a woman nor a woman and man and that includes shaking hands. Refusing to eat food set before you is almost always seen as a rejection of hospitality, so take at least one bite. What is the proper role of men and women? What is appropriate dress? The list is nearly endless. Give some thought to your own cultural norms. Remember our goal is to bring the gospel to people. If their culture needs to change, then let the Holy Spirit and the Bible drive the change, but accept that whatever culture develops it likely will not look like yours.

- **How can you prepare yourself to adapt to other cultures?** Are you going to reach the homeless. Hindus, college students, others? Take some time to investigate what their cultural practices are. In most cases you will never entirely fit-in a different culture, but you can anticipate and adapt so that you are not offensive.

- **Separate religious culture from the presentation of the gospel.** This means to separate the religious culture that we personally are comfortable with from the presentation of the gospel. This is accomplished by using the scriptures without additional written materials or teachings.

The gospel, however, must be contextualized into the receiving culture. This is one of the roles that the Discovery Groups naturally play. As they study and then apply what they learn using "we will" statements, they will modify practices in their culture that are not compatible with the words of the Bible.

Contextualizing, however, does not mean changing their cultural or religious practices to match ours; see figure 1.1. Rather, as the new believers discover and obey what they learn in the Bible, they are the ones to identify what and how their culture needs to be modified to conform to the words they have read. If a custom or practice is not contrary to the scriptures, it remains, even if it is unacceptable to us.

The simplest way of doing our part of deculturing the gospel is to stick to reading and discovery from the Bible itself. Make sure that the facilitator can give you the Biblical basis for all of the practical applications of their discovery group. If there is need for a broader understanding by the group, then direct them to additional passages. But leave the discovery and modifications to them. The only standard you should hold them to, is that they can point to a solid Biblical explanation to their practices, even if you disagree with their interpretation.

Here is an example from Afghanistan where a group of men who were new believers were discussing how they should treat their wives and children. They asked their mentor to explain the way that believers should do this. Their new faith in Christ had not changed any of their family behavior, but they sensed that it should. Rather than teach them, their mentor led them to Genesis 2 and several passages in the Epistles. The result was that after much discussion and discovery, the group of men decided that since God created woman to be their help-mate, they needed to involve their wives in their lives and ministries in a more respectful way.

Over several weeks, they came up with several "we will" and "I will" statements and they reported on the impact it was having with their families. Their conformance was to the standards of the Bible, not to the standards of the mentor who was working with them. A second benefit was they learned how to seek answers to their questions in the Bible and how to apply them to their lives.

One of my favorite expressions applies here, "before you go, be prepared and when you are there be aware." When you begin working with a person of peace, be prepared to be surprised and to hold your words of correction before they come out of your mouth. Rather than give advice, seek for scripture passages to have them study. As you hear what the group discovers about God and man in the Bible, you will discover more about their culture.

In India, as in many cultures, people in non-family situations are segregated according to age, gender, and class. If there is a mixed group of youth, men, women, and old, it is possible that only the men may speak and the older men will have priority. Even though this type of segregation may offend our Western sense of equality, our job is to work with the culture, not to change it. In the case where it is clear that participation is being affected, it may be better to separate the men from the women and even older from younger, so that everyone can share. Train the facilitator to make sure everyone in his study group is sharing. Ask him how the group dynamics are going. If there are deficiencies in this area, explore ways to resolve them within the context of their culture.

One of the things I have done when training in India is to watch the way people sit in the group and interact. People who are not fully involved tend to sit just outside the circle. Also watch and see what people are talking and their gender and age. If there is a pattern of gender or age segregation, then have the facilitator explore ways to reorganize the discovery group.

Americans are committed to integrating the church, at least in words. As we see in Revelations, trying to make one of many may be working against the cultural identities that God has established .

> After this I looked, and behold, a great multitude that no one could number, from every nation, from all tribes and peoples and languages, standing before the throne and before the Lamb,
> — Revelations 7:9

One Latino pastor was explaining to me the challenge of pastoring a multi-national Hispanic church. He said the church splits along three lines, those who do not eat tamales and those that do, and then again between those who wrap tamales in corn husks and those who wrap them in banana leaves. The point he was making is that culture is not just a language or racial matter and that there is no one right culture!

**10. Cultural adaptation

As a group, discuss the results of your personal written assignment 5 in chapter 9. Next discuss :

• What are your experiences with different cultures? Are there any ideas or general principles that you can draw from them? How could you apply them in the future?

• How can you separate the gospel from aspects of your culture such as eating, clothing, family, individual identity?

• Who can coach you in reaching into a different culture? Often the person of peace can fulfill this role. Even people in your own neighborhood or extended family have different social practices. Ask about: how people celebrate birthdays and holidays, who are the family authorities, how they govern, and the work ethic of the family. These questions can both help you understand the people you are trying to reach and build your relationship with the person of peace.

• What are some of your cultural additions (music, order of service, etc.) to the Bible's model of the church? Are any of these essential? As a group, make a list of the absolute essentials for a church to function. Think through what you can

recall from the Bible.

• As a group, make a list of the absolute essentials for a church to function. Think through what you can recall from the Bible.

Written Discovery Assignments

In the next chapter we will look at what skills a Disciple Maker needs in a new culture and the model that Paul of Tarsus used. Do written Discovery Studies on the following three short passages.

Philippians 2:1–5 — Paul's model for cultural flexibility — how did this influence Paul's approach to cultures? How does this demonstrate Paul's application of what he learned as a disciple of Jesus?

I Corinthians 9:19–23. — Paul's orientation to different cultures

Acts 17:22–27 — Example of Paul's transcultural practice. What do you learn about Paul's contextualization and the proclamation of the truth?

Supplemental Reading:

Miraculous Movements, by Jerry Trousdale:
Ch. 10 — "The Hardest People Yield the Greatest Results"

Contagious Disciple-Making, David L. and Paul D. Watson:
• Ch. 5 — "Disciple Makers Realize the Structure of the Community Determines the Strategy Used to Make Disciples", and
• Ch. 6 — "Disciple Makers Realize Their Culture and Religious Experience Can Negatively Influence Their Disciple-Making Unless They Are Very Careful"

Chapter Twelve

What is a Disciple Maker?

As important as it is to focus on finding people of peace, developing relationships, and encouraging them to start and facilitate their discovery groups, we also need to focus on our role as Disciple Makers.

A key component of engaging people is a compatibility with the person you are trying to reach. This includes age, education, interests, and marriage status. In general, being a few years older is helpful. Having the same level of education helps communication. Sharing general interests and marital status allows deep discussions and empathetic understanding. Even though there are cultural differences, these common experiences greatly facilitate developing a long-lasting relationship with the person of peace.

These natural bridges are not absolute requirements, but in general give some guidance to looking for and training Disciple Makers. If the population that you desire to reach is young, then young men and women make the best people to send. If the population is highly educated, then sending people who are educated is pref-

erable. God is in control and can establish whatever relationships he wants, but since he created us with certain characteristics, he usually will work along those lines.

The Disciple Maker from outside the culture faces a different set of challenges and opportunities. Most cross-culture Disciple Makers stand out and attract attention. In many cultures a Westerner enjoys a special status. In open cultures, a Westerner enjoys a position of esteem. In others he is greeted with suspicion. In many poorer societies, Westerners are seen as opportunities for personal enrichment, jobs, or other opportunities. Generally, age confers respect and an older Disciple Maker's words hold more value than those of a younger.

A Disciple Maker Is Not:

Depending on our personal sense of worth, ability, or understanding we may take on more or less responsibility for the work than God expects from us. Preconceptions about the qualifications that are needed can intimidate some people. Following is a list of things that a Disciple Maker is not:

He or she is **not Superman or Super-woman**. It is likely that the Disciple Maker will see or participate in many miraculous things. But these are not the work of the Disciple Maker; rather it is the Holy Spirit who is working unseen alongside him.

There are two dangers in seeing ourselves in the role of an "anointed" minister of God or superman. The first is that our ego will swell and we can become susceptible to seeking the praises of men. The second danger is that we can begin to believe that the outcome of the disciple-making depends on us. If our person of peace fails to respond, we may try to work harder or apply pressure. Remember, we are in a partnership with Jesus and the Holy Spirit. Nothing happens apart from what God is doing in the hearts of people we are working with. Disciple-making is Jesus' project in which we are privileged to participate.

With one of the first people of peace I had, the person missed several appointments and I began to try to figure out ways to make it more convenient to meet. I rearranged locations and times. When that did not work, I doubled down on prayer. Finally, during one of those times of prayer, I heard that little voice I associate with God ask me the question, "whose project is this person?" I laughed and quit pursuing. Two days later I received a phone call from my person of peace asking to get together.

A Disciple Maker **does not need formal education**. It is not academic education that prepares a person to be a disciple maker. It is the relationship with Jesus.

Education can be an asset when working with educated people, but also a liability. Since most people are not highly educated and communication is key to building relationships, being able to talk at the same level as the people you want to reach is very important. I recall talking at a bridge inspector conference some years ago when I was working as a structural engineer. Afterwards one of the burly inspectors said, "I really liked what you were trying to tell us, but I didn't know half the words you were using."

In contrast to my technical speech in the above story was the experience at a training event I recently did in Mexico. My American colleague Kevin, was a Minnesotan farmer who spoke Spanish with a heavy Scandinavian brogue. He could not conjugate Spanish verbs. But because he used very simple language to communicate, the Mexicans understood and loved him. Even children understood him.

Education is more than vocabulary and grammar. Even the way uneducated and educated people think differs. This means that people with similar educational backgrounds and experiences generally will be best able to relate and identify with one another.

A Disciple Maker is **not given credentials** by a certifying body. A degree in discipleship does not make you a Disciple Maker. Jesus is looking for people he can work with. The most important thing you can do to become a Disciple Maker is to become a disciple of Jesus yourself. Jesus will bring people to you. Our role is to invite and guide people of peace to Jesus in the

What is A Disciple Maker?

scriptures so they can form groups where Jesus and the Holy Spirit can do the teaching.

Our youngest daughter has mental and physical delays. Intellectually she operates at about a five-year old level, so we watch a lot of "Thomas the Tank Engine" videos. One of the consistent themes of these videos and the greatest words of praise, is to be "a very useful engine." Being "a very useful disciple of Jesus" is not a bad compliment either.

A Disciple Maker is **not a CEO.** Even the executives of mission organizations are not necessarily good Disciple Makers. Seek to find your identity in being a disciple of Jesus. Beware of people exalting your success. Being a CEO of an organization does not mean you cannot be a Disciple Maker, but rather your position in society, ministry, or business is not what qualifies you.

A Disciple Maker is not **powerful or influential** in the organizational or popularity sense. Whatever power or influence that a Disciple Maker has, it flows from his relationship with Jesus. There are callings and giftings that we receive from God that the Holy Spirit will use (Romans 11:29). Growing and maturing in these callings and giftings is part of what living as a disciple is about. Obviously Peter had certain leadership gifts from the beginning, but it took intensive training by Jesus and an infilling of the Holy Spirit to render him fully effective. There are people with strong charismatic gifts, whom people tend to follow, but that in itself does not make them effective Disciple Makers.

A Disciple Maker is **not a pastor,** in the sense of the meaning in a western institutional church. In our western church model, a pastor is the head of the church organization or a sub-organization within the church, such as Senor Pastor, or Youth Pastor. The role of a pastor as we in the western church have defined it is to care for people, to teach, to preach, and to administer an organization. There is, however, another way to think about what it means to be a pastor.

I had an interesting encounter with God one morning a few years ago. A small voice inside my head asked me "What is a pastor?" I answered, "A pastor is a man who cares for the people in his church and feeds them the Word of God." The same small voice said, "I don't mean in the church, I mean among sheep in the pasture."

When I was a young man I spent a summer surveying roads on a ranch in Wyoming. During this time, I had the opportunity to talk to one ranch foreman who ran a mix of cattle and sheep. This was one of the largest ranches in the state and it had several flocks of 1000 sheep. Each flock had a Basque shepherd who was brought over from northern Spain. Each shepherd lived in a little domed trailer which was moved with the flocks to the different pastures. It seemed to me to be the most boring job in the world to sit out on the prairies of Wyoming every day and watch the sheep eat grass.

I had a couple of conversations with the rancher about shepherding.

Me: "Why do you hire Basque to be shepherds?"

"Because they are used to living in solitude and have experience working with dogs. This is a very lonely job. They come over on a two year contract and save up enough money to start a life in their country."

Me: "What are the most difficult duties of a shepherd?"

"Lambing season; with 1000 ewes, lambing is a 24 hour a day job for more than two weeks. The shepherd sleeps and eats with the sheep during this time."

Me: "What are the main duties of the shepherd?"

"The shepherd needs to keep an eye on the pasture, once it is nearing depletion, he must identify the next pasture and make plans to move them there. This can mean arranging trucks and extra help. I check on the shepherds from time to time to see what they need. We move the flocks from the prairies in the middle of the summer when the grass dries up here and truck them to the mountains until the winter starts. Then we bring them back here for the winter"

On a daily basis, every morning the shepherd needs to watch when the sheep rise up."

Me: "Why?"

"Old ewes often will not get up with the flock."

Me: "So, what difference does that make? Won't they eventually get up when they are hungry?"

"No, they will stay down and die in a few days."

Me: "What do you do?"

"See these pointy-toe boots (lifting one of his cowboy boots), you walk over and kick the ewe as hard and long as necessary until she gets up. Every morning you watch and repeat the process. After the third or fourth time, when she sees you coming, she will get up on her own. A ewe will live two or three more years with proper-attention."

So, that morning when the voice said "I don't mean in the church, I mean among sheep in the pasture," I knew first off that a true shepherd, a pastor, never feeds the sheep. His job is to get the sheep to the pasture and make sure they feed themselves. When Jesus told Peter to "feed my sheep" he would have known that that meant to make sure they were in a place where they could feed themselves. I think we in the church have spiritualized things to the point that a culture has developed in which the "sheep" cannot feed themselves.

In context of Disciple Making Movements, there is a need for shepherds, pastors, to make sure the members of a Discovery Group are studying the right passages in the Bible that both address their needs and move them along into a deeper relationship with Jesus.

As mentioned earlier, when things occur among the members of a discovery group, it may be necessary to modify what the group studies until the need is met. To assure that everyone discovers and applies the truths in the Bible, the facilitator needs learn how to pastor the people to find needed passages in the Bible to study.

What is A Disciple Maker?

This process produces people who know how to feed themselves from the Bible. This is quite different from what we find in the Western church. Comparing the two models it is easy to see why the standards and expectations of most churches are not producing strong disciples.

A Disciple Maker is not **"The Answer Person."** If you, like me, have grown up in a teaching-oriented culture, there is a trained disposition to provide the answers to a person's question. There is a sense of superiority or at least satisfaction, in being able to answer a person's question.

Good questions come along every so often. If the answer comes directly from God, it will not only change the person's life, but also the world around them.

I have been in some countries where it is considered impolite or the person would lose face, if they did not answer a stranger's question, even if the answer given is wrong. Good questions come along every so often in people's lives. If they receive the answer to these questions directly from God it will not only change the person's life, but also the world around them. Good questions are those that the person is wrestling with in their understanding of life, the scriptures, or God.

The role of the Disciple Maker is to train people to look to God for their directions and answers directly in prayer and in the Bible. A Disciple Maker needs to learn how to answer a question by asking another question or to lead the person to a passage in the Bible that pertains to their question. This is a skill that takes time to master.

A Disciple Maker is not the **Controller** of what happens in people's lives. We talked briefly in chapter 10 that Disciple-Making Movements are high accountability but low control organizations. As groups grow larger there is an increasing tendency to set up government and for the governing authorities to begin to exert more and more control. Government like this does provide stability and dependability for a group of people. In general, the larger the group, the more government is needed. The cost is that people shift their allegiance to people with the authority, the government or organization, and away from God.

Remain faithful. God will make you fruitful.

The goal of disciple-making movements is that Jesus and the Holy Spirit will be the controlling and directing authority of every disciple. This is not a new problem. We see the same tension in Israel in 1 Samuel 8 and 9, when the people asked Samuel to choose a king for them. Whatever the merits or problems of human control over a society or group of people, as Disciple Makers our role is to assure that it is Jesus and the Holy Spirit working through discovery in the Bible, are the ones in control. Our role of holding people accountable to what God is calling them to do is critical in the process.

My personal observations are that people who are internally governed by God according to the Bible, need much less external government than those who are not.

This is one reason why it is valuable and important for parents to raise children who are disciples of Jesus rather than merely believers.

Discipleship is a relational process, not an organizational or hierarchical

Finally, a Disciple Maker is **not focused on position.** This is somewhat related to not being a salaried position. I have friends who are missionaries in other countries. They have established or are part of ministries or mission bases that are intcndcd to be permanent stations in the country. These ministries serve many needed functions, but in themselves, are not adequate for the task of Disciple Making. They may train and send out Disciple Makers, but need to keep a hands-off policy as to what happens with the Discovery Groups. The Holy Spirit can best work when people know that it is he, not a human being who is in control.

In order for a movement conformable to the culture and with indigenous leadership to start and grow, it is important that the Disciple Maker have as little direct visible connection with what is happening as possible. Leaving early needs to be one of the goals of the Disciple Maker!

Jesus Modeled Leaving Early
I used to think about how much better things would have been if Jesus had been physically involved in planting and forming the first churches, clarifying things like baptism, communion, and salvation by grace

However, like everything else he calls us to do, Jesus modeled how to raise up dis-

ciples who were able to facilitate his building churches and then he modeled leaving early. As soon as he had disciples with the ability to hear from his father in heaven, he began planning and executing his exit (Matthew 16:13. –21).

Disciple-making is a relational process, not an organizational or hierarchical one. Our role is to equip the person of peace, who has the position and relationships in his or her community to function as the worker in the field. If a church emerges, then it should be one that is faithful to the Bible, but conforms in every way possible to the surrounding culture.

A Disciple Maker Is:
Having looked at what a Disciple Maker is not, let us turn the tables and look at the essential characteristics of a Disciple Maker.

First, please keep in mind that being a disciple-maker means that you are in process yourself. It does not mean that you have mastered everything. Peter provides a great example of the imperfection of a disciple in the sixteenth chapter of Matthew. After his proclamation of the identity of Jesus that earned him the name Peter, within a couple of verses Jesus calls him a son of Satan. Most of us Christians would have been so offended that we would have left and told everyone what a terrible person Jesus was. But Peter knew that it was Jesus who had the words of life, so he stayed and failed again at Jesus' trial. Yet he was there by the Sea of Galilee and became the first among equals in the leadership of the church. If you fall short, follow

What is A Disciple Maker?

Peter's example and remain faithful. God will make you fruitful.

A disciple-maker is first **a disciple of Jesus.** On a regular basis he or she personally spends time doing Discovery Studies: memorizing, discovering, applying it to his own life in obedience and telling it to other people. His readings include both Old and New Testament with thought given to understanding and applying Jesus' interpretation. He has at least one other person with whom he can discover more about God weekly and will hold him accountable to complete his promises to God.

One of the wonderful things about introducing people to the Disciple-Making Process is that each new disciple has the potential to change the world around him or her. Disciples make disciples who will continue to multiply. Jesus' original disciples changed our world. Continuing to make disciples will fulfill the Great Commission, so the entire world will hear and know.

A Big Caution: It is easy to become too busy doing things for God and fail to do the work of building and maintaining your own relationship with Jesus.

A Disciple Maker is **passionately in love with Jesus.** One of the most satisfying results of living a disciple of Jesus is that your love for him grows continually. There is a connection between love and obedience and obedience and love. As Jesus said, "If you love me you will obey my commandments," and "he who obeys my commandments abides in my love, even as I obey the commandments of my father and abide in his love." (John 14:15 and John15:10).

A Disciple Maker is a **servant of Jesus** for anyone who Jesus brings to him or sends him to (Matthew 23:11). The heart of a servant rejoices in meeting the needs of others because that is the heart of Jesus. Jesus lives to make intercession for us (Isaiah 53:12). If you enjoy helping others, then you indeed have the heart to be a servant of Jesus.

A Disciple Maker is **obedient to the Word of God and listens to the guidance of the Holy Spirit.** Everything we are doing is centered upon the words in the Bible. However, it is also important that a Disciple Maker learn to hear from God directly. Peter gave us this example in his professing that Jesus was the messiah, the Son of the living God (Matthew 16:16). Cultivating the ability to hear God takes time, but is possible for any believer to do. Be humble enough to receive God's word from unlikely sources, even as the eleven did in obeying Mary Magdalen and the other Mary (Matthew 28:10).

A Disciple Maker is a **life-long learner.** As long as we live, Jesus and his Holy Spirit will teach us though the words of the Bible. But God also teaches us through our experiences, through the words and experiences of others, and from direct revelation. There are many things that give value in our lives by being disciples of Jesus. The continual learning about God and his purposes for our lives is one of them.

A Disciple Maker is **an insider.** So how does that work when we are outsiders to most of the groups that we want to reach?

First, we need to recognize that once we move outside of our own cultural group, we will be the outsider. Our access is through the insider, the person of peace. If we want to practice facilitating, it will be with other believers in our social network.

Second, as we develop the person of peace to become a skilled facilitator and a disciple of Jesus, he or she will be the one who will be able to make disciples within his own social group. He will become a Disciple Maker as well. The most productive time a person of peace will have in reaching his own community will be in the first few months of his own his beginning in his own discovery and discipling process.

An outside Disciple Maker's time with a community is **short term.** Our goal is to see self-replicating indigenous groups that can become actual churches as God directs. Our role as an outside disciple-maker is to catalyze movements within a group of people. It is the person of peace we are working with who as a member of his Oikos, who is the long term disciple-maker.

A Disciple Maker is **one who leads through influence rather than position.** Anyone who has a clear vision and a way of accomplishing it has influence in the lives of those who have similar interests, but lack the vision and a way of accomplishing it.

Many churches believe that discipleship is of value. Yet they don't know what a disciple is, why making them is important, and how to make them. As a disciple of Jesus you have the knowledge and the vi-

sion. When you share with them, you will have influence among these people.

An "Influencer" is a person with vision and knowledge of how to accomplish it.

You will also have a lot of influence in the life of the person of peace, since you have a vision for his life and a way for him to draw closer to God who is actively calling him.

A Disciple Maker is a **lover of people.** The connection that Jesus makes about loving God with all our hearts, souls, minds, and strength; and loving our neighbor as ourselves is tied to Jesus' mission and his reason for coming to earth, as we will see in Philippians 2:1–8. One of the five disciplines of a first century disciple that Ed Gross described is imitating the rabbi. That is especially true in making Jesus' mission, his love, and his passion our own.

> No greater love has any man than he lay down his life for his friends" (
> — John 15:13

A Disciple Maker is a **catalyst to church planting.** As we saw in the discovery study on Matthew 16:13–21, the foundation that Jesus promises to build his church upon is the bedrock of disciples. Just as we are called as Disciple Makers to train those who facilitate the Discovery Process, it is this same process that we use to catalyze the planting of churches.

In other words, just as we direct a study of the Bible to discover God and Jesus, so working through the facilitator, we continue to direct other studies of the Bible, so the group can discover what it means to become a church. (See Appendix 2) In both the discovery of God and the discovery of church, we rely on the Holy Spirit to teach.

**11. Discovery Group Exercise:

Watch video 11, "Disciple Maker," by Richard Williams and 5f, the Conclusion of Ed Gross' series on First Century Discipleship (Appendix 6).

With your discovery group, complete the entire group process using the following three passages for your discovery study. The Philippians passage not only lays out the mission and sacrifice of Jesus, but it also gives a clear picture of what Paul used as the model for his own interactions with different cultures. In the 1 Corinthians passage Paul explains his general philosophy which reflects his understanding of what Jesus modeled. The Acts passage gives a graphic example of how Paul implemented his vision for reaching the lost.

As you study these three passages, in addition to the standard three discovery questions, discuss Paul's focus on Jesus as a model. What was Paul's philosophy, and how do you see it at work in his address in the Areopagus? As the final part of the study of this passage, discuss how you can apply this to your work with the people that you are trying to reach.

How did Jesus model contextualization?

> Have this mind among yourselves, which is yours in Christ Jesus, who, though he was in the form of God, did not count equality with God a thing to be grasped, but emptied himself, by taking the form of a servant, being born in the likeness of

men. And being found in human form, he humbled himself by becoming obedient to the point of death, even death on a cross.
—Philippians 2:5-8

- What do we learn about God and man?

- Describe the cross-cultural model that Paul saw in Jesus

Paul's orientation to different cultures

> For though I am free from all, I have made myself a servant to all, that I might win more of them. To the Jews I became as a Jew, in order to win Jews. To those under the law I became as one under the law (though not being myself under the law) that I might win those under the law. To those outside the law I became as one outside the law (not being outside the law of God but under the law of Christ) that I might win those outside the law. To the weak I became weak, that I might win the weak. I have become all things to all people; that by all means I might save some. I do it all for the sake of the gospel, that I may share with them in its blessings.
> — I Corinthians 9:19–23

- What do we learn about God and man?

— Paul was a disciple of Jesus. How did he apply Jesus model in Philippians 2:5–8 to his philosophy?

— What do we learn about how a disciple models his life after that of Jesus?

— What do we learn about adopting the model of Jesus into our own lives?

— What changes can you make in your own life to adopt the model of Jesus?

Acts 17:22–27 — Paul Addresses the people at the Areopagus

So Paul, standing in the midst of the Areopagus, said: "Men of Athens, I perceive that in every way you are very religious. For as I passed along and observed the objects of your worship, I found also an altar with this inscription, 'To the unknown god.' What therefore you worship as unknown, this I proclaim to you. The God who made the world and everything in it, being Lord of heaven and earth, does not live in temples made by man,

nor is he served by human hands, as though he needed anything, since he himself gives to all mankind life and breath and everything. And he made from one man every nation of mankind to live on all the face of the earth, having determined allotted periods and the boundaries of their dwelling place, that they should seek God, and perhaps feel their way toward him and find him. Yet he is actually not far from each one of us,

In this passage we see one application of Paul's philosophy.

- What do we learn about God and man?

- What do we learn about how Paul researched a new culture?

- How did Paul apply what he learned?

- How did Paul balance contextualization with truth?

- How can we apply this to our own outreach?

What is A Disciple Maker?

In your Discovery Group discuss how to develop a relationship with people of peace. Then discuss how to guide them to starting their own discovery group.

Written Discovery Assignment

Complete two Discovery Studies —

2 Timothy 2:1–7; 14–16 — Key to replication
John 15:1–11 — Call to be fruitful

Look at:
Genesis 1:1–25 — How to establish a foundation

Supplemental Reading:

Miraculous Movements, Jerry Trousdale

- Ch. 7 — "Simple Churches, Dramatic Transformation, Rapid Replication"

Contagious Disciple-Making, David L. and Paul D. Watson

- Ch. 2 — "Disciple Makers Deculture, Not Contextualize, the Gospel"

- Ch. 16 — "Establish Churches"

Are you a Christian or a Disciple? by Ed Gross Ch. 6 — "Jesus and Evangelism,"

Chapter Thirteen

Replication and Getting Started

We are at the end of the beginning. The question is what do you do now? What should be your next steps?

Purpose of Planning

We have talked about developing action plans of various types during this study. It is not so much the written plan that matters as it is the mental process you go through to develop it.

In one essay about military strategy and planning it was said that no battle has ever been won without a plan, but once the battle starts the plan goes out the window and the successful general must adapt quickly. Under stress, any logical plan is better than no plan.

So it is with these plans of yours. Without plans of: with whom, when, and how you will share a passage; without a plan for prayer; and without a plan for implementing what you have learned, the chances of success are small. Once implemented, plans give you a basis to start but they will need to be updated regularly as the unexpected happens.

We have been looking at the "Discovering Disciple-Making" series so that you can develop as Disciple Makers (See appendix 2). The passages you have been studying would not mean much to anyone who was not already a believer and follower of Jesus Christ, so as you move forward, take a look at the first discovery series, "Discovering God".

Finally, we will start applying what you have already learned with people who are not yet believers. For this last study we will look at developing an implementation plan that you can use with your Disciple-Making group in the future.

Multiplication and Replication:

In a conversation with Roy Moran the pastor of Shoal Creek Church near Kansas City, Missouri, he explained the difference between multiplication and replication. Multiplication implies a maturation process that takes time. Animals multiply and people multiply. Replication on the other hand is what viruses do. From the moment a virus is created, it is looking for another cell to enter and cause a replication of the virus.

Once I adjusted my initial revulsion about tying spiritual principles to organic concepts, particularly viruses, I was able to see the difference in the scriptures. The church in Antioch sent out Paul after it had developed leadership and structure. The result was multiplication, planting more churches. In John's account of the first disciples, the first thing Andrew and Philip did was to go and call others to follow Jesus, replication. Churches multiply. Disciples replicate. The rate of growth is entirely different. Disciple-making has the significant advantage of apparent miraculous growth in comparison to anything possible with church multiplication.

Another example of replication is Saul of Tarsus, who was blinded on the road so that he might receive new sight in Damascus. Following a few days with the disciples there, he began to proclaim that Jesus was the Son of God (Acts 9:20). Replication is most robust during the first hours, days, and weeks of a disciples life because he is in contact with the greatest number of people who don't yet know the Messiah.

Churches multiply, but disciples replicate.

There is another aspect to replication verses multiplication that is worth considering. Multiplication is a matter of numbers, whereas replication is a matter of DNA. The multiplication of numbers does not in itself guarantee we will see the same life replicated in future generations.

Maintaining fidelity to the basic principles requires that people regularly complete all of the critical components of the Discovery Process. They are: obedience, committing to memory the scripture stories to tell others, knowledge of the Old Testament and understanding Jesus' teachings about it, adoption of Jesus' mission of reconciling the world to God, and the making of disciples of Jesus.

It is easier to count numbers than it is to determine fidelity to being disciples of Jesus. In Paul's second letter to Timothy that you will study in this chapter, Paul writes with the expectation that his time of ministry on this earth is coming to a close. Timothy, who is his closest associate, disciple, and personal friend, is receiving what might be Paul's final counsel. Paul is concerned that the work that he has accomplished would not perish with Timothy. Replication of the same DNA depends on the character, faithfulness, and training of the people who will carry on. It is having the same Disciple Making DNA which allows the Holy Spirit to use men and women to complete Jesus' Great Commission.

Developing Faithful Men and Women Who Can Teach Others

Developing a relationship of accountability with the person of peace from the beginning is important. As the relationship develops, taking note of both his character and abilities is a continual part of the training process. Notice how he responds to the challenges he faces, how he interacts with you and other people, and what he is learning.

In the previous chapter, the characteristics of a Disciple Maker are also the characteristics and attitudes that you are looking for and are trying to develop in your person of peace. Once the new Discovery Group is underway, your first goal in training the facilitator is to encourage growth in each of these areas:

- Be a disciple of Jesus

- Be passionately in love with Jesus

- Be a servant of Jesus

- Be obedient to Jesus' commands

- Be continuously learning

- Be influential

- Be a lover of people

- Be a catalyst for planting churches

As Jesus shared in the parable of the talents (Matthew 25:14–30), each person is given a different quantity of abilities. Part of your job as a Disciple Maker is to recognize the facilitator's abilities and to help him or her use what he has to the best advantage. In this parable the servant who was punished, was punished for his failure to use what he had, not for what he lacked. Like the parable, if a person refuses to extend themselves, investing time in them is of little use. Instead invest in people who are willing to develop the talent they have and are willing to step out and invest what they learn with others.

Critical Elements of Multiplication and Replication

To assure that groups both multiply and replicate each facilitator must faithfully follow all of the key parts of the discovery-group process. It is a serious mistake to leave out any of the three critical parts of the Discovery Process at the beginning

thinking that they can be added back in later.

Without telling the passage with others there is no replication and without obedience there is little spiritual growth and personal transformation. These are the elements that transform a Bible study into a Disciple-Making Process and enable the members of the group to become disciples of Jesus and fulfill the Great Commission.

When a group of non-believers is just beginning, obedience may be sporadic, but the facilitator needs to hold to the standard. It takes about four or five times using the Discovery Process to become comfortable with it. A good thing about non-believers is that they usually don't have preconceptions. In this regard, believers who have been in Bible studies may prove to be more difficult, as they have to unlearn and adjust their expectations.

When you meet with the facilitator to prepare for the next study, have him give you an update on what happened in the Discovery Group the last meeting and assure that the three critical elements of the Discovery Process (memorize, obey, tell) are adhered to consistently.

You need to know if there are any difficulties that arise in the group and any questions that the facilitator may have. You should learn the names of each of the people in the facilitator's Discovery Group. If there are specific personal needs in the group, you should learn about them as well. Prayer is a critical part of this process and praying together with the person you are training and mentoring for the needs of the people in his group should become part of your training time. Even before he has discovered the need for prayer himself, you can model it for your person of peace by praying for the needs that he relates to you.

Moving past the first generation of discovery groups, it is important to assure that the next two generations remain faithful to the basics of the process. When the person of peace you have been mentoring, starts training and mentoring other facilitators, he needs to brief you on what the other facilitators are doing with their groups. This is in addition to reporting about his own group. Just as you are assuring compliance with the critical elements of his group, you should have him brief you on what he has learned from the facilitators he is mentoring and that they in turn are doing the same. Tracking the compliance of three generations of discovery groups is the easiest way to assure that groups carry the same DNA are equipped to continue to multiply.

Another way to maintain fidelity of the groups is to make occasional visits. These should be very infrequent. Your role is simply to be an observer. People in the group should see you simply as an interested visitor. While you are there, note the dynamics of the group. Is everyone participating? How is the facilitator doing? Is he using questions to draw people out? Is he assuring that the main lessons in the passage are being discovered? (These major points should be discussed in your meeting with the facilitator before each of his Discovery Group meetings.)

After visiting the discovery group, debrief and share your observations. Ask the facilitator to evaluate what you observed. Are there scripture passages that can be used to give understanding? Together decide what he can do to improve the dynamics of his discovery group. Remember this is a collaborative process. Especially as you are starting, you will both be learning together.

**12. Discovery Group Exercise: 2 Timothy 2:1–7; 14–16

Watch videos 12a, "Lack of Obedience" and 12c, "Multiplication," by Jim Yost (Appendix 6).

In your group, do another discovery study focusing on 2 Timothy 2:1–7; 14–16.

In addition to the questions about God and man, discuss how this advice to Timothy would apply to what you need to do. Read through the following passages and discuss their application to training a new facilitator as well as your own group's goals.

- Matthew 13:3–23 — Sower of seed, pathway, rocky, thorns, good ground

- Matthew 21:19 — Cursing the fig tree

- Matthew 13:31–33 — Mustard seed

- Colossians 1:6–7 — Epaphras a faithful brother

- John 1:35–51 — Come and see

Ephesians 6:10–20 — Spiritual Armor — (This is a good addition to your own group's prayer).

Role Play: Review the Kingdom Circles and role play explaining the Kingdom of

God as Jesus' message to a potential person of peace. On a piece of paper, draw the circles as you explain Jesus' message.

Develop your skills as a facilitator
As you conclude your own Discovery Group time, take a few minutes to discuss what you have learned about facilitating a discovery group.

The first obstacle in the Discovery Process is becoming comfortable with both the order of the process and in your ability to facilitate groups. Helping each other improve in facilitating a Discovery Group and understanding group dynamics is essential if you are going to lead a group of not-yet believers yourself or train a person of peace.

The Disciple-Making Movement Cycle

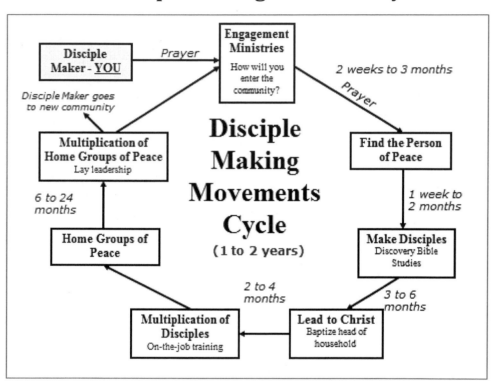

Fig 13.1 — The Disciple-Making Movement Cycle — *Cityteam, International*

Become a Disciple Maker
Making disciples is a process that involves several steps. The first one in which you are engaged is to live as a disciple yourself.

Where is Jesus Working?
The second step is to find out where Jesus intends to visit; what group that he is sending you to. This is accomplished both by prayer and investigation. The

Community Prayer Guide you have worked on is the tangible fruit of this work.

Engagement Ministries
The third step is the engagement of the people you want to reach. The final question in the Discovery Process, "Do you know anyone who needs help?" is part of this step. This is effective when reaching neighbors, family members, or

coworkers. It can be applied to reach into any community of people you are trying to reach.

Reaching out to a group with whom you do not already have some social contact, requires initiating some type of engagement ministry. Many of these ministries focus on social services, medicine, language acquisition, educational help, etc. One of my colleagues is assisting an immigrant family who is having medical problems.

If there are already engagement ministries involved with the people you want to reach, joining either as a volunteer or disciple trainer of the engagement ministry staff is the quickest way to put your Disciple-Making skills to work.

Find a Person of Peace

The next step is to find a person of peace. As Jesus instructed us, we are to pray that the Lord of the harvest sends workers into the field. As we have discussed in Chapters 8 and 9, this is the critical step prior to finding a person of peace.

Starting Discovery Studies

In Chapter 10, we discussed that the next critical step in the process is to coach the person of peace in starting a Discovery Group in his field; which is his family or social network. This will involve developing his or her skills in facilitating a discovery group.

Making Disciples

The process of the group member coming to Christ is part of the Discovery Studies. Your role as the disciple-maker is to coach and work through the person of peace.

Lead to Christ - Baptism

Baptism is a critical step and is intimately connected to being a disciple. It marks the point at which a non-believer publically declares himself to be a believer and full disciple of Jesus. Depending on the culture this can put people at risk of retribution from their native culture. This is true even in Europe, the United States, and Canada. It can mean social shunning, physical attack, or even death. Normally, the Disciple Maker would baptize the head of the Discovery Group and coach that person to baptize the remainder of the group. Baptism normally occurs as the result of personal "I will" or corporate "we will" statements.

Making Disciple Makers

At this point the group should be studying the "Discovering Obedience" series and then move on to the "Church Planting" series. During this time, the members of the group will both begin to develop an identity as a group and develop more expertise in initiating other groups.

Your relationship with the person of peace will change throughout the entire process. As he matures, you may meet less frequently. As the group progresses through the multiplication step, he should be developing his own team of facilitators.

Groups and Churches

It is normal and desirable that some of the home groups will develop into churches. As this happens they may combine or meet together periodically. Our role as Disciple Maker with the groups and churches is strictly relational and confined to the emerging leaders of the group.

In open societies home churches of 20 to 40 people are generally the most sustainable number of people. This size of group normally has enough social interaction to support growing families yet still fits into a home. Over time, members of groups that do not reach this size often drift away looking for a more diverse fellowship. As long as the members take with them the same DNA of a discovery group, each one can start other groups which utilize the same principles of disciple-making and replication.

In societies with significant levels of persecution typically will have smaller numbers to minimize detection. Greater persecution means smaller size groups.

Moving from a Discovery Group format to a house church format can be accomplished in several ways. Let the groups work out their own method of transitioning and forming a service based upon what they discover in the scriptures. Appendix 2 contains lists of scriptures that will provide insight and guidance in transitioning from a discovery group to a church.

It is important that these new churches look for opportunities to multiply by starting other churches. Multiplication may slow down, but it should not stop when a group becomes a church.

Multiplication and Sending

If the Discovery Group Process has been diligently followed and members have been faithful to share and apply what they have learned, they should arrive at the point of both reengaging their own community and sending out others to adjoining communities. These other communities should be identified in the Community Prayer Guide that you should be regularly using for prayer and updating.

Getting Started — Engaging the Lost

The passages that you have been studying in this book have been selected to help you to discover the Disciple-Making Process. Sharing these passages with believers is a good recruiting tool to find people who can join you in becoming and making disciples. However, to engage those who are not yet believers or followers, you will need to know and be able to share some more basic passages.

When God began giving mankind his revelation, he started with the words in Genesis. Starting here has proven to be very productive in making disciples. Shortcutting the process and going immediately to the gospels or epistles may rapidly produce converts or believers, but rarely provides sufficient foundation for people to become productive disciples of Jesus. The stories in the Old Testament also have a universal appeal, so are excellent ways to build bridges into people's lives.

As you and the members in your Discovery Group proceed to reach out to others, you will need to have a foundational knowledge of a few key Old Testament passages. That means that you need to include them in your personal and group Discovery Studies.

Impact of Old Testament Discovery
I have been deeply impacted by my studies of the Discovering God series. Moving

beyond knowing and learning about the stories of the Old Testament, to making them part of my own identity has enriched my reading of all the other parts of the Bible.

Understanding the identity of Jesus and the orientation of writers of the Epistles has its foundation in the stories of the first five books of the Bible. Having made some of the stories part of me, I now not only have an understanding of God's purposes, but also personally identify with those purposes. Jesus' purpose of reconciling the world to himself and his father has become my purpose. When Paul says that it is no longer he that lives, but that Christ lives in him, I also share those sentiments and feelings.

In the seven appendices that follow, there are resources for you to use. The first one is a format for implementation workshops. This document like all of those in the appendices is meant as a source of suggestions and as a guide. You should use these workshops as opportunities to transition your own Discovery Group from a training group to actually beginning to engage in reaching the lost. Feedback from your outreach, prayer, and strategizing, should be regular parts of your meeting times together.

It is important that the disciple-making efforts of your Discovery Group continue on beyond the training phase. Doing this requires implementing what you have learned by reaching out to others and looking for people of peace. Networking disciple-making Discovery Groups

together is valuable for both prayer support and counsel when encountering challenging situations.

The phenomenal success of disciple-making movements in Sub-Saharan Africa has been the result of the partnership of more than 300 churches and ministries in more than 19 countries. There are great advantages to linking up with other groups or organizations who are engaged in initiating disciple-making movements. Even though the Discovery Process is simple, it is not easy. It takes commitment, effort, flexibility, as well as knowledge and experience. Working with others of like mind and commitment will make a difference.

**13. Discovery Group Exercise: John 15:1–11

Watch video 1, "Cityteam's Animated Overview" (Appendix 6).

The final study for your introduction to Disciple-Making is John 15:1–11, in which Jesus strongly links abiding in him with fruitfulness and Disciple-Making. Nowhere in the gospels does Jesus specifically define what he means by fruitfulness, but here it is obvious that it characterizes the life of all of his disciples. It is abundant and it abides, enduring forever.

With your group discuss what it might mean for you to be fruitful.

Engagement Partnerships

If you wish to engage a large people-group, assembling or becoming a part of team of people who engage their physical needs is best.

What other ministries or groups are working with the people you want to reach? Write names and contact information:

Establish Prayer Networks

Of primary importance is to seek to establish prayer networks. The best people to engage in this work are people who have a burden for the particular group that you are trying to reach. Join with other groups who are working to reach the same or similar groups of people to pray regularly.

Who can you invite to begin praying for you and the people you want to reach? This can be individuals or existing prayer groups. For instance you may want to approach your church's mission board or prayer ministry. Write their names and contact information.

Starting to Reach Out

At this point you and your small group should be prepared to focus on fulfilling the Great Commission by making disciples wherever you go. When you have completed this lesson, take some time to discuss how you will implement what you have learned. Read the "Great Commission Outreach Guidelines" in Appendix 1. Schedule your next meeting to begin finding people of peace.

Written Assignment: As you begin reaching out, start with the Discovering God Scripture Series in Appendix 2 and be prepared to share these passages from memory. Additional and specialized study passages can be found in *Appendices 2 and 7.*

REVIEW: It is by cooperating with the Holy Spirit and applying the five disciplines of a first century disciple which are given in Chapter 2 and below, that we arrive at the point where we become fruitful in making disciples who make other disciples. All of this flows naturally as we learn and teach others how to obey Jesus' commandments and teachings.

Since one of the roles of the Holy Spirit is to bring to mind all that Jesus has taught, we must have intimate knowledge of all of Jesus' major teachings.

FIVE DISCIPLINES OF A DISCIPLE

A disciple of Jesus would endeavor to:

1. **Obey** all of the commands of Jesus

2. Have an intimate knowledge of and ability to **tell others from memory** all of the key teachings and commands of Jesus.

3. Have a solid knowledge of the **Old Testament** and to know and accept all of Jesus' teaching about it.

4. **Imitate and conform** every aspect of the disciple's life to that of Jesus. This especially means adopting Jesus' mission as the disciple's own. This will result in seeing, treating, and speaking with people and God as Jesus did.

5. **Make disciples** of all the ethnic groups in the world including your own. And as Jesus commanded his disciples, baptizing them, and teaching them to obey all the commandments he gave them.

Jesus limited our role in the Disciple-Making Process to assisting the Holy Spirit by baptizing, teaching obedience, and being a brother and servant to others who are called to be disciples of Jesus (John 14:26, Matthew 23:8–11).

So what are Jesus' major teachings? We often refer to the words written in the Bible as the word of God. Jesus is also referred to as "The" Word of God. Obviously they are not identical, but they are intimately connected. God the Father is the Author, and Jesus the Son is both the medium of communication and the incarnation of the word of God. Jesus, "the words that you have heard from me are not mine, but the Father's who sent me." Because they are the Father's words, all the words of the Bible are intimately Jesus' as well (cf. John 14:24)..

To live in the kingdom of God under the lordship of Jesus requires a foundation built upon the words of the Old Testament. To properly do this we must understand all of the teaching of the Old Testament through the lens of Jesus' teachings. This is the third discipline of a first century disciple of Jesus. Guiding people through the Old Testament to establish a foundation then, is an essential requirement for being a disciple-maker.

The fourth discipline, to imitate and conform to Jesus life cannot be better described than in the John 15 passage you have just studied. If we abide in him, he will abide in us. If we obey his commandments, we will abide in his love. In all of this we will come to abide in the Father's love. In John 14 we learned that the Holy Spirit will be in us and the Father and Jesus will make their home in us.

This is the grace and power that works in and through us to transform and accomplish the purposes of God in us and in the world. We are indeed "saved by grace through faith" (Ephesians 2:8). That grace both transforms us and enables us to work in an intimate partnership with Jesus and the Holy Spirit in establishing a bedrock, a foundation of disciples upon which Jesus can build his church.

We learned in the study of Matthew 16 that his church will attack and prevail against even the gates of hell. We also learned that as disciples who learn to hear directly from Jesus' heavenly father, we have tremendous authority both here on earth and in heaven. In the last verses of Matthew 28, we learn the reason that we have such authority is because Jesus is with us always until the end of the age and he has been given all authority both in heaven and earth.

Discovery Studies:

In Appendix 2 are lists of the six different Discovery Studies which are arranged in order that they would normally be studied:

Discovering God

Discovering Obedience

Discovering Church Planting

Discovering Equipping Leaders

Discovering Leadership

Discovering Disciple-Making

For most people whose orientation is to believe in one God, such as those who come from a Jewish, Christian, or Muslim background, the standard "Discovering God" series gives a solid basis to understand God and his purpose in sending his son Jesus. However, for those who believe in pantheism or polytheism, such as Hindus, Shinto, Mormons, Animists and New Age believers, extra passages about God's unity and distain for polytheism may need to be incorporated. A couple variations on the "Discovering God" series are included for Hindu and young urban professionals.

Part of your planning should be to evaluate the people you are guiding to a relationship with Jesus. Are there other passages that they should study that will give them the ability to fully discover God? The standard "Discovering God" series is an excellent place to begin and if you don't know what else to add or omit, you will have reasonable success using it.

The question now is how do you plan on growing as a disciple of Jesus and making other disciples? Take a few minutes to review the first Appendix, "Implementation Workshops." The most important thing to keep in mind in context of the Great Commission is that it is your growing relationship with Jesus as his disciple that will enable you to best fulfill it.

The minimum size of your group should be two people. If you are married, your spouse counts as the second person. The optimum group size is six to eight people.

This will provide prayer, personal and outreach support, discernment, and continuity in making a disciple of the person of peace in case you are not available for a time.

Engagement Partnerships

If you wish to engage a large people-group, assembling or becoming a part of team of people who engage them is best. These teams need to pray for these people, meet some of their needs, and get to know them individually. Look for other ministries who are reaching this group of people and form partnerships with them. As you are able and are open, introduce them to disciple-making concepts. It is valuable if you establish a communications and accountability process with these networks of partnerships.

Establish Prayer Networks

Of primary importance is to seek to establish prayer networks. The best people to engage in this work are people who have a burden for the particular group that you are trying to reach. Join with other groups who are working to reach the same or similar groups of people to pray regularly.

Starting to Reach Out

At this point you and your small group should be prepared to focus on fulfilling the Great Commission by making disciples wherever you go. The Outreach Guidelines in Appendix 1 provide assistance to help you get started. As you begin reaching out start with the Discovering God Series in Appendix 2 and be prepared to share these passages from memory.

- Genesis 1:1–25 — God Creates the World

- Genesis 2:4–24 — God Creates Man and Woman

- Genesis 3:1–13 — Man and Woman Eat the Fruit

- Genesis 3:14–24 — God's Curses

Supplemental Reading:

There are a small, but growing, number of books addressing Disciple-Making Movements. I have found the following four to be extremely important. I have included quotations from each of them in this book to give you an idea of their content as well as to share a few of their important insights.

Miraculous Movements, How Hundreds of Thousands of Muslims Are Falling in Love with Jesus, by Jerry Trousdale, Thomas Nelson Publishing, ISBN: 978-1-4185-4728-8

Contagious Disciple-Making, Leading Others on a Journey of Discovery, by the father-son team of David L. and Paul D. Watson, Thomas Nelson Publishing ISBN: 9780529112200.

Are You a Christian or a Disciple?, Rediscovering and Renewing New Testament Discipleship, by Edward N. Gross, Xulon Press, ISBN:9781629523491

A Movement of God Among the Bhojpuri of North India, David L. and Paul D. Watson (p. 697ff "Perspectives on the World Christian Movement, A reader, 4th edition (Winter, RD and Hawthorne, SC editors). William Cary Library, ISBN 978-0-87808-390-9

This last article is from the textbook used in the course, "Perspectives on the World Christian Movement." For the person who wants to understand the basics of missions, I recommend that you register and take this course. It was through one of these training courses that my wife Cindy and I were introduced to David Watson's work in India.

The course covers in fifteen lessons: the Biblical perspective of missions, the historical perspective of missions, the cultural perspective, as well as the strategic perspective.

You can find information about online and local offerings of the course at: www.perspectives.org

Additional books:

These following three books provide additional insights in Disciple-Making and I recommend that you read each as you have time.

Poised for Harvest, Braced for Backlash, Birthing New Testament Movements When Jesus Disrupts the Systems, by Timothy Miller

The Father Glorified, True Stories of God's Power through Ordinary People, by Patrick Robertson and David Watson, with Gregory C. Benoit. Is filled with extended testimonies.

Spent Matches: Igniting the Signal Fire for the Spiritually Dissatisfied (Refraction), by Roy Moran.

Spent Matches explores the possibility that a few paradigm shifts within the church might make the difference between extinction and effectiveness.

Appendix 1:
Great Commission Outreach Guidelines

Purpose:
Everything you have learned so far has been to prepare you to fulfill Jesus' final command as outlined in Matthew 28:16–20. Your group's focus should now shift from preparation to implementation, from becoming disciples to making disciples who in turn can make disciples. Just as the Apostles operated in teams, so you should continue to operate as a team.

The Discovery Process is simple, but implementing it takes commitment, prayer, work, and flexibility. As you have learned, it is a partnership with Jesus by means of his word, and the Holy Spirit. Your responsibilities are limited and well defined: pray the Lord of the Harvest to send laborers; as you go, with prayer and blessings, look for and find them; bring your person of peace to Jesus and his word where Jesus promises to be there (two or more gathered), teach him or her to teach his group to obey all that Jesus' Spirit commands them.

Goal:
That you and your group will find one or more people of peace who will become the worker or workers to lead his or their family and or social group into the kingdom of God and will in turn replicate by reaching others within their communities.

General: Plan on a minimum of 12 to 14 implementation sessions with your group of Disciple Makers. The meeting times and dates need to fit your schedules. I suggest meeting bi-weekly or monthly to give yourselves time to implement what your group decides to do. Following are only suggestions, but may give you a place to start your own planning.

First meeting: Determine the group of people you want to reach. Complete or review your "Community Prayer Guide" that you should have started during this training (see Appendix 4). Determine what additional information you need about this group and how you will obtain it. If you have sufficient information, review the six Discovery Series in Appendix 2 and determine what series of scriptures would work best to engage them. Depending on the underlying belief system of the group you are trying to engage, you may need to modify the discovery passages. (In addition to the standard Discovering God series, there are some topical studies that can be used to engage people which are available in Appendix 7.)

Sample Meeting Agenda:

Follow the five part Discovery Group Guide:

1. **COMMUNITY — Opening questions:** In addition to focusing on your individual needs, include questions about finding people of peace and developments in the new discovery groups. This builds strong relationships with your team with a focus on your mission.

2. **SHARE EXPERIENCE – Review Questions** is the place you can report progress with reaching people of peace as well as each member's "I will" and the groups "we will" statements. If there are difficulties in finding or working with people of peace, the group can work out solutions or approaches.

3. **DISCOVERY – Bible Study** should have two parts. The first is a review of one of the passages from the training seminar. The second is a full discovery study on one of the passages you have selected to connect with people in your selected outreach community.

> With **the review passage**, (from the Discovering Disciple-Making series) focus on how you can implement this passage in your own lives as well as reaching others.

> With **the outreach passage**, (from the discovering God series) identify the essential elements of the passage, so that the facilitator (person of peace) of the community Discovery Group can be prepared to draw out his group members. These leading questions assure that the basics in each passage will be discovered. This is especially important as the new Discovery Group starts.

4. **OBEDIENCE** — is time for brain storming and to make personal commitments on how to reach your target community. Don't neglect your own growth as disciples. Develop "I will" and "we will" statements from each of the Discovering God passages you study.

5. **OUTREACH**, is the time to discuss your plans to share the passage you are memorizing and make plans to better connect with your outreach community. Identify the needs and ways to meet those needs is a good place to start.

Close your time with a time of prayer for the needs of your group and particularly for the needs of the community you are trying to reach.

As you continue to meet you may need to adjust the time and frequency of your meetings. Always confirm the next meeting with everyone.

Appendix 2: The Discovery Series

When developing lists of scripture passages to study, there is no one-size-fits-all approach. There are topical studies such as marriage, parenting, and finances in Appendix 7. The following sets of basic Discovery Studies have been field tested. They have been adequate in guiding people from most backgrounds to discover Jesus and provide direction to help them form a church as well as reaching out to replicate the process in other places.

The following sets of passages are to be used with the Discovery Group Process which is outlined in Appendix 5 and explained in Chapters 3 and 4. They are designed to move people step by step into a deeper understanding of God's kingdom and purposes. . In general, they are designed to take a group of people with no belief in Jesus and by means of a Biblically based discipling process, lead them into a personal relationship with Jesus and then on to forming a church and continuing to reach out to other groups and cultures.

All of these series except: Discovering Spiritual Community, Hindu Passages, Shame and Honor, and Disciple-Making were developed and used by permission of Cityteam International and are available at http://www.Cityteam.org/dmm/.

Discovering God: (Focuses on Old Testament leading into the gospels) — The initial process of discipling people to Jesus begins with discovering God using select passage from Genesis through Acts 2. Depending on the background of the group of people being reached, these lists may vary somewhat from the list of passages included here, but the goal remains the same, establish the practice of applying and sharing what the members of the group discover in what they read, and laying a foundation of understanding for the mission and accomplishments of Jesus.

Discovering God: This series is the standard one used for reaching people from a monotheistic world view such as Jews, Muslims, and cultural Christians. It has proved effective in most of these cultures.

Discovering Spiritual Community: An alternate series for college students and young professionals. It appeals to those looking for a sense of community and family. This series was developed by Andrew Hocking.

Discovering God – Hindu Passages: This series was developed by Roy Wingerd and is commonly used in India where polytheism is the prevalent mindset

Shame and Honor: These three lists of passages are useful to reach people with Islamic Shame and Honor based world views. The first two lists have a bridge passage from the Quran.

Discovering Obedience: (Focuses on the gospels) Once a person has completed the Discovering God series and has committed his or her life to becoming His disciple, the second step is to discover what it means it means to live in obedience to Jesus.

Discovering Church Planting — (Covers material from both the Old and New Testament) — This series leads to a discovery of the essential components of becoming a church. It is this series that will lead many groups to actually become simple churches.

Discovering Equipping Leaders — (Uses a broad spectrum of scriptures from both the Old and New Testaments) — This series presents Jesus as the model of leadership in order to form leadership skills.

Discovering Leadership — (Focuses on Matthew) — This series is designed to prepare people to fulfill the Great Commission

Discovering Disciple-Making — This is the series that you have covered in this book.

Discovering God

God Creates — Genesis 1:1–25

God Creates Man and Woman — Genesis 2:4–24

Man and Woman Eat the Fruit — Genesis 3:1–13

God's Curses — Genesis 3:14–24

God Regrets His Creation — Genesis 6:5–8

God Saves Noah and His Family — Genesis 6:9–8:14

God's Covenant with Noah — Genesis 8:15–9:17

God's Covenant with Abram — Genesis 12:1–8, 15:1–6, 17:1–7

Abraham Gives His Son as an Offering — Genesis 22:1–19

God Spares His People — Exodus 12:1–28

The Commands of God — Exodus 20:1–21

The Sin Offering — Leviticus 4:1–35

God's Righteous Servant — Isaiah 53

Jesus is Born — Luke 1:26–38, 2:1–20

Jesus is Baptized — Matthew 3; John 1:29–34

Jesus is Tested — Matthew 4:1–11

Jesus and the Religious Leader — John 3:1–21

Jesus and the Samaritan Woman — John 4:1–26, 39–42

Jesus and the Paralyzed Man — Luke 5:17–26

Jesus Calms the Storm — Mark 4:35–41

Jesus and the Man with Evil Spirits — Mark 5:1–20

Jesus Raises a Man from the Dead — John 11:1–44

Jesus Talks about His Betrayal and the Covenant — Matthew 26:17–30

Jesus is Betrayed and Faces Trial — John 18:1–19:16

Jesus is Crucified — Luke 23:32–56

Jesus is Resurrected — Luke 24:1–35

Jesus Appears to the Disciples and Ascends to Heaven — Luke 24:36–53

Enter the Kingdom of God — Acts 2:25–41

Justified by God's Grace — Romans 3:21–31

Discovering Spiritual Community – Young Professionals

Genesis 2:4–25 God Creates People

Genesis 3:1–24 God hold People responsible

Genesis 12:1–8, 15:1–6, 17:1–7 Covenant with Abraham

Exodus 1:1–14, 2:11–25 God hears the Defenseless

Exodus 3:1–22 God Responds to the Defenseless

Exodus 14:5–31 God defends his people

Leviticus 19:1–18 The Commands of God

Nehemiah 9:5–31 The People take Responsibility

Isaiah 61:1–9 The Promise of a New Day

Jeremiah 31:31–34 God's Covenant with People

Luke 4:14–21 Jesus announces His purpose

John 3:1–21 Jesus and the Religious Leader

John 4:1–26, 39–42 Jesus and the Samaritan Woman

Mark 6:30–44 Jesus Feeds the Five Thousand

Luke 5:17–26 Jesus and the Paralyzed Man

Matthew 22:34–40 The Great Commandment

Matthew 26:17–30 Jesus Tells of his Covenant

Matthew 26:47–57 Jesus is Arrested

Luke 23:32–56 Jesus is Crucified

Luke 24:1–35 Jesus is Resurrected

Acts 1:3–11 Jesus Ascends to Heaven

Acts 2:22–41 People respond to the Message

Acts 2:42–47 People create new community

Appendix 2 — Discovery Series

Discovering God – Hindu Passages

Genesis 1:1–25 God created the world

Genesis 2:4–24 God created man and woman

Genesis 3:1–24 Man and woman disobey God

Genesis 3:14–24 Judge disobedience

Genesis 6:5–8:14 Grief - disobedience

Genesis 6:9–18; 7:11–2 The flood

Genesis 8:13, 18–22 God saves Noah

Genesis 12:1–8, 17:1–8 Abram

Genesis 18:9–14; 17–19 promised son

Genesis 21:1–7; 22:1–19 The test

Exodus 1:7–14; 2:23–25Slavery

Exodus 12:21–23; 29–32God rescues

Exodus 20:1–21Gods commandments

Leviticus 4:1–35 Offerings for sins

Judges 2:10–23 Continual sin

Isaiah 53:1–9 Suffering Saviour

Matthew 1:1; 1–17 Genealogy

Luke 1:26–38 Angel appears to Mary

Matthew 1:18–25 Angel appears Luke 2:1–20 Jesus is born

Matthew 3:1–6; 13–17 baptism

John 1:29–34 John testifies

John 3:1–21 Jesus to save the world

John 4:1–26, 39–42 Jesus Messiah

Luke 5:17–26 Jesus' authority to heal

Mark 4:35–41 Authority over nature

Mark 5:1–20 Authority over spirits

John 11:1–44 Jesus Authority over death

Matthew 26:17–30; Jesus' betrayal

John 18:1–19:16 Jesus is betrayed

Luke 23:32–56; 24:1–12 Resurrected

Luke 24: 36–53 Jesus back to life

Acts 2:25–47 Becoming believers

Great Commission Disciple Making

Shame and Honor Bible and Quran Passages

From Randy Torpen

- The Fall   AQ Al Aaraf 7:9–27, Genesis 3
- Jacob getting rid of foreign gods   Genesis 35:1–5
- The Bronze Serpent   Numbers 21:4–9
- The temptation of Isa by Satan   Matthew 4:1–11
- Isa exalted in the AQ   Al Imran 3:45–55
- Isa casting out a demon in the synagogue Mark 1:21–28
- An evil spirit bringing 7 more   Matthew 12:43–45
- The Storm   Mark 4:34–41
- The Demoniac   Mark 5:1–20
- The woman with the flow of blood   Mark 5:25–34
- The Syrophoenician Woman   Mark 7:24–37
- The Widow of Nain   Luke 7:11–17
- Lazareth raised   John 11:1–44
- The Sons of Sceva   Acts 19:11–20

Shame/Honor stories to Jesus

- Adam and Eve   Al Aaraf 7:11–26, Gen 3
- God Promising Honor to Abraham   Genesis 12:1–3
- The Sinful Woman in Simon's house   Luke 7:36–50
- The Priest and the Samaritan   Luke 10:25–37
- Mary & Martha   Luke 10:38–42
- The Prodigal   Luke 15:11–32
- The Rich Man and Lazarus   Luke 16:19–31
- The Pharisee and the Tax Collector   Luke 18:9–14
- The Sheep and the Goats   Matthew 25:31–46
- The Gift of the Poor Widow   Mark 12:41–44
- Jesus shame and honor   Phil 2:5–11

Bible Stories with Shame and Honor Themes

From: The Ephesus Team

1. Naked and Unashamed   (Shame/Cover-Ups)   Genesis 2:18–3:11
2. Joseph in Potiphar's House   (Honor: Fear of God)   Genesis 39:1–23
3. Moses/Miriam/Aaron (Sibling Honor/Shame)   Numbers 12:1–15
4. Korah's Rebellion   (Usurping Honor)   Numbers 16:1–50
5. Deborah/Barak/Jael   (Honor for Bold Obedience)   Judges 4:1–24
6. Hannah   (From Dishonor to Honor)   I Samuel 1:1–28
7. Ahab/Jehoshaphat/Micaiah (Dishonor: Alignments)   2 Chronicles 18:1–34
8. Mary and Joseph (Lineage: Cultural Shame/Honor)   Matthew 1:1–25
9. Jesus and Fasting   (Ceremonial Honor/Dishonor)   Matthew 6:16–24
10. Elisabeth and Zacharias (From Dishonor to Honor)   Luke 1:5–25
11. The Prodigal Son (Honor by Grace for the Dishonorable)   Luke 15:11–32

12. Rich Man and Lazarus (Status and Honor)	Luke 16:19–31
13. Honor of Jesus (God's Honor)	John 1: 1–18
14. Incarnation of Christ (From Dishonor to Honor)	Philippians 2:4–11
15. Woman at the Well (Cultural Dishonor/Honor)	John 4:4–42
16. Jesus Washes Disciples' Feet (Countercultural Honor)	John 13:1–17
17. Judas (Shame that Leads to Death) 50; 27:1–10	Matthew 26:14–16, 47–
18. Jesus on the Cross (Countercultural Honor)	Matthew 27:27–54
19. Jesus' Resurrection (Dishonor/Honor)	Matthew 28:1–20

*For those **from an honor/shame-oriented culture**, this story list can be used with just the usual DS questions.*

*To focus on honor/shame issues with **those not from an honor/shame-oriented culture**, you might want to add one extra question (besides the usual DS questions) for these studies:*

1. What does this teach us about God?

2. What does this teach us about ourselves / people?

2a. **Who is honored or put to shame in this story? Why?**

3. What do you need to apply / obey? ("I will…")

4. Is there some way we could apply this as a group? ("We will…")

5. Who are you going to tell? ("I will…")

Discovering Obedience

Matt 4:1–11 Facing temptations

Lk 5:1–11, Matt 4:18–22, Mk 1:16–2 Immediate obedience

John 1:35–51 Introduction obedience

Matt 10:16–23 Relating to unbelievers

John 15:18–25 Persecution is normal

Matt 10:23–31, Mk 13:9–13 Don't be fear persecution

Matt 10:18–22, Mk 13:11–13 God's provision in persecution

Matt 5:10–12 Rejoicing in persecution

Matt 5:13–16 The life that make a difference

Matt 5:17–23 Reconciling relationship

Matt 7:17–23 Nature of sin

Matt 19:1–6 Marriage for life

Matt 5:33–37 Keeping our word

Matt 5:38–42 Revenge

Matt 5:43–48; Luke 6:27–36 Loving our enemies

Matt 7:12 Relating to others

Luke 6:27:38; Matt 5:38–42 Giving to others

Matt 6:1–4, Lk 12:33–34 Do good to please God

Matt 6:5–8 Praying with sincerity

Matt 6:5–13, Luke 11:1–4 God as Father

Matt 6:5–13, Luke 11:1–4 Worshiping God in prayer

Matt 6:5–13, Luke 11:1–4 Surrender

Matt 6:5–13, Luke 11:1–4 God is my provider

Matt 6:5–13, Luke 11:1–4 Surrender

Matt 6:5–13, Luke 11:1–4 Forgiveness

Matt 6:5–13, Luke 11:1–4 God is our protector

Matt 18:21–22 Forgive always

Appendix 2 — Discovery Series

Discovering Church Planting

It is not necessary to do complete full Discovery Studies on each of these passages, but Discovery Groups should select passages in each section to do Discovery Studies on. They should review and discuss the others. This series allows people to discover the basics of what it means to be a church.

Matthew 22:34--40; Deuteronomy 6:1–6; and John 14:15–26. Love and Obey
Matthew 28:16–20: Great Commission

The Holy Spirit

Acts 3:1–10 The Holy Spirit at work through Peter and John and the church
Acts 2:1–47 How the Holy Spirit was at work in birthing the church?
John 15:26– 16:15 — Act of the Holy Spirit in disciple's lives
Acts 1: 4–9 Importance of the Holy Spirit
Acts 5:12–16; 9:31, 9:40–42 — Working of the Holy Spirit
Acts 16:6–10 Guidance of the Holy Spirit
Acts 15: 28 — Seeking unity and guidance in solving difficult problems

All Authority — Prayer

Matthew 6:5–18	Psalm 88:1–2	Luke 18:1–7
Luke 11:1–13	Psalm 107:6	Luke 20:45–47
Matthew 7:7–11	Psalm 116:1–2	John 14:12–14
John 17	Psalm 118:5–6	Acts 12:5–16
John 15:4–10		2 Corinthians 12:8–10
Genesis 18:23–32	Ecclesiastes 5:2	Hebrews 4:15–16
Joshua 7:6–12	Matthew 26:39–46	James 5:16
Job 30:20–23	Matthew 18:18–20	1 John 3:21–22
Psalm 5:1–3	Matthew 21:21–22	
Psalm 28:6–7	Luke 11:5–13	

All Authority — Intercession

2 Chronicles 20:1–30 — Mobilizing Prayer	Ezra 9:1–15
	I Kings 18:30–39
Exodus 32:7–14	Luke 23:24
Daniel 9:1–27	Acts 11
Nehemiah 1:1–11	Acts 7:60
John 17:6–26	Ephesians 3:14–20
Romans 8:26–39	
Genesis 18:20–33	Philippians 1:9–11
Exodus 32:19–32	Colossians 1:9–17

All Authority — Hindrances to Intercession

Psalm 66:16–20	Luke 20:46–47

Great Commission Disciple Making

Mark 11:22–25
James 1:5–7
James 4:3
John 15:16–17
Psalm 66:16–20 sin

Luke 20:46–47 pride

Mark 11:22–25 lack of faith and forgiveness
James 1:5–7 doubt and not asking
James 4:3 motives
John 15:16–17 not asking and lack of love

All Authority — Practice Praying Scripture:

Deuteronomy 4:29
1 Chronicles 28:9
Psalms 9:10
Psalms 19:1–3
Proverbs 8:17
Isaiah 55:6

Colossians 1:9–14

Jeremiah 29:13
Matthew 7:13–14
Luke 13:24

John 6:65
Romans 2:4
2 Corinthians 2:11

2 Corinthians 4:4
2 Corinthians 7:10
1 Timothy 2:4
2 Timothy 2:26

Go — Be Like Christ

John 12:20–33
John 20:21,
Philippians 2:1–11.

Go — Overcoming

John 4:1–42 — Barriers between Jesus and the woman
Acts 10:9–48 and Acts 1:8.
Matthew 28:16–20 and Acts 17:15–34.
Mark 16:15–16 and Acts 28:1–10.
Luke 24:45–49 and Luke 24:13–27.
John 20:21 and Acts 13:1–4.

Go — Spiritual Warfare

Daniel 9–10
Ephesians 6:10–18
Matthew 10:16–25

2 Corinthians 10:3–6.
2 Chronicles 20:1–30
Exodus 17:8–16

Effects of prayer: Acts: 1:14 / 1:24 / 2:42 / 6:6 / 8:15 / 9:11 / 9:40 / 10:2 / 10:9 / 10:30 / 11:15 / 12:5 / 12:12 / 13:3 / 14:23 / 16:16 / 16:25 / 20:36 / 21:5 / 22:17 / 27:29 / 28:8

Make Disciples — Do What Jesus Did

John 20:21 — As the Father sent me, so I send you.
Matthew 3:11–17 — Jesus obeyed God through baptism.
Matthew 4:1–11 — Jesus resisted temptation.
Matthew 4:12–17 — Jesus declared 'The Kingdom of Heaven is near.'

Matthew 4:18–22 — Jesus called others to follow Him.
Matthew 5:1–29 — Jesus taught them how to live.
Matthew 8:1–17 — Jesus healed the sick.
Matthew 5:28–34 — Jesus drove out evil spirits.
Matthew 10:1–42 — Jesus sent out the disciples.
Matthew 14:13–21 — Jesus fed the hungry.
Matthew 17:24–27 — Jesus obeyed the law.
Matthew 10:1–35 — Jesus taught using stories.
Matthew 26:36–46; 27:32–56 — Jesus obeyed God to the point of death.
Matthew 28:16–20 — Jesus commanded His disciples to teach others to obey.

Make Disciples — How We Are Sent
Luke 10:1–20
Matthew 9:35 — 10:16

Make Disciples — Find the Person of Peace
Luke 9:1–16,
Luke 10:1–20,
Matthew 10:5–20
Acts 13:1–4,
Acts 16:11–15

Make Disciples — Appropriate Evangelism
Acts 2 Peter's Sermon to Jews in Jerusalem on the Day of Pentecost
Acts 17:18–34 Paul's Sermon to pagans in Athens
I Cor. 9:19–23
John 4:1–30, 39–42

Make Disciples — Make Disciples of All People
Matthew 28:16–20
Matthew 24:14
Revelation 7:9–12
Galatians 3:26–29
Genesis 12:1–3 God's promise to Abraham
I Corinthians 9:19–23
Acts 15:1–29

Basics: Baptized

Matthew 28:19–20;
1 Corinthians 12:12
Romans 6:1–14
Baptized — Metaphors of the Church
Ephesians 1:15–23 / Romans 12:3–8 / 1
Corinthians 12:12–31 (Body of Christ)
Ephesians 5:22–32 (Bride of Christ)
1 Timothy 3:14–15 (God's Household, Pillar)
1 Corinthians 3:9–17 (Temple of the Holy Spirit)
1 Peter 2:4–10

Baptized — Nature of the Church
Matthew 16:18 (Belongs to Christ)
Matthew 16:18 / Ephesians 2:19–22 (Built on Foundation of Apostles, Prophets, & Christ)

Great Commission Disciple Making

Matthew 18:15–18 / Acts 5:11 / 1 Corinthians 1:2 / Ephesians 5:22–32 (Holy)
Galatians 3:26–28 / Revelation 5:9 / Revelation 7:9 / Ephesians 2:11–22 (Universal)
John 17:20–23 / 1 Corinthians 1:10 / Ephesians 4:1–6 (United)
Acts 13:1–3 / 1 Corinthians 12:1–30 (Led, Empowered, and Gifted by the Holy Spirit)

Baptized — Functions of the Church

1. Teaching: Matthew 28:18–20 / Acts 2:42–47 / 1 Corinthians 14:26 / 2 Tim. 2:2 / 2 Tim. 4:2
2. Fellowship and Encouragement: Acts 2:42–47 / 1 Thessalonians 5:11 / Hebrews 10:24–25
3. Caring for each other: 1 Corinthians 16:1–4, 2 Corinthians 8:1–5, Galatians 6:9–10
4. Praying: Acts 12:5 / Acts 14:23 / James 5:14
5. Fasting: Matthew 6:16–18 / Matthew 9:14–15 / Acts 13:1–3 / Acts 14:2
6. Worship: Acts 13:1–3 / 1 Peter 2:1–10
7. Reverence and Awe: 1 Corinthians 11:17–34 / Hebrews 12:28–29
8. Miraculous Signs and Wonders — Acts 5:12, Acts 19:11, 2 Corinthians 12:12
9. Lord's Supper: 1 Corinthians 10:14–22 / 1 Corinthians 11:17–34
10. People Saved: Acts 5:14, 8:12, 9:42, 11:21, 14:2, 17:12
11. Discipline: Matthew 18:15–18 / 1 Corinthians 5:1–13 / 2 Corinthians 2:5–11
1 Chronicles 16 — make list of everything the people of God are supposed to do

Leadership in the Church

Ezekiel 34
Matthew 23:1–39
1 Peter 5:1–11,

Teach to Obey — Scripture

Nehemiah 8:1– 9:1, 2 (covenant following obedience)
Acts 8:26–40
Acts 2 (mixture of the Holy Spirit and Word)
Acts 17:10–15
Hebrews 5:12–14

Obey and Teach Obedience

1 Samuel 15:1–35
Deuteronomy 6:1–8;
Matthew 28:16–20
Matthew 22:36–40,

John 15:4–14
Deuteronomy 28:1–14
Psalm 1:1–3

Rediscovering Church: Church

John 20:21–23;
Philippians 2:1–11;
1 Corinthians 9:19–23;

Matthew 23:8–15;
Amos 5:21–24

Appendix 2 — Discovery Series

Rediscovering Church: Make Disciples, Not Converts

Matthew 28:16–20;

Matthew 15:1–20;

Matthew 23:1–36;

Luke 18:18–30

1Corinthians 11:1

2Timothy 3:10–12;

Matthew 4:18–22;

Mark 1:14–20

Rediscovering Church: Five-fold leadership

Ephesians 4:11–15

Galatians 2:8;

1 Corinthians 12:4–31

Rediscovering Church: Tent-making

1 Corinthians 9:1–23;

Acts 20:32–35;

2 Thessalonians 3:6–15;

1 Timothy 5:17–18

Jesus as carpenter (Mark 6:3)

Acts 4:34–37

Acts 5:1–11

Acts 21:16

Acts 28:7–10

Acts 1:1; see also Colossians 4:14; 2 Timothy 4:11

Acts 6:8–10

Acts 8:4–5

Acts18:24–28),

Acts 8:26–40),

Acts 8:3; 9:1–2; 26:9–11

Acts 13:6–12

Acts 16:22–34

Acts 17:34

Acts 18:8

Acts 9:36–43

Acts 10:1–48

Acts 12:12–17).

Acts 16:13–15, 40

Acts18:1–3

Discovering Equipping Leaders

It is not necessary to do complete full Discovery Studies on each of these passages, but Discovery Groups should select passages in each section to do Discovery Studies on. They should review and discuss the others. The goal here is to train leaders within the church and prepare them to impact the world around them.

Acts 9:26–27
Acts 11:25–26
Acts13:1–13
Acts13:46–14:20
Acts 14:8–18
Acts 15:1–4, 12

•Acts 15:36–39
2 Timothy 4:11
Exodus 18
Deuteronomy 31:1–8;
34:9
Judges 4:4–16

Ruth 1:1–4
1 Samuel 1:1–3
1 Samuel 9–15
1 Samuel 16; 19:18–24
Esther 1–10

God's Glory

Revelation 7:9–12
John 17:1–5
Isaiah 43:6–7
Ephesians 1:4–6
Isaiah 49:3
Psalms 106:7–8
Ezekiel 20:14

2Samuel 7:23
Romans 9:22–23
Ezekiel 36:22–23

John 7:18
Mat 5:16
John 5:44
John 14:13

John 12:27–28
Romans 15:7
John 16:14
Romans 15:8–9
1Corinthians 10:31
1Peter 4:11

Outside and Inside Leaders

Acts 16:1–5; 17:14–15; 19:22
1Timothy 1:18–20; 3:1–15; 4:11–16; 2
Timothy 2:1–2
Matthew 28:18–20; John 16:5–15

Acts 14:21–28; Acts 20:17–38; Titus 1:4–5
Exodus 18:13–26; Joshua 1:1–9; 2 Kings 2:1–14

Reaching All

Acts 1:8
Acts 2:5–12, 37–41
Acts 6:1–7
Acts 8:1, 4
Acts 8:5–8
Acts 8:14–17, 25
Acts 8:26–40.
Acts 10:1–48

Acts 11:19–26
Acts 13:1–14:26
Acts 15:1–33
Acts 16:1–4
Acts 17:16–34
Acts 18:5–11
Acts 21:17–36
Acts 28

Matthew 28:16–20;
Acts 1:1–11
Luke 10:25–37
1 Thessalonians 1:2–10;
Matthew 8:5–13;
John 4:4–42;
Acts 16:9–10,
Acts 1

Redeem Local Culture

John 20:21–23;
Philippians 2:5–11
Acts 17:16–34;
Acts 19:11–20
1 Corinthians 9:19–23
Matthew 22:15–22;

Acts 17:22–23:
Acts 15:5–22;
Galatians 2:11–14; 1
1 Thessalonians 1:9–10;
1 Corinthians 2:1–5

Church Planting Strategy: Reproducing

John 1:35–51
Acts 2:41; 4:4; 6:7; 8:1,14; 9:31; 15:7–9; 17:4,12 and 18:8
Matthew 25:14–30;
Matthew 13:3–23;
Matthew 21:19; Matthew 13:31–33; 2 Timothy 2:2; Colossians 1:6–7

Spiritual Warfare

Ephesians 6:10–20

The Rightful Order

Daniel 7:13–14
John 17:1–6
John 12:31–32
Colossians 2:14–15
2 Corinthians 10:3–6

2 Corinthians 5:18–20
Ephesians 1:19–23
Ephesians 3:5–12
1 Corinthians 15:22–25
Philippians 2:9–11

God's Work and Our Response

2 Kings 6:15–23
2 Chronicles 20:15–26
Isaiah 57:14–19
Isaiah 60:1–5
Isaiah 61:1–4
Luke 6:12
Luke 9:18
Ezekiel 22:30
Romans 8:26 — 35
Acts 17:26–31
Hebrews 7:25
Hebrews 10:19–25
Hebrews 11
Attacks of the Enemy
Matthew 13:24–30, 36–43

Discovering Leadership

Matt 4:18–22 Leaders Call Other to Follow Christ

Matt 5:1–16. Matt 6:33–34 Leaders Teach Attitudes That God Blesses

Matt 6:1–8. Matt 6:16–18 Leaders Seek to Please God, Not Man

Matt 6:19–34 Leaders Serve God

Matt 7:1–6. Matt 18:15–20 Leaders Judge Rightly

Matt 7:7–12 Leaders Seek God

Matt 7:21–28 Leaders Obey God

Matt 9:9–13 Leaders Work with Social Outcasts

Matt 9:18–33. Matt 10:1 Leaders Use Jesus' Power

Matt 9:35–38 Leaders Model Kingdom Strategy

Matt 10:1–16 Leaders Implement Kingdom Strategy

Matt 10:16–31. Matt 5:43–48 Leaders Prepare for Persecution

Matt 11:25–30 Leaders Offer Rest to the Weary

Matt 13:3–9. Matt 13:18–23 Leaders Are Fruitful

Matt 14:13–21. Matt 20:29–34 Leaders Meet People's Needs

Matt 16:13–28 Leaders Accept the Cost

Matt 17:1–13 Leaders Listen to Jesus

Matt 17:14–21 Leaders Teach About Faith

Matt 18:15–35 Leaders Deal with Sin

Matt 19:3–9 Leaders Honor God's Design for Marriage

Matt 20:20–28 Leaders are Servants

Matt 25:14–30 Leaders Invest Faithfully

Matt 25:31–46 Leaders Serve the Needy

Matt 28:16–20 Leaders Teach Others to Obey

Discovering Disciple-Making

This is the series that we study in this book.

Luke 10:1–11 — Disciple-Making Process

John 14:15–27 — Obedience—our instructor

John 1:35–51 — Calling disciples

Matthew 23:8–11 — Our role in Disciple-Making

Luke 11:1–13 — Focus and persist in prayer

Deuteronomy 6:1–15 — Internal and External

Acts 16:25–34 — People of Peace

Matthew 9:35–10:16 — Compare to Luke 10:1–11

Matthew 28:16–20 — Disciples' commission

Matthew 16:13–21 — Planting churches

Philippians 2:1–8 — Model for Paul's and our actions

1 Corinthians 9:19–23 — Cultural relevance

Acts 17:22–27 — Where to start

2 Timothy 2:1–7; 14–16 — Key to replication

John 15:1–11 — Fruit, love, obedience

Appendix 3: Scripture Questions

These questions are meant to stimulate you to think about the passages being studied during your personal study time. They are not meant to be written out nor shared in the discovery group. Read the verses and then ask yourself the questions.

These do not replace the six basic questions: What is this passage about? What do we learn about God? What do we learn about man? If this passage is true what will you change in your life? Who will you tell? And who will you help?

Luke 10:1–11 — Disciple-Making Process

After this the Lord appointed Seventy-two others and sent them on ahead of him, two by two, into every town and place where he himself was about to go.

   i.   After what? (Take a look at chapter 9.)

   ii.   Where might the Seventy-two have come from, how were they recruited and developed?

   iii.   How were they to go out? Was there any hierarchy in how they were sent out?

   iv.   Where were they to go? How did they know?

   v.   How can you know where to go?

² And he said to them, "The harvest is plentiful, but the laborers are few. Therefore pray earnestly to the Lord of the harvest to send out laborers into his harvest.

   vi.   Who were they praying for, themselves or others?

   vii.   If God was to send out laborers, who might they be?

   viii. What did Jesus mean by "harvest?"

   ix.   What should be a regular part of your prayer life?

³ Go your way; behold, I am sending you out as lambs in the midst of wolves.

   x.   What does this indicate about the assignment?

   xi.   How does Jesus expect the Seventy-two to operate?

   xii.   How could the Seventy-two get through the midst of the wolves?

   xiii. What should you do when confronting challenges and dangers?

⁴ Carry no moneybag, no knapsack, no sandals, and greet no one on the road.

   xiv.   What did they have to rely upon?

   xv.   What might be some of the reason for Jesus to instruct them to "greet no one?"

xvi.   What should you do to obtain sufficient resources?

⁵ Whatever house you enter, first say, 'Peace be to this house!'

xvii.   Where was the ministry of the Seventy-two to start?

xviii.   What is the first thing to say when entering a place on ministry?

⁶ And if a son of peace is there, your peace will rest upon him. But if not, it will return to you.

xix.   What does it mean, "Your peace will rest upon him?" What might this look like?

⁷ And remain in the same house, eating and drinking what they provide, for the laborer deserves his wages. Do not go from house to house.

xx.   How does this compare with general "evangelism" that is practiced today?

xxi.   What does "hospitality" look like here?

xxii.   How should you react to hospitality?

xxiii.   What does this say about ongoing relationship with the "person of peace"?

xxiv.   How could you do this?

⁸ Whenever you enter a town and they receive you, eat what is set before you.

xxv.   When might this be a challenge?

xxvi.   What if you don't like what is set before you?

xxvii.   What do you learn about working in a different culture?

⁹ Heal the sick in it and say to them, 'The kingdom of God has come near to you.'

xxviii.   How are you called to heal the sick?

xxix.   What are you called to proclaim?

xxx.   Is this the same as proclaiming salvation?

xxxi.   What might be the connection between healing the sick and saying the "kingdom of God has come near?"

¹⁰ But whenever you enter a town and they do not receive you, go into its streets and say,
¹¹ 'Even the dust of your town that clings to our feet we wipe off against you. Nevertheless know this, that the kingdom of God has come near.'

xxxii.   What does this tell you about where you expend your time and efforts?

xxxiii.   What is the consistent message that we are to proclaim whether we are received or not?

xxxiv.   How many commands of Jesus are there in this passage (verses 1–11)? What are they?

What other questions could you ask about this passage?

The six basic questions: What is this passage about? What do we learn about God? What do we learn about man? If this passage is true what will you change in your life? Who will you tell? And who will you help?

John 14:15–27 — Obedience and our instructor

"If you love me, you will keep my commandments.

    i.   Is it possible to love Jesus and not obey his commands?

    ii.   How can you "keep" the commandments of Jesus?

    iii.   What are some of the ones you know?

[16] And "I will" ask the Father, and he will give you another Helper, to be with you forever, [17] even the Spirit *of truth, whom the world cannot receive, because it neither sees him nor knows him.*

    iv.   Who will send the helper, the spirit of truth?

    v.   What are the preconditions for Jesus to ask the Father?

    vi.   What do we learn about the Spirit of truth?

    vii.   What does Jesus mean by "the world?"

    viii.   What do we learn about what the world understands of spiritual matters?

You know him, for he dwells with you and will be in you.

    ix.   Jesus makes a statement here and gives a promise. What are they and what does this mean?

[18] "I will not leave you as orphans; "I will" come to you.

    x.   Is Jesus still with us?

    xi.   What does this mean to us as disciples?

[19] Yet a little while and the world will see me no more, but you will see me.

    xii.   What did this mean to the original disciples?

    xiii.   What does this mean to us?

Because I live, you also will live. [20] In that day you will know that I am in my Father, and you in me, and I in you.

    xiv.   How important is Jesus' resurrection?

    xv.   What does this mean to you personally?

[21] Whoever has my commandments and keeps them, he it is who loves me. And he who loves

me will be loved by my Father, and "I will" love him and manifest myself to him."

xvi.   How can we have Jesus' commandments?

xvii.   What does it mean to "keep" the commandments?

xviii.   How is obedience connected to loving Jesus?

xix.   If we do these things what can we expect Jesus to do?

xx.   What can we expect to experience from the Father?

[22] *Judas (not Iscariot) said to him, "Lord, how is it that you will manifest yourself to us, and not to the world?"*

xxi.   What do we learn about the way our mind works compared to that of God?

[23] *Jesus answered him, "If anyone loves me, he will keep my word, and my Father will love him, and we will come to him and make our home with him.* [24] *Whoever does not love me does not keep my words.*

xxii.   What is the result of Jesus' Father loving us?

xxiii.   Why doesn't Jesus manifest or show himself to everyone?

And the word that you hear is not mine but the Father's who sent me.

xxiv.   If we memorize all of Jesus words and share them, whose words are we sharing?

xxv.   If memorizing-to-tell is a discipline of a disciple, what is Jesus modeling for us?

xxvi.   What then is Jesus asking us to do?

[25] *"These things I have spoken to you while I am still with you.* [26] *But the Helper, the Holy Spirit, whom the Father will send in my name, he will teach you all things and bring to your remembrance all that I have said to you.*

xxvii.   What is the role of the Holy Spirit?

xxviii.   There are two related things that the Holy Spirit is to do, what are they? How do they differ?

xxix.   What is required for the Holy Spirit to "bring to [our] remembrance?" What are we responsible to do?

[27] *Peace I leave with you; my peace I give to you. Not as the world gives do I give to you. Let not your hearts be troubled, neither let them be afraid.*

xxx.   What is the difference between the peace of the world and Jesus' peace?

xxxi.   What should be the result of the peace of Jesus when we are in difficult or dangerous situations?

xxxii.   If our hearts are troubled or afraid, what are we lacking? Where should we turn to get it? How can we do that?

What other questions could you ask about this passage?

The six basic questions: What is this passage about? What do we learn about God? What do we learn about man? If this passage is true what will you change in your life? Who will you tell? And who will you help?

John 1:35–51 — Living as a Disciple of Jesus

35 The next day again John was standing with two of his disciples, 36 and he looked at Jesus as he walked by and said, "Behold, the Lamb of God!"

    i.   What was John's role in Jesus' ministry?

    ii.   What might he have been doing for his disciples?

37 The two disciples heard him say this, and they followed Jesus. 38 Jesus turned and saw them following and said to them, "What are you seeking?" And they said to him, "Rabbi" (which means Teacher), "where are you staying?" 39 He said to them, "Come and you will see." So they came and saw where he was staying, and they stayed with him that day, for it was about the tenth hour.

    iii.   What might be the unspoken communications between Jesus and the two disciples of John?

    iv.   The two are simply referred to as disciples not at disciples of John. What might this tell us about the general practice of being a disciple?

40 One of the two who heard John speak and followed Jesus was Andrew, Simon Peter's brother. 41 He first found his own brother Simon and said to him, "We have found the Messiah" (which means Christ).

    v.   What was the first response of Andrew?

    vi.   What does this tell us about inviting people to join us in becoming disciples of Jesus?

    vii.   Who might have been the second disciple of John?

42 He brought him to Jesus. Jesus looked at him and said, "You are Simon the son of John. You shall be called Cephas" (which means Peter).

    viii. Simon means "one who hears." The meaning of Simon's name gives underlying content to some of the conversations between Jesus and Simon Peter. Also, note that Simon's father is John. This will provide more understanding when you study Matthew 16.

    ix.   Who normally names a person? What does this tell about the new relationship between Jesus and Peter?

Appendix 3: Scripture Questions

43 The next day Jesus decided to go to Galilee. He found Philip and said to him, "Follow me."

    x.   In John's account of the gospel, Philip is the first person Jesus called.

    xi.   What do we learn about being called verses choosing to follow Jesus as Andrew and the other disciple did?

44 Now Philip was from Bethsaida, the city of Andrew and Peter. 45 Philip found Nathanael and said to him, "We have found him of whom Moses in the Law and also the prophets wrote, Jesus of Nazareth, the son of Joseph.

    xii.   Philip like Andrew immediately went and called his brother. Was Andrew's call of Simon and Philip's call of Nathanael a valid call to become a disciple of Jesus?

"46 Nathanael said to him, "Can anything good come out of Nazareth?" Philip said to him, "Come and see."

    xiii.   What can we infer about the men of the region of Bethsaida in terms of their expectations for the messiah?

    xiv.   What was Nathaniel's response to Phillip's skepticism? How can this apply to us?

47 Jesus saw Nathanael coming toward him and said of him, "Behold, an Israelite indeed, in whom there is no deceit!" 48 Nathanael said to him, "How do you know me?" Jesus answered him, "Before Philip called you, when you were under the fig tree, I saw you." 49 Nathanael answered him, "Rabbi, you are the Son of God! You are the King of Israel!"

    xv.   What do we see in the way Jesus was working through Philip? Does this support or change your earlier decision about the validity of coming to Jesus via an invitation of another disciple? (Question xii.)

    xvi.   What role does the supernatural play in these five men becoming disciples of Jesus?

50 Jesus answered him, "Because I said to you, 'I saw you under the fig tree,' do you believe? You will see greater things than these." 51 And he said to him, "Truly, truly, I say to you, you will see heaven opened, and the angels of God ascending and descending on the Son of Man."

    xvii.   What is Jesus preparing the disciples for?

    xviii.   What should we be prepared for?

What other questions could you ask about this passage?

The six basic questions: What is this passage about? What do we learn about God? What do we learn about man? If this passage is true what will you change in your life? Who will you tell? And who will you help?

Matthew 23:8–11 — Our role in Disciple-Making

But you are not to be called rabbi, for you have one teacher, and you are all brothers. [9] And call no man your father on earth, for you have one Father, who is in heaven. [10] Neither be called instructors, for you have one instructor, the Christ. [11] The greatest among you shall be your servant.

> i. In terms of Disciple-Making, who is to be our teacher and instructor? (ref John 14:26)
>
> ii. What is our role in the Disciple-Making Process?
>
> iii. What does this mean practically for us in the Disciple-Making Process? How do we implement this?

What other questions could you ask about this passage?

The six basic questions: What is this passage about? What do we learn about God? What do we learn about man? If this passage is true what will you change in your life? Who will you tell? And who will you help?

Deuteronomy 6:1–15 — Internal and External

"Now this is the commandment—the statutes and the rules—that the Lord your God commanded me to teach you, that you may do them in the land to which you are going over, to possess it, [2] that you may fear the Lord your God, you and your son and your son's son, by keeping all his statutes and his commandments, which I command you, all the days of your life, and that your days may be long.

> i. What are God's expectations for our response to what he teaches us?
>
> ii. What does it mean to "fear the Lord your God?"
>
> iii. What is the focus and duration of God's commands? "How many generations are included?" How should this influence our plan for training and reaching people?
>
> iv. What is the promise of obedience to God's commands?

[3] Hear therefore, O Israel, and be careful to do them, that it may go well with you, and that you may multiply greatly, as the Lord, the God of your fathers, has promised you, in a land flowing with milk and honey.

> v. How seriously does God intend us to obey his commands?
>
> vi. What are the outcomes of obedience in this verse?

[4] "Hear, O Israel: The Lord our God, the Lord is one.

> vii. How do we reconcile the Father, Son, and Holy Spirit to this statement?

Appendix 3: Scripture Questions

⁵ You shall love the Lord your God with all your heart and with all your soul and with all your might.

viii.   How do you understand the difference between the heart, soul, and might?

⁶ And these words that I command you today shall be [graven] on your heart.

ix.   How can we make sure that God's words are [engraved] on our hearts?

⁷ You shall teach them diligently to your children,

x.   What is God's generational perspective?

and shall talk of them when you sit in your house, and when you walk by the way, and when you lie down, and when you rise.

xi.   What should be the focus of all of our conversations?

xii.   How would you talk of them when you walk by the way? (Important to finding a person of peace.) Give and practice some examples.

⁸ You shall bind them as a sign on your hand, and they shall be as frontlets between your eyes. ⁹ You shall write them on the doorposts of your house and on your gates.

xiii.   What way can you "bind" God's commands as a sign on your hand? (Hint: what do you do with your hands?)

xiv.   What way can God's word symbolically be "as frontlets" (hint: what is the first thing people see when they meet you?)

xv.   What ways, physically and symbolically can God's commands be written on the door posts of our house?

xvi.   What is the significance of writing God's law on the "gates [of your city]?

¹⁰ "And when the Lord your God brings you into the land that he swore to your fathers, to Abraham, to Isaac, and to Jacob, to give you—with great and good cities that you did not build, ¹¹ and houses full of all good things that you did not fill, and cisterns that you did not dig, and vineyards and olive trees that you did not plant—and when you eat and are full, ¹² then take care lest you forget the Lord, who brought you out of the land of Egypt, out of the house of slavery.

xvii.   What is the danger of abundance?

¹³ It is the Lord your God you shall fear. Him you shall serve and by his name you shall swear. ¹⁴ You shall not go after other gods, the gods of the peoples who are around you—

xviii.   What are some of the characteristics of an "other god?"

xix.   What "other gods" rule in materialistic societies? In Muslim, Hindu, and Animist societies? In intellectual societies?

xx.   What "other gods" most often allure and temp you?

^{15} for the Lord your God in your midst is a jealous God—lest the anger of the Lord your God be kindled against you, and he destroy you from off the face of the earth.

xxi.   What is the threatened outcome of going after other gods?

xxii.   How might this appear in the life of a person we meet and work with?

What other questions could you ask about this passage?

The six basic questions: What is this passage about? What do we learn about God? What do we learn about man? If this passage is true what will you change in your life? Who will you tell? And who will you help?

Luke 11:1–13 — Focus and persist in prayer

Now Jesus was praying in a certain place, and when he finished, one of his disciples said to him, "Lord, teach us to pray, as John taught his disciples." ^{2} And he said to them, "When you pray, say:

xvii.   What was a characteristic of Jesus that the disciples noticed here?

xvii.   What did disciples expect from their rabbi? How does that apply to Disciple Makers today?

xvii.   Is this a commandment of Jesus? What does that mean to a disciple?

"Father, hallowed be your name.

xvii.   What is the relationship of Jesus' disciples to God?

xvii.   What is the purpose of a disciple's prayer (and action)

Your kingdom come.

xvii.   What is the first request?

xvii.   What did Jesus come to proclaim?

xvii.   What is our mission?

^{3} Give us each day our daily bread,

xvii.   What is included in this request?

xvii.   Why is it second?

xvii.   Who are we to rely upon for our physical needs?

^{4} and forgive us our sins, for we ourselves forgive everyone who is indebted to us.

xvii.   What is the precondition for our forgiveness?

xvii.   If we have not forgiven someone what happens to God's forgiveness for our sins?

And lead us not into temptation."

> xvii.   What does "lead us not into temptation" mean?

> xvii.   What does this tell us about the temptations that we face?

⁵ And he said to them, "Which of you who has a friend will go to him at midnight and say to him, 'Friend, lend me three loaves, ⁶ for a friend of mine has arrived on a journey, and I have nothing to set before him'; ⁷ and he will answer from within, 'Do not bother me; the door is now shut, and my children are with me in bed. I cannot get up and give you anything'? ⁸ I tell you, though he will not get up and give him anything because he is his friend, yet because of his impudence he will rise and give him whatever he needs.

> xvii.   What do we learn about people's initial response to our request?

> xvii.   What is Jesus trying to tell us about prayer?

⁹ And I tell you, ask, and it will be given to you; seek, and you will find; knock, and it will be opened to you. ¹⁰ For everyone who asks receives, and the one who seeks finds, and to the one who knocks it will be opened.

> xvii.   What are the three components of prayer that Jesus is presenting here?

> xvii.   What is included in asking, in general and in the context of this passage?

> xvii.   What is included in seeking; what are some of the things you might seek?

> xvii.   What might you want to be opened to you?

¹¹ What father among you, if his son asks for a fish, will instead of a fish give him a serpent; ¹² or if he asks for an egg, will give him a scorpion? ¹³ If you then, who are evil, know how to give good gifts to your children, how much more will the heavenly Father give the Holy Spirit to those who ask him!"

> xvii.   What can you be sure of when you pray?

> xvii.   What is the most important thing that we can ask for according to this passage?

> xvii.   Why is it important?

What other questions could you ask about this passage?

The six basic questions: What is this passage about? What do we learn about God? What do we learn about man? If this passage is true what will you change in your life? Who will you tell? And who will you help?

Acts 16:25–34 — People of Peace

About midnight Paul and Silas were praying and singing hymns to God, and the prisoners were listening to them,

> i.   Why were Paul and Silas behaving this way?

ii.   What was the effect on the other prisoners?

iii.   What do you learn from this?

26 and suddenly there was a great earthquake, so that the foundations of the prison were shaken. And immediately all the doors were opened, and everyone's bonds were unfastened.

iv.   Was this just a "natural" event and why do you say so?

v.   What do we learn about God's intervention?

27 When the jailer woke and saw that the prison doors were open, he drew his sword and was about to kill himself, supposing that the prisoners had escaped. 28 But Paul cried with a loud voice, "Do not harm yourself, for we are all here."

vi.   What was Paul's attitude toward the jailer?

vii.   What do think Paul's goal was during this entire event?

viii.   How should we look at our adversaries, opponents and jailers?

29 And the jailer called for lights and rushed in, and trembling with fear he fell down before Paul and Silas. 30 Then he brought them out and said, "Sirs, what must I do to be saved?"

ix.   What do you think was motivating the Jailer? Was this a "natural response" by the jailer?

31 And they said, "Believe in the Lord Jesus, and you will be saved, you and your household." 32 And they spoke the word of the Lord to him and to all who were in his house.

x.   What is the key thing that Paul and Silas were looking for in a response?

xi.   What was the focus of their presentation?

xii.   What is different between this approach of Paul and Silas and our current evangelism styles?

33 And he took them the same hour of the night and washed their wounds; and he was baptized at once, he and all his family.

xiii.   When were they baptized? How much instruction was given?

xiv.   This was a group profession of faith rather than individual, was it valid?

xv.   How do you think that this family would have continued in faith?

34 Then he brought them up into his house and set food before them. And he rejoiced along with his entire household that he had believed in God.

xvi.   The jailer is a person of peace. List some of the characteristics that he demonstrated?

xvii.   Paul and Silas are Disciple Makers and church planters. List some of the characteristics you see that they demonstrated.

Appendix 3: Scripture Questions

What other questions could you ask about this passage?

The six basic questions: What is this passage about? What do we learn about God? What do we learn about man? If this passage is true what will you change in your life? Who will you tell? And who will you help?

Mt. 9:35–10:16 — Compare Luke 10:1–11

And Jesus went throughout all the cities and villages, teaching in their synagogues and proclaiming the gospel of the kingdom and healing every disease and every affliction.
³⁶ When he saw the crowds, he had compassion for them, because they were harassed and helpless, like sheep without a shepherd.

 i. What did Jesus do?

 ii. What did he proclaim? What did this mean?

 iii. What is Jesus' attitude toward people?

³⁷ Then he said to his disciples, "The harvest is plentiful, but the laborers are few;
³⁸ therefore pray earnestly to the Lord of the harvest to send out laborers into his harvest."

 iv. Look at the comparable verse in Luke 10 below.

 v. What significance can be applied to the fact that they are identical?

[² *And he said to them, "The harvest is plentiful, but the laborers are few. Therefore pray earnestly to the Lord of the harvest to send out laborers into his harvest.*]

10 And he called to him his twelve disciples and gave them authority over unclean spirits, to cast them out, and to heal every disease and every affliction. ² The names of the Twelve apostles are these: first, Simon, who is called Peter, and Andrew his brother; James the son of Zebedee, and John his brother; ³ Philip and Bartholomew; Thomas and Matthew the tax collector; James the son of Alphaeus, and Thaddaeus; ⁴ Simon the Zealot, and Judas Iscariot, who betrayed him.

 vi. Looking at the comparable verse in Luke 10 — how does it differ?

[¹ . . . *After this the Lord appointed Seventy-two others* . . .]

⁵ These twelve Jesus sent out, instructing them, "Go nowhere among the Gentiles and enter no town of the Samaritans, ⁶ but go rather to the lost sheep of the house of Israel.

 vii. Looking at the comparable verse in Luke 10? How does it differ?

 viii. In our context (the church), who would be the "lost sheep"?

[*and sent them on ahead of him, two by two, into every town and place where he himself was about to go.*]

 ix. Why might Jesus have sent the Twelve to one group and the Seventy-two to different groups of people?

[7] And proclaim as you go, saying, 'The kingdom of heaven is at hand.' [8] Heal the sick, raise the dead, cleanse lepers, cast out demons.

x. Looking at the comparable verse in Luke 10? How does it differ?

[[9] Heal the sick in it and say to them, 'The kingdom of God has come near to you.']

You received without paying; give without pay. [9] Acquire no gold or silver or copper for your belts, [10] no bag for your journey, or two tunics or sandals or a staff, for the laborer deserves his food.

xi. Looking at the comparable verses in Luke 10? How do they differ?

[[4] Carry no moneybag, no knapsack, no sandals, and greet no one on the road. [7] And remain in the same house, eating and drinking what they provide, for the laborer deserves his wages.]

[11] And whatever town or village you enter, find out who is worthy in it and stay there until you depart. [12] As you enter the house, greet it. [13] And if the house is worthy, let your peace come upon it, but if it is not worthy, let your peace return to you.

xii. Looking at the comparable verse in Luke 10? How does it differ?

[[5] Whatever house you enter, first say, 'Peace be to this house!' [6] And if a son of peace is there, your peace will rest upon him. But if not, it will return to you... [7] Do not go from house to house.]

[14] And if anyone will not receive you or listen to your words, shake off the dust from your feet when you leave that house or town. [15] Truly, I say to you, it will be more bearable on the day of judgment for the land of Sodom and Gomorrah than for that town.

xiii. Looking at the comparable verses in Luke 10? How do they differ?

[[10] But whenever you enter a town and they do not receive you, go into its streets and say, [11] 'Even the dust of your town that clings to our feet we wipe off against you. Nevertheless know this, that the kingdom of God has come near.']

[16] "Behold, I am sending you out as sheep in the midst of wolves, so be wise as serpents and innocent as doves.

xiv. Looking at the comparable verse in Luke 10? How does it differ?

[[3] Go your way; behold, I am sending you out as lambs in the midst of wolves.]

*Luke 10: 8

There is one command unique for the Seventy-two, it is verse 8

xv. Why would Jesus tell this to the Seventy-two and not to the Twelve? What type of people would Jesus have to instruct them to eat what is set before them?

[^{8} Whenever you enter a town and they receive you, eat what is set before you.]

xvi.   The Twelve were sent out first, where might the Seventy-two have come from?

xvii.   What might be the purpose that Jesus first sent the Twelve to the "lost sheep" and then the Seventy-two more broadly?

xviii.   What can we learn from this and how can we apply it?

What other questions could you ask about this passage?

The six basic questions: What is this passage about? What do we learn about God? What do we learn about man? If this passage is true what will you change in your life? Who will you tell? And who will you help?

Matthew 28:16–20 — Disciples' commission

^{16}*Now the eleven disciples went to Galilee, to the mountain to which Jesus had directed them.*

i.   Why did they go?

^{17}*And when they saw him they worshiped him, but some doubted.*

ii.   How many doubted?

iii.   If we have doubts about Jesus what is the best course of action?

^{18}*And Jesus came and said to them,*

iv.   What is Jesus' response to obedient doubt?

"All authority in heaven and on earth has been given to me.

v.   What does this mean to us as we go out to obey the Great Commission?

^{19}*Go therefore and make disciples of all nations,*

vi.   What is the extent of our charge and commission?

vii.   What does the word nations ("ethne" — Greek) mean? (The word "ethnic" is derived from it.)

viii.   Looking at Matthew 10 and Luke 10, what might be Jesus' discipling and sending strategy?

ix.   Who is this command given to (ref vs. Matthew 28:16)?

baptizing them in the name of the Father and of the Son and of the Holy Spirit,

x.   Who is to baptize? What qualifications are needed?

xi.   How soon should someone be baptized?

xii.   How many names are used to baptize? How many Gods?

²⁰ teaching them to observe all that I have commanded you.

    xiii.   What are we to teach?

    xiv.   How do we teach people to observe (obey)?

And behold, I am with you always, to the end of the age."

    xv.   What is this promise conditional upon?

    xvi.   How will you know if Jesus is with you in this process?

What other questions could you ask about this passage?

The six basic questions: What is this passage about? What do we learn about God? What do we learn about man? If this passage is true what will you change in your life? Who will you tell? And who will you help?

Matthew 16:13–21 — Planting churches

This takes place somewhere between 2-1/2 and 3 years into Jesus' public ministry.

¹³ Now when Jesus came into the district of Caesarea Philippi, he asked his disciples, "Who do people say that the Son of Man is?" ¹⁴ And they said, "Some say John the Baptist, others say Elijah, and others Jeremiah or one of the prophets."

    i.   What were people's perceptions of Jesus?

    ii.   What were the people hoping for?

    iii.   Why did Jesus start the conversation this way?

    iv.   Can we apply this method as we engage people?

¹⁵ He said to them, "But who do you say that I am?"

    v.   Why would the perspective of the disciples be different than that of the people?

    vi.   What does this tell you about what you can expect as you grow as a disciple of Jesus?

¹⁶ Simon Peter replied, "You are the Christ, the Son of the living God." ¹⁷ And Jesus answered him, "Blessed are you, Simon Bar-Jonah! For flesh and blood has not revealed this to you, but my Father who is in heaven.

    vii.   What is Jesus' emotional response; how would you describe his response to Simon's profession?

    viii.   (The name Simon means "one who hears." Bar means "son of.") Based on these definitions, what is Jesus saying to and about Simon?

    ix.   What is the critical thing that has happened with Simon at this moment?

    x.   How would you describe Simon-Peter before he started following Jesus?

xi.   What did he become when he began to follow Jesus?

xii.   Do you have to be a believer before you become a disciple?

xiii.   What did Simon demonstrate in these verses that elicited this response from Jesus? What do you think is Jesus' desire for all of his disciples?

¹⁸ And I tell you, you are Peter, and on this rock "I will" build my church, and the gates of hell shall not prevail against it.

xiv.   Who will build Jesus' church?

xv.   (Peter — "petros" means "stone" or "small rock"; rock — "petra" means "bedrock,") Reflecting on these two words, what is the foundation upon which Jesus will build his church?

xvi.   Recalling Jesus' command in Matthew 28:19, what is our responsibility in building Jesus' church?

xvii.   What is the relationship between the church and hell?

xviii.   How and where does this apply today?

¹⁹ "I will" give you the keys of the kingdom of heaven, and whatever you bind on earth shall be bound in heaven, and whatever you loose on earth shall be loosed in heaven."

xix.   Where does it appear that the "kingdom of heaven" lies and what is the effect of disciples hearing from God?

xx.   What is the source of the "keys" that lock and unlock entrance into the kingdom of heaven?

xxi.   What are the criteria indicated to receive these keys? (ref. vs. 17)

²⁰ Then he strictly charged the disciples to tell no one that he was the Christ. ²¹ From that time Jesus began to show his disciples that he must go to Jerusalem and suffer many things from the elders and chief priests and scribes, and be killed, and on the third day be raised.

xxii.   What changed in Jesus' ministry following Peter's profession and what had it been?

xxiii.   What goal did Jesus have to achieve before he focused on redeeming the world?

xxiv.   What does this tell us of the importance that Jesus placed on making disciples?

What other questions could you ask about this passage?

The six basic questions: What is this passage about? What do we learn about God? What do we learn about man? If this passage is true what will you change in your life? Who will you tell? And who will you help?

Philippians 2:1–8 — Model for our actions

So if there is any encouragement in Christ, any comfort from love, any participation in the Spirit, any affection and sympathy, ² complete my joy by being of the same mind, having the same love, being in full accord and of one mind.

    i.   What are some of the sources to be able to be of the same mind, have the same love, and be in full accord?

    ii.   Where this unity is lacking what is the solution?

³ Do nothing from selfish ambition or conceit, but in humility count others more significant than yourselves. ⁴ Let each of you look not only to his own interests, but also to the interests of others.

    iii.   How is "humility" demonstrated?

    iv.   What are some of the causes of selfishness?

⁵ Have this mind among yourselves, which is yours in Christ Jesus, ⁶ who, though he was in the form of God, did not count equality with God a thing to be grasped, ⁷ but emptied himself, by taking the form of a servant, being born in the likeness of men. ⁸ And being found in human form, he humbled himself by becoming obedient to the point of death, even death on a cross.

    v.   How did Jesus model reaching to another culture?

    vi.   What does it mean for you to "empty" yourself?

    vii.   What are some of the obstacles that keep you from reaching out to others?

    viii. What was Jesus mission to us? What should yours be?

What other questions could you ask about this passage?

The six basic questions: What is this passage about? What do we learn about God? What do we learn about man? If this passage is true what will you change in your life? Who will you tell? And who will you help?

1 Corinthians 9:19–23 — Cultural relevance

For though I am free from all, I have made myself a servant to all, that I might win more of them.

    i.   Why has Jesus given us freedom?

    ii.   How is this connected to fulfilling the Great Commission (Mt 28:16–20)

²⁰ To the Jews I became as a Jew, in order to win Jews.

    iii.   Paul was a Jew, what did he mean that he "became as a Jew?"

To those under the law I became as one under the law (though not being myself under the law) that I might win those under the law.

    iv.   What is the difference between being a Jew and being under the law?

    v.   How is it possible to submit to "the law" without being "under the law?"

[21] To those outside the law I became as one outside the law (not being outside the law of God but under the law of Christ) that I might win those outside the law.

    vi.   What do we learn about the law of Christ from this verse?

    vii.   Are believers free from all Law? How should this affect the way we live?

[22] To the weak I became weak, that I might win the weak.

    viii.   What are the different type of weaknesses with which Paul might identify?

I have become all things to all people, that by all means I might save some.

    ix.   How flexible was Paul in his approach to reaching people?

    x.   What was Paul's sole goal in all that he did?

    xi.   How do you think people might react to this flexibility?

    xii.   What is the counterbalance to prevent inappropriate compromise (syncretism)? (see verse 21)

    xiii.   How can we maintain maximum flexibility without compromise?

[23] I do it all for the sake of the gospel, that I may share with them in its blessings.

    xiv.   What does Paul mean, by "share with them" in the blessings of the gospel?

What other questions could you ask about this passage?

The six basic questions: What is this passage about? What do we learn about God? What do we learn about man? If this passage is true what will you change in your life? Who will you tell? And who will you help?

Acts 17:22–27 — Where to start

So Paul, standing in the midst of the Areopagus, said: "Men of Athens, I perceive that in every way you are very religious. [23] For as I passed along and observed the objects of your worship, I found also an altar with this inscription, 'To the unknown god.' What therefore you worship as unknown, this I proclaim to you.

    i.   What is Paul demonstrating here?

    ii.   What does this challenge you to do when you are entering a different culture?

[24] The God who made the world and everything in it, being Lord of heaven and earth, does not live in temples made by man, [25] nor is he served by human hands, as though he needed anything, since he himself gives to all mankind life and breath and everything. [26] And he

made from one man every nation of mankind to live on all the face of the earth, having determined allotted periods and the boundaries of their dwelling place, ²⁷ *that they should seek God, and perhaps feel their way toward him and find him.*

    iii.   What is Paul presenting here?

    iv.   What do we learn from this about the simple church in contrast to temples?

    v.   What do we learn about our involvement in God's timing and places?

    vi.   How can you be prepared to address people in different cultures?

Yet he is actually not far from each one of us,

    vii.   What is Paul saying about God?

    viii.   How might he demonstrate God's nearness?

What other questions could you ask about this passage?

The six basic questions: What is this passage about? What do we learn about God? What do we learn about man? If this passage is true what will you change in your life? Who will you tell? And who will you help?

2 Timothy 2:1–7; 14–16 — Key to replication

You then, my child, be strengthened by the grace that is in Christ Jesus,

    i.   If grace is defined as "God's power working in us and through us, to accomplish his purposes for his glory," what does this tell us we need to have?

    ii.   How can we receive this? What can you do to receive more of this grace?

² *and what you have heard from me in the presence of many witnesses entrust to faithful men who will be able to teach others also.*

    iii.   What are three keys to replication given in this verse?

    iv.   How do we test a man to see if he is faithful?

    v.   What does this imply about our ongoing relationship with him or her?

³ *Share in suffering as a good soldier of Christ Jesus.* ⁴ *No soldier gets entangled in civilian pursuits, since his aim is to please the one who enlisted him.* ⁵ *An athlete is not crowned unless he competes according to the rules.* ⁶ *It is the hard-working farmer who ought to have the first share of the crops.*

    vi.   What do we learn about maintaining focus on our goals?

    vii.   How does this affect our involvement with the "faithful men" with whom we are working?

    viii.   What might be the "first share of the crops?"

⁷ Think over what I say, for the Lord will give you understanding in everything.

    ix.   What is the relationship between thinking and prayer?

¹⁴ Remind them of these things, and charge them before God not to quarrel about words, which does no good, but only ruins the hearers.

    x.   What is the difference between quarreling and discussing?

    xi.   What does it mean to quarrel about words?

    xii.   About what are we to remind the people with whom we work?

    xiii.   What does this tell us about the nature of our ongoing relationship with the people we coach in the Disciple-Making Process?

¹⁵ Do your best to present yourself to God as one approved, a worker who has no need to be ashamed, rightly handling the word of truth.

    xiv.   What does this tell us about our own self-conduct as disciples of Jesus?

    xv.   How are the best ways to handle the "word of truth"?

¹⁶ But avoid irreverent babble, for it will lead people into more and more ungodliness

    xvi.   What are some of the types of "irreverent babble" that we should avoid?

    xvii.   Overall the first 16 verses of this chapter, what are some of the practical lessons that you can apply to assuring that the Discovery Groups and churches that emerge from the Disciple-Making Process continue to replicate accurately?

Make a list of all the components to replication that you find here

    xviii.   How will you do this in your own work?

What other questions could you ask about this passage?

The six basic questions: What is this passage about? What do we learn about God? What do we learn about man? If this passage is true what will you change in your life? Who will you tell? And who will you help?

John 15:1–11 — Being Fruitful as Proof of Disciple-Making

15 "I am the true vine, and my Father is the vinedresser.

- What does this tell us about the relationship between Jesus and the Father?

- What do we learn about Jesus' role in our lives?

² Every branch in me that does not bear fruit he takes away, and every branch that does bear fruit he prunes, that it may bear more fruit.

- What do we learn about Jesus' expectations for us?

- What do we learn about failure to meet Jesus' expectations?

- What do we learn about the role that trials and difficulties serve in our lives?

- Why doesn't Jesus tell us what it means to be fruitful?

³ Already you are clean because of the word that I have spoken to you.

- What do we learn about the effect of memorizing Jesus' words?

⁴ Abide in me, and I in you. As the branch cannot bear fruit by itself, unless it abides in the vine, neither can you, unless you abide in me. ⁵ I am the vine; you are the branches. Whoever abides in me and I in him, he it is that bears much fruit, for apart from me you can do nothing.

- What do we learn about our ongoing relationship with Jesus?

- How can we abide in Jesus and what will you do to make this happen?

- What role does having a Discovery Group have in this (Matthew 18:20)?

⁶ If anyone does not abide in me he is thrown away like a branch and withers; and the branches are gathered, thrown into the fire, and burned.

xi. What does this indicate about the need to be fruitful?

⁷ If you abide in me, and my words abide in you, ask whatever you wish, and it will be done for you. ⁸ By this my Father is glorified, that you bear much fruit and so prove to be my disciples.

xii. What is the effect of having Jesus' words abide in us and how does this affect our freedom to "ask whatever we wish?"

xiii. What is the proof that we are disciples of Jesus?

xiv. What is the purpose of being a disciple of Jesus and bearing fruit?

xv. What then is the ultimate purpose of all that a disciple of Jesus does?

⁹ As the Father has loved me, so have I loved you. Abide in my love.

- What is the ultimate effect of abiding in the love that Jesus has for us as disciples?

¹⁰ If you keep my commandments, you will abide in my love, just as I have kept my Father's commandments and abide in his love.

- What condition do we need to fulfill to abide in the love of Jesus?

- A disciple models and obeys. Whose disciple was Jesus?

- By being a disciple of Jesus, whose disciple do we ultimately become?

¹¹ These things I have spoken to you, that my joy may be in you, and that your joy may be full.

Appendix 3: Scripture Questions

- What is the result of being a disciple of Jesus, based on this passage?

- What have you noticed about your own joy as you have become a disciple of Jesus?

What other questions could you ask about this passage?

The six basic questions: What is this passage about? What do we learn about God? What do we learn about man? If this passage is true what will you change in your life? Who will you tell? And who will you help?

Appendix 4: Prayer Guides

Community Prayer Guide –

(Developed by Andrew and Heather Hocking)

Examples include a specific neighborhood, company, ethnicity, organization, affinity group, etc.

Thank God for what He is doing in the Community — Identify what God is doing.

Continue steadfastly in prayer, being watchful in it with thanksgiving. (Col 4:2)

Pray for Laborers to Partner with You

And He was saying to them, "The harvest is plentiful, but the laborers are few; therefore beseech the Lord of the harvest to send out laborers into His harvest." (Luke 10:2)

Pray for someone to join you and for God to raise up workers from the harvest.
Write down names of people who can partner with you in prayer and reaching the community:

_____   _____   _____

_____   _____   _____

Pray for Guidance in Reaching the Community

Ask God, and write down any insight that God gives you for reaching the community:

Pray for Open Doors to the Gospel

At the same time, pray also for us, that God may open to us a door for the word, to declare the mystery of Christ, on account of which I am in prison- that I may make it clear, which is how I ought to speak. (Col 4:3–4)

Pray for natural opportunities to discuss Christ and spirituality with people in the community.

Pray for Individuals

Write down individuals that you know in community:

_____   _____   _____

_____   _____   _____

_____   _____   _____

Pray for Persons of Peace

And if a son of peace is there, your peace will rest upon him. But if not, it will return to you. (Luke 10:6)

Persons of Peace are insiders in the community who are spiritually hungry and will share spiritual things with others. Pray that God would connect you with persons of peace. Make note of the individuals that fit this description and pray for them.

_____   _____   _____

_____   _____   _____

Pray God would Demolish Strongholds in the Community

For the weapons of our warfare are not of the flesh but have divine power to destroy strongholds. (2 Cor 10:4)

Write down worldviews contrary to the Gospel and pray God reveals truth. Write down problems in the community and pray God brings transformation in these areas:

Pray for Multiplication Inside and Out from the Community

Write down other communities to which the Gospel can spread:

_____   _____   _____

Great Commission Scripture Prayer

Praying through the scriptures is a powerful way to connect ourselves with God's heart and mind. The center of making disciples is responding to the Great Commission using the process that Jesus gave his disciples to make other disciples. The following two passages, Matthew 28:16–20 and Luke 10:1–11 encapsulate our mission as Disciple Makers. You can use this in both your personal prayer as well as in group prayer sessions.

Matthew 28:16–20 (ESV)

[16] Now the eleven disciples went to Galilee, to the mountain to which Jesus had directed them.

- *Thank God for Jesus, his sacrificial work of reconciliation*
- *Thank him for allowing us to be disciples of his son Jesus.*
- *Pray your fellow Disciple Makers by name*
- *Thank him for the directions that Jesus gives us.*

Example: *Father God, we thank you for the directions of your son Jesus. We thank you and praise you for offering him as a sacrifice to pay the price of our redemption and to reconcile us to you through him. We thank you Jesus, that you have called us to yourself to live fully as your disciples by giving us you Word and asking your father to send your Holy Spirit to abide in us, to teach us, and guide us.*

[17] And when they saw him they worshiped him, but some doubted.

- *Worship God the Father, the Son, and the Spirit for his greatness, steadfast love, etc.*
- *Confess your doubts, failures, and sins.*
- *Ask for his assurance, direction, and forgiveness*

[18] And Jesus came and said to them, "All authority in heaven and on earth has been given to me.

- *In silence: Seek to dwell in Jesus' presence and allow him to talk to you.*
- *Make note of anything he tells you, be it words, a sense, or a scripture.*
- *Out loud: ask Jesus to assure you of his direction for your life and to allow you to work in that authority that he has.*

[19] Having gone make disciples of all people groups (languages and cultures),

- *Pray for the people groups and / or the communities to which he is sending you. Use whatever "Community Prayer Guide" you have prepared. [There are 299 languages spoken in homes of the diverse population in Minnesota.]*
- *Ask God to use you to bring others to his son Jesus.*

Baptizing them in the name of the Father and of the Son and of the Holy Spirit,

- *Ask God to direct you so that you will operate in the fullness of his person.*
- *Ask the Holy Spirit to use you to bring others fully into becoming disciple of Jesus.*

²⁰ teaching them to obey all that I have commanded you.

- *Commit yourself to teaching those who seek God, to obey all of the commandments of Jesus.*

- *Ask the Holy Spirit for guidance and his presence in doing this effectively.*

And behold, I am with you always, to the end of the age."

- *Thank and praise Jesus for his presence and guidance*

- *Acknowledge that it is Jesus and not you who is making disciples.*

Luke 10:1–11 (ESV)

¹ After this the Lord appointed Seventy-two others and sent them on ahead of him, two by two, into every town and place where he himself was about to go.

- *Pray for the other disciples Jesus is sending out, your three and your twelve.*

- *Ask Jesus to join you with other Disciple Makers, his Seventy-two.*

- *Thank Jesus for calling and appointing you to continue the work of fulfilling the Great Commission.*

- *Ask Jesus to direct you where he is manifesting his presence and to open your eyes to recognize the people in whom he is working.*

² And he said to them, "The harvest is plentiful, but the laborers are few. Therefore pray earnestly to the Lord of the harvest to send out laborers into his harvest.

- *Acknowledge that God is the Lord of the harvest.*

- *Beseech him to send out additional laborers and to prepare them and you.*

- *Ask God to open your eyes to see and recognize the harvest and identify the existing laborers who are there.*

³ Go your way; behold, I am sending you out as lambs in the midst of wolves.

- *Pray for protection for yourself and your family against the physical, spiritual, and relational attacks of the enemy.*

- *Pray that the Holy Spirit guides you pass people, and bureaucratic, religious, and spiritual obstacles.*

- *Pray for discernment of spirits and the authority and wisdom in dealing with them.*

⁴ Carry no moneybag, no knapsack, no sandals, and greet no one on the road.

- *Pray for God's financial, housing, and clothing provision.*

- *Ask God to guide your tongue and give you discernment about whom you make your ally.*

- *Resolve to keep focused and not allow yourself to become distracted.*

⁵ Whatever house you enter, first say, 'Peace be to this house!' ⁶ And if a son of peace is

there, your peace will rest upon him. But if not, it will return to you.

- *Ask Jesus for his peace to abide in you and empower you.*

- *Pray for the peace of God for each person and their Oikos with whom you are in contact.*

- *Ask God to confirm the person of peace or lead you to the one who is.*

[7] And remain in the same house, eating and drinking what they provide, for the laborer deserves his wages. Do not go from house to house.

- *Ask God for the grace to receive hospitality*

- *Ask for God's patience and endurance as you work with individual people of peace.*

- *Ask God to strengthen and develop long lasting relationships with people of peace.*

- *Pray for those who are difficult and to establish and strengthen your relationship with those people of peace whom God desires to use for bringing in the harvest.*

- *Commit yourself to coach, mentor and befriend those whom God sends into your life.*

- *Ask God to provide for all physical and spiritual needs as you work with the people of peace God has appointed to bring in the harvest.*

[8] Whenever you enter a town and they receive you, eat what is set before you.

- *Ask God to help you accept people where they are and then letting God make the changes needed in their lives.*

- *Ask God for wisdom on what you say and how to act.*

[9] Heal the sick in it and say to them, 'The kingdom of God has come near to you.

- *Ask God to empower you to heal the sick, cast out evil spirits, break addictions, and encourage the broken hearted.*

- *Commit yourself to focus on God's kingdom and nothing else (no doctrine or practices).*

[10] But whenever you enter a town and they do not receive you, go into its streets and say, [11] 'Even the dust of your town that clings to our feet we wipe off against you. Nevertheless know this, that the kingdom of God has come near.'

- *Ask God for discernment of when to persevere and when to leave.*

- *Ask God how to leave an open door for the kingdom in the hearts of the people.*

Matthew 28:20b

And behold, I am with you always, to the end of the age."

- *Once again thank and praise Jesus for his presence and guidance*

- *Acknowledge that it is Jesus and not you who is making disciples.*

Praying Paul's Epistles

As you focus your prayer to individuals or groups of people, you may find the following passages from Paul's epistles useful.

Ephesians 1:15–23

Ephesians 1:15–23 is a good passage to pray for people who need to be delivered from demonic influences:

[15] For this reason, because I have heard of your faith in the Lord Jesus and your love toward all the saints, [16] I do not cease to give thanks for you, remembering you in my prayers, [17] that the God of our Lord Jesus Christ, the Father of glory, may give you the Spirit of wisdom and of revelation in the knowledge of him, [18] having the eyes of your hearts enlightened, that you may know what is the hope to which he has called you, what are the riches of his glorious inheritance in the saints, [19] and what is the immeasurable greatness of his power toward us who believe, according to the working of his great might [20] that he worked in Christ when he raised him from the dead and seated him at his right hand in the heavenly places, [21] far above all rule and authority and power and dominion, and above every name that is named, not only in this age but also in the one to come. [22] And he put all things under his feet and gave him as head over all things to the church, [23] which is his body, the fullness of him who fills all in all.

Father God, I pray that _____ (each person you are reaching out to) may come to faith in your son Jesus and know him as Lord and savior. That you would give _____ the spirit of wisdom and of revelation in knowledge of you. Enlighten ____ eyes that ____ might know the hope to which you have called ____ and the riches of your glorious inheritance with the saints. Reveal the immeasurable greatness of your power into ___ li(fe-ves), so that ___ might know and believe that you raised Jesus from the dead and have seated him at your right hand in the heavenly places.

Father, place all of the authorities, powers, and dominions that have control in _____ li(fe-ves) beneath the feet of your son Jesus, so that he might be the head over everything in ____ li(fe-ves), until ____ is(are) fully united with your son as part of his body, his church and grow(s) into his fullness. AMEN!

Ephesians 3:14–21

Ephesians 3:14–21 — Is a good passage to pray for your fellow workers.
(Substitute individual names)

[14] For this reason I bow my knees before the Father, [15] from whom every family in heaven and on earth is named, [16] that according to the riches of his glory he may grant you to be strengthened with power through his Spirit in your inner being, [17] so that Christ may dwell in your hearts through faith—that you, being rooted and grounded in love, [18] may have strength to comprehend with all the saints what is the breadth and length and height and depth, [19] and to know the love of Christ that surpasses knowledge, that you may be filled with all the fullness of God.

[20] Now to him who is able to do far more abundantly than all that we ask or think, according to the power at work within us, [21] to him be glory in the church and in Christ Jesus throughout all generations, forever and ever. Amen.

Lord God, heavenly father, I bow my knees before you, from whom every family in heaven and on earth is named. Strengthen (each of your workers) in their inner being according to the riches of your glory, so that Christ may live in (their) heart(s) through faith. So, (each of them) being rooted and grounded in love, may have strength to comprehend with all of the saints, what is the breadth and length and height and depth and to know the love of your son Jesus that surpasses knowledge. Let (them) be filled with all your fullness, heavenly father. For you are able to do far more abundantly than all we ask or think, according to the power that is at work within us. Father, may you be glorified in the church and in your son Jesus throughout all generations, forever and ever. Amen!

Philippians 1:9–11

[9] And it is my prayer that your love may abound more and more, with knowledge and all discernment, [10] so that you may approve what is excellent, and so be pure and blameless for the day of Christ, [11] filled with the fruit of righteousness that comes through Jesus Christ, to the glory and praise of God.

2 Thessalonians 1:11–12

[11] To this end we always pray for you, that our God may make you worthy of his calling and may fulfill every resolve for good and every work of faith by his power, [12] so that the name of our Lord Jesus may be glorified in you, and you in him, according to the grace of our God and the Lord Jesus Christ.

2 Thessalonians 2:16–17

[16] Now may our Lord Jesus Christ himself, and God our Father, who loved us and gave us eternal comfort and good hope through grace, [17] comfort your hearts and establish them in every good work and word.

Philippians 1:9–11 and the two 2nd Thessalonians passages are good to pray together for yourself and your ministry team:

(Substitute individual names)

Father God, I pray that (our) love may abound more and more with knowledge and all discernment, so that (we) may approve what is excellent, and so be pure and blameless for the day of Christ. May (we) be filled with the fruit of righteousness that comes through your son Jesus to glorify and praise your name.

Father, to this end I pray that you will make (us) worthy of the calling that you have given (us) and fulfill every resolve for good and every work of faith by your power, so that the name of your son Jesus may be glorified in you, and you in him, according to your grace and that of your son Jesus.

Father, we ask that your son Jesus himself and you who have loved us and given (us) eternal comfort and good hope through your grace will continue to comfort (our) hearts and establish (us) in every good work and word.
Amen!

Colossians 1:9–14

[9] And so, from the day we heard, we have not ceased to pray for you, asking that you may be filled with the knowledge of his will in all spiritual wisdom and understanding, [10] so as to walk in a manner worthy of the Lord, fully pleasing to him, bearing fruit in every good work and increasing in the knowledge of God. [11] May you be strengthened with all power, according to his glorious might, for all endurance and patience with joy, [12] giving thanks to the Father, who has qualified you to share in the inheritance of the saints in light. [13] He has delivered us from the domain of darkness and transferred us to the kingdom of his beloved Son, [14] in whom we have redemption, the forgiveness of sins.

Colossians 1:9–14 **is** good to pray for lost family members

"Dear Heavenly Father, I pray for _____ today. I ask that you would fill _____ with the knowledge of your will with all spiritual wisdom and understanding, so that _____ will walk in a manner worthy of you and please you in everything and bearing fruit in every good work. I ask that _____ might increase in knowledge of you. May _____ be strengthened with all power, according to your glorious might, so that _____ might have full endurance and patience joyfully giving thanks to you, Father, for qualifying _____ to share in the inheritance of the saints in light. I ask that you would fully deliver _____ from the domain of darkness and transfer _____ to the kingdom of your beloved Son Jesus in whom we have redemption, the forgiveness of sin. Amen.

Appendix 5: Discovery Group Questions

1) COMMUNITY — Opening Questions:

• What are you thankful for this week?

• What problems do you have this week? *(Counseling should take place outside group time.)*

• Is there any way this group can help you? *(Help physically or pray for these.)*

2) SHARE EXPERIENCES —Review Questions: *(These start second time.)*

• With whom did you share last week's passage?

• Did you apply what you learned since our last meeting and how did it go?

• What has happened with the people you helped?

• How have you experienced God since the last time that we met?

3) DISCOVERY — Bible Study: (Read, Reread, Retell, Details)

Read the passage at least twice. The second time one person can reread it while the others just listen. Then take turns trying to retell the passage in each person's words covering all of the main points, the group should add missing parts. The **goal** is to learn together and be able to share this passage with someone outside the group in your own words by memory.

Details: Discuss the passage: Participants are required to confine their remarks to the passage being studied (no preaching or teaching or outside materials.) Challenge question: "Where does it say that in this passage?"

• What happens in this scripture passage?

• What do we discover about God from it?

• What do we discover about people from it?

4) OBEDIENCE — "I Will" and "We Will" Statements must be practical and able to be started in 24 to 48 hours. *(Record these for next meeting.)*

Now that the group members have discovered truths from God's Word, identify what difference this makes in each of your lives.

I will change my daily life to reflect the reality that I have learned. (I will)

• If this scripture passage is true, how does it change how we see God?

• If this is true, how does this change how we treat others?

• If it is true, how does it change what we do? (We will)

5) OUTREACH—Concluding Questions:

• What other questions do you have about this passage?

• With whom will you share this story, when, and how? *(Record these for next meeting)*

• Do you know anyone who needs help? What can this group do to help them?

For believers: Pray for needs from 1) and the people with whom you will share and help.

LAST QUESTION — When do you want to meet again?

Appendix 5: Discovery Group Questions

Small Group Acrostic — LOOP Format

This acrostic is designed to aid in remembering the Discovery Process and covers the same materials as in the regular Discovery Group Process

1) 𝕷ive the Word: (Start the *Review Questions the second time.*)
COMMUNITY — Opening Questions:
• What are you thankful for this week?

SHARE EXPERIENCES —Review Questions: *(Start at second meeting)*
> • *With whom did you share last week's passage?*
> • *Did you apply what you learned since our last meeting?*
> • *How have you experienced God since the last time that we met?*

• What challenges do you have this week? *(Any counseling should take place outside group time.)*
• Is there any way this group can help you? *(Help physically or pray for these.)*

2) 𝕺pen the Word: DISCOVERY STUDY:
(Read, Reread, Retell, Details)
Read the passage at least twice. The second time one person can reread it while the others listen. Then take turns trying to retell the passage in each person's words covering all of the main points, the group should add missing parts. The **goal** is to learn together and be able to share this passage with someone outside the group in your own words by memory.

Details: Discuss the passage. Participants are required to confine their remarks to the passage being studied (no preaching or teaching or outside materials.) Challenge question: "Where does it say that in this passage?"
• What happens in this scripture passage?
• What do we discover about God from it?
• What do we discover about people from it?

3) 𝕺bey the Word: "I will and we will statements" must be practical and something that can be started in 24 to 48 hours. *(Record these for next meeting.)*

Now that the group members have discovered truths from God's Word, identify what difference this makes in each of your lives. The individual application "I will" statements should be each person's response to what they discover personally and not directed by others. Group "we will" statements should be by consensus of the entire group. Individual "I will" statements should happen weekly. "We will" statements only happen when there is a consensus. *Metanoia (Greek) - repentance, a change of mind and actions.)*
I will change my daily life to reflect the reality that I have learned. (I will)
• If this scripture passage is true, how does it change how we see God?
• If this is true, how does this change how we treat others?
• If it is true, how does it change what we do? (We will)

4) 𝕻ass on the Word:
Concluding Questions for Outreach:
• What other questions do you have about this passage?
• With whom will you share this story, when, and how? *(Record these for next meeting)*
• Do you know anyone who needs help? What can this group do to help them?
Pray for needs from 1) and for the people with whom you will share and help.
LAST QUESTION: When do you want to meet again? What do we change?

Appendix 6
Video Training Resources — Current in 2016

It is recommended that you download the below videos to use in your training. You can also download one large zip file (takes over an hour to download) containing all videos here: http://tinyurl.com/nskxkv4 (1.9 GB)

1. Cityteam — DMM Overview (5 min.): https://www.youtube.com/watch?v=29b-KlAFr28

2. Act Beyond — Introduction

    a. Disciple-Making Training (8 min.): http://vimeo.com/84442681

    b. Awareness Training (6 min.): https://vimeo.com/76341533

3. Jerry Trousdale — What are DMM (3 min.): https://www.youtube.com/watch?v=6xlVhXw9G4A

4. Richard Williams — Disciple (5.5 min.): https://www.youtube.com/watch?v=JidJe9PkmOE

5. Ed Gross — First Century Discipleship

    a. Introduction (4 min): https://www.youtube.com/watch?v=qlREyeb671g

    b. Part 1: The Foundation (12 min.): https://www.youtube.com/watch?v=x_Ma5fwYaYM

    c. Part 2: Follow Me (12 min.): https://www.youtube.com/watch?v=tUY8JQ0WkKI

    d. Part 3: Fruit That Remains (13 min.): https://www.youtube.com/watch?v=ArIo9uy7W8o

    e. Part 4: The Form (13 min.): https://www.youtube.com/watch?v=HvMc3VsMNq8

    f. Conclusion (13 min.): https://www.youtube.com/watch?v=UqjIXWYJs-0

6. Dave Hunt — Group Process (4 min.): https://www.youtube.com/watch?v=dHggzCWYL-Q

7. Dave Hunt — Bible Study Process (5 min.): https://www.youtube.com/watch?v=azJq4McK7uc

8. Jerry Trousdale — Obedience (4.5 min.): https://www.youtube.com/watch?v=bvQJdKCHn2M

9. Jerry Trousdale — Prayer (4 min.) https://www.youtube.com/watch?v=hzgWV4i8tEs

10. Dave Hunt — Group Process (4 min.): https://www.youtube.com/watch?v=dHggzCWYL-Q

11. Dave Hunt — People of peace (3 min.): https://www.youtube.com/watch?v=m_lvX5UfM3Q

12. Richard Williams — Disciple Maker (6 min.): https://www.youtube.com/watch?v=V5zA9FaLn-E

13. Jim Yost — Inhibitors to DMM

    a. Part 1: Lack of Obedience (3 min.): https://www.youtube.com/watch?v=tjgfU4XKgAw min.) https://www.youtube.com/watch?v=hzgWV4i8tEshttps://www.youtube.com/watch?v=UqjIXWYJs-0

    b. Part 2: Preparing a PoP (2 min.): https://www.youtube.com/watch?v=ia8OvFtd6Tw

    c. Part 3: Multiplication (2 min.): https://www.youtube.com/watch?v=aSdf-wD5EMg

Appendix 7: Topical Discovery Studies

PURPOSE (This series of topical studies was developed by Jim Yost.)

Because people do not always want to commit to a 25-week study of Creation to Christ, we have designed Trial Discovery Bible Studies that ask people to only commit to 6 weeks (or 6 sessions) and are designed with the felt-needs of the group in mind. Among the 9 Major Categories you will certainly find one that fits your target audience. The point is not to do all of these studies like a curriculum. The point is to find just one that fits your target group of people and do it for six sessions in order to find who the Person of Peace actually is. Then you can move into a longer series introducing them to who Jesus is. Nearly all of the scriptures used in these DS's are narrative in nature which makes it easier for not-yet believers to enter into discussion and makes is conducive to 'story-telling'. Our desire is to get people quickly into scripture that's relevant to their lives in order to see who is responding to God.

Table of Contents

Great Commission Disciple Making

MEN — MASCULINITY — "I get mixed messages about what a man should be — somewhere between macho and passive. I know Jesus is God, but is he also someone I can look to as the ultimate man?"

1 — The Divine Jesus	"God with us"	Matthew 1:18–25
2 — The Human Jesus	"Isn't this Joseph's son?"	Luke 4:14–30
3 — The Initiated Jesus	Baptized and tempted	Matthew 3:13–4:11
4 — The Tough Jesus	Temple cleansing time	Mark 11:12–19
5 — The Tender Jesus	"Jesus wept"	John 11:1–44
6 — The Triumphant Jesus	Jesus' death	Luke 23:44–49

MEN — ACCOUNTABILITY — "It's about time men got together and got real. I know what's right and what I need to do. I don't need advice, but I do need a group of guys to listen, keep what I say to themselves, and hold me accountable."

1 — Our Need for Others	Raising the roof for a friend	Mark 2:1–12
2 — Our Need for Accountability	Gehazi caught red–handed	2 Kings 5:1–27
3 — Our Need for Support	David's mighty men	2 Samuel 23:8–23
4 — Our Need for Counsel	Rehoboam needs advice	I Kings 12:1–24
5 — Our Need for Correction	Nathan rebukes David	2 Samuel 12:1–14
6 — Our Need for Mentoring	Moses commissions Joshua	Numbers 27:12–23

MEN — DISCIPLE MAKING — "Could anyone tell me what it means to be a man of God? I'm tired of pious Jesus talk and Sunday Christians. If I'm going to commit to this, I'm going all the way."

1 — Fighting Spirit	David and Goliath	I Samuel 17:12–50
2 — Total Commitment	The rich young man	Mark 10:17–31
3 — Obedience	Abraham's greatest test	Genesis 22:1–19
4 — Teachable Spirit	Peter's stretching vision	Acts 10:1–23
5 — Spreading the Word	Don't just stand there	Acts 1:1–11
6 — God's Man at Home	"As for me and my house"	Joshua 24:1–27

MEN — ATTITUDE ADJUSTMENT — "Pressure is closing in on me. Too many demands; Not enough time; Money; My job; My kids; My marriage. Things are out of control and getting worse. I can't take this rat race anymore."

1 — Pressures	Three men and a furnace	Daniel 3:1–30
2 — Demands	Moses and spoiled Israel	Numbers 11:4–34
3 — Chaos	Paul and Silas in prison	Acts 16:16–40
4 — Blowing It	Peter denies Jesus	Luke 22:54–62
5 — Family Stress	Fractured family	Luke 15:11–32
6 — Moving On	Peter steps out of the boat	Matthew 14:22–33

MEN — PERFORMANCE ANXIETY — "I constantly feel like my job is on the line. I'm always afraid I'm not measuring up. Even when I'm home I worry about work."

1 — Who Is The Boss?	Workers in the vineyard	Matthew 20:1–16
2 — What's My Responsibility?	Parable of the talents	Matthew 25:14–30
3 — What's God's Responsibility?	God fights Gideon's battle	Judges 7:1–25
4 — Working for Tyrants	Bricks and straw	Exodus 5:1–21
5 — Worry is Overwhelming	Moses under stress	Exodus 5:22–6:12
6 — Being Content	Abram gives Lot a choice	Genesis 13:1–18

Appendix 7: Topical Discovery Studies

MEN — ISSUES MEN FACE — "There are some things I need to talk about, although it won't be easy. I'm sure other guys fight the same battles. We just don't tell each other. I think I'm ready to talk."

1 — Opening Up	A Pharisee and a tax collector	Luke 18:9–14
2 — Fatal Attraction	David and Bathsheba	2 Samuel 11:1–27
3 — My Dark Side	Dirty dancing	Mark 6:14–29
4 — My Doubts	I believe, help my unbelief	Mark 9:14–29
5 — Authority Figures	King Saul fails badly	I Samuel 13:1–15
6 — Spiritual Responsibility	Eli: A failure at home	I Samuel 2:12–26

WOMEN — REAL BEAUTY — "It's a constant battle! My hair, my shape and my clothes are never quite right. I know I don't need to measure up to the glamorous stereotype, but where can I find a role model for real beauty?"

1 — I Don't Measure Up	Amazing affirmation	John 7:53–8:11
2 — Struggle to Stay in Shape	Leah and Rachel	Genesis 29:31–30:24
3 — Keeping Up My Image	Queen of Sheba	I Kings 10:1–13
4 — Finding My Own Style	Stylish love	Luke 7:36–50
5 — Staying Focused	Wealthy woman focused	2 Kings 4:8–37
6 — Achieving Real Beauty	Mary's song	Luke 1:39–56

WOMEN — WHEN LIFE IS NOT A PARTY — "I never thought my life would be like this. I've had so many disappointments and unfulfilled expectations. I try so hard, but things just don't go the way I've hoped. What am I doing wrong?"

1 — Where's The Romance?	Rachel and Leah	Genesis 29:1–30
2 — Grown Up, and Doing This?	Swallowing pride	Jonah 1:1–17
3 — Where's My Dream House?	The house built on rock	Matthew 7:24–29
4 — Where's My Dream Family?	Rebekah tricks Isaac	Genesis 27:1–40
5 — Weren't We Best Friends?	Hagar's favor turns sour	Genesis 16:1–16
6 — No More Goodbyes!	Mary must say goodbye	John 20:1–18

WOMEN — BEING A GODLY WOMAN — "What does God want me to be like? How can I apply what the Bible says about women to real life today?"

1 — Seeking God's Truth	Queen of Sheba	I Kings 10:1–13
2 — Using My Gifts	Priscilla	Acts 18:1–4, 18–28
3 — Caring for Others	Shunammite woman	2 Kings 4:8–37
4 — Being Bold, Yet Wise	Esther	Esther 4:6–17; 7:1–10
5 — Trusting God in the Unknown	Ruth	Ruth 1:1–22
6 — Giving God the Glory	Mary, mother of Jesus	Luke 1:39–56

WOMEN — COPING WITH CHANGE — "My head is spinning. Last year we moved. I went back to work. My youngest child is starting school. Can somebody throw me a life jacket to survive all the emotions that go along with change?"

1 — My Changing Relationships	Ruth chooses a new family	Ruth 1:1–22
2 — My Changing Home	Abram and Sarai on the move	Genesis 11:27–12:9
3 — My Changing Career	First disciples called	Luke 5:1–11
4 — My Changing Children	Mary's changing child	Luke 2:41–52
5 — My Changing Age	Sarah receives a promise	Genesis 18:1–15
6 — My Changing Spiritual Life	Woman gets "living water"	John 4:7–30

Great Commission Disciple Making

WOMEN — HOLDING YOUR OWN — "I feel like I'm giving and always giving in. I want to be a giving person, but I have needs too. How and when do I speak up for myself?"

1 — Empathy vs. Obsession	Jesus mourns with friends	John 11:1–44
2 — Servanthood vs. Setting Limits	Mary chooses not to serve	Luke 10:38–42
3 — Caring for Myself	Accepting help from others	Exodus 18:1–27
4 — Speaking Up	Esther speaks for her people	Esther 4:6–17; 7:1–10
5 — A Strong Woman	Deborah guides Israel	Judges 4:1–24
6 — At Peace with Myself	Jesus at peace in the temple	Luke 2:41–52

WOMEN — ISSUES WOMEN FACE — "I wish I could talk to other women about some things I can't escape. Like questions and feelings about career vs. family. About roles at home and in the community. And issues that require trust to even bring up."

1 — To Work...or Not to Work	Lydia the businesswoman	Acts 16:11–15
2 — What About Submission?	One flesh	Genesis 2:4–25
3 — My Role in the Community	Priscilla's gift	Acts 18:1–4, 18–28
4 — Can I Love Too Much?	Learning not to do it all	Exodus 18:1–27
5 — Why Didn't God Help?	Amnon rapes Tamar	2 Samuel 13:1–22
6 — Recovering From Abuse	Jesus heals a bleeding woman	Mark 5:24–34

SINGLES — LOVE AND LONELINESS — "I often go for days without a hug or meaningful conversation. Sometimes singleness is like being a social leper. How can I deal with this isolation?"

1 — I Don't Fit Anywhere	Elijah in the wilderness	1 Kings 19:1–18
2 — My Need for a Loving Touch	A touching act	Luke 7:36–50
3 — My Need for Communication	Early connections	Acts 2:42–47
4 — My Need for Companionship	God provides a companion	Genesis 2:4–25
5 — Busyness vs. Loneliness	Jesus' life of balance	Mark 1:29–39
6 — Making the Most of My Life	Lydia: a servant open to God	Acts 16:11–15

SINGLES — PRESSURES — "Panic attack . . . Dirty laundry. Leaking plumbing. Broken car. Checkbook a disaster. Health problems. I'm a capable person, but how can I survive on my own?"

1 — Making My Own Living	Widow become salesperson	2 Kings 4:1–7
2 — Coping With Crisis	Joseph stands under pressure	Genesis 39:1–23
3 — Dealing With My Health	Jesus heals a long sickness	John 5:1–15
4 — Managing My Finances	Making the most of what I have	Mat. 25:14–30
5 — Dealing With Family Issues	God supports Hagar	Genesis 21:1–21
6 — Handling My Emotions	Paul's vision brings comfort	Acts 18:5–17

SINGLES — BEING A COMPLETE PERSON — "Jesus was single. Is it possible God wants me to remain single for life? How can he call singleness a 'gift'? Couldn't I serve him better with a partner? How can I be 'whole' for him now as a single?"

1 — Did Jesus Ever Feel Lonely?	Alone in the wilderness	Matthew 3:13–4:11
2 — The 'Gift' of Singleness	A high calling	I Corinthians 7:25–35
3 — Am I called to be Single?	Each has his own gift	I Corinthians 7:36–40
4 — How Can I Best Serve?	The Greatest servant	Mark 10:35–45
5 — How Should I Pray?	Jesus prays for God's will	Mark 14:32–42
6 — A Whole in One	"I can do everything"	Philippians 4:10–23

Appendix 7: Topical Discovery Studies

SINGLES — HOW TO FIND A PARTNER — "The singles bar is a drag . . . but the church scene isn't much better. I'm about ready to give up on a real relationship and forget the whole dating game."

1 — Where Should I Look?	Isaac looks for love	Gen 24:1–29, 50–67
2 — Staying Disciplined	Samson loses control	Judges 14:1–20
3 — Finding the Right Fit	Priscilla and Aquila	Acts 18:1–4, 18–28
4 — Making Myself "Right"	Solomon desires God's best	I Kings 3:1–28
5 — What About My Fears?	Gideon overcomes his fears	Judges 6:1–40
6 — When God Says "Wait"	Jacob and Rachel wait	Genesis 29:1–30

SINGLES — SEXUALITY — "The whole world tells me to do it. God gave me these desires. What does he expect me to do with them? Is there anyone out there who struggles with the stuff I struggle with?"

1 — Are My Desires Normal?	David is tempted	2 Samuel 11:1–27
2 — What Are God's Standards?	Nathan rebukes David	2 Samuel 12:1–14
3 — Isn't Sex an Act of Love?	"Love" takes over Samson	Judges 16:1–22
4 — How Long Can I Wait?	Jacob puts in his time	Genesis 29:1–30
5 — What If I've Made Mistakes?	Jesus forgives a prostitute	Luke 7:36–50
6 — Dealing With Frustrations	A greater power for Elisha	2 Kings 6:8–23

SINGLES — ISSUES SINGLES FACE — "What kinds of friends do I look for? How do I keep from being burned again? Should I live in community or alone? Should I go back to school or volunteer overseas? What does God want me to do?

1 — Whom to Pick for Friends	David's friendship of character	I Samuel 20:1–42
2 — When to Risk With Others	Seventy-seven times	Matthew 18:21–35
3 — Where to Live	Israel's cloud of guidance	Numbers 9:15–10:36
4 — How to Spend My Life	The Good Samaritan	Luke 10:25–37
5 — Where to Use My Talents	David in Saul's service	I Samuel 16:14–23
6 — What About the Future?	Noah waits on God	Genesis 8:1–22

MARRIAGE — GETTING ALONG AT HOME — "We don't have a bad relationship, but why isn't marriage more fun? I want to be my spouse's best friend — as well as lover. How can I do a better job of living with the one I married?"

1 — In Good Times and Bad	Isaac and Rebekah; 1st love	Gen. 24:1–29, 50–67
2 — Love, Honor and Cherish	Ruth and Boaz; mutual respect	Ruth 2:1–23
3 — 'Til Death Do Us Part	Jacob and Rachel; worth the wait	Genesis 29:1–30
4 — Serving One Another	Footwashing; whose job is it?	John 13:1–17
5 — Friends	Adam and Eve; one flesh	Genesis 2:4–25
6 — And Lovers	Celebrate difference!	Songs 6:13–8:4

MARRIAGE — BALANCING WORK AND HOME — "We both have so many demands for our time and energy. How can we give our best to our work without it coming at the expense of our family? I don't want to lose what we're supposed to be working for!"

1 — Teammates	Adam and Eve; one flesh	Genesis 2:4–25
2 — Roommates	Martha in the kitchen	Luke 10:38–42
3 — Work and Stress	Workers in the vineyard	Matthew 20:1–16
4 — Stress management	Jesus deals with demands	Mark 1:29–39
5 — Serving Each Other	Footwashing	John 13:1–17
6 — Faithful and Fulfilled	Priscilla and Aquila	Acts 18:1–4, 18–28

Great Commission Disciple Making

MARRIAGE — COMMUNICATION CONFLICT — "Whether it's how to guard an evening or how to spend our income — we have a different point of view. How can we relate to each other in a way that pulls us together instead of apart?"

1 — Power of Commitment	Joseph marries Mary	Matthew 1:18–25
2 — Power of Words	David and Michal: cutting words	2 Samuel 6:1–23
3 — Acting on Impulse	Abram, Sarai and Hagar	Genesis 16:1–16
4 — Dealing with Conflict	Abraham and Sarah disagree	Genesis 21:1–21
5 — Pulling Apart	Adam and Eve blame each other	Genesis 3:1–24
6 — Pulling Together	Mutual respect	Eph. 5:22–6:9

MARRIAGE — INTIMACY — "The world exalts sex as the ultimate high. But we both have different needs. We'd like more romance and sizzle in our love life. How does God want us to enjoy this gift?"

1 — God's Gift	Delighting in love	Song of Songs 1:1–14
2 — Sharing Yourself	Wooing words	Song of Songs 1:15–2:15
3 — The Rhythm of Romance	Absence grows love	Song of Songs 2:16–3:11
4 — Only You	Can't keep my eyes off you	Song of Songs 5:9–6:9
5 — Sensitive Sex	Celebrate difference!	Song of Songs 6:13–8:4
6 — Committed Love	The power of love	Song of Songs 8:5–14

MARRIAGE — SPIRITUALLY SINGLE — "Since we've been married, my husband won't come to church with me. I want our children to grow up with Christian teaching, but he doesn't back me up. How can I please God and my husband?"

1 — Don't Give Up	A household conversion	Acts 16:16–40
2 — God's Love and Ours	Abraham pleads for Sodom	Genesis 18:16–33
3 — Trusting God	Abraham's greatest test	Genesis 22:1–19
4 — Who's Number 1?	Take a warning from Solomon	1 Kings 10:23–11:13
5 — God is at Work	Praying for Peter in prison	Acts 12:1–19
6 — Your Spiritual Family	Mary and John at the cross	John 19:16–27

MARRIAGE — MISCARRIAGE — "It tears me up to walk past the baby's room. Now I wish we hadn't gotten so excited and made so many plans. I'm dying inside, and I've got to talk to someone who has gone through this."

1 — When Life Falls Apart	Job's life collapses	Job 1:1–22
2 — Shattered Dreams	Elisha and a grieving woman	2 Kings 4:8–37
3 — Marital Stress	Jacob and Rachel under stress	Genesis 29:31–30:24
4 — Releasing the Pain	Hannah pours out her soul	1 Samuel 1:1–28
5 — God Cares	Jesus weeps over death	John 11:1–44
6 — Life Goes On	David pleads, then accepts	2 Samuel 12:15–25

PARENTING — HOW IT'S DONE — "I got into parenting before I was ready. Other people make it sound so easy. My mother just laughs. My grandmother says everything will be okay. But I'm trying to raise my kids without a map. Please help."

1 — Preparation	Mary and Joseph become parents	Luke 2:1–20
2 — Dedication	Jesus presented in the temple	Luke 2:21–40
3 — Expectations	A mother's high hopes	Mat. 20:20–28
4 — Confrontation	Eli's failure to restore his sons	I Samuel 3:1–21
5 — Consecration	Abraham's greatest test	Genesis 22:1–19
6 — Celebration	Homecoming party	Luke 15:11–32

Appendix 7: Topical Discovery Studies

PARENTING — FAMILY TIME — "We want to create memories as a family. Will our kids remember their childhood in a way that feels good to them and honors God?"

1 — Proper Priorities	God commands a day off	Exodus 16:1–35
2 — Time Together	Supper time	John 13:1–17
3 — Family Traditions	Passover: a family ritual	Exodus 12:1–30
4 — Family Vacations	A "vacation" with 5000 surprises	Mark 6:30–44
5 — Worshiping Together	The fellowship of believers	Acts 2:42–47
6 — Lasting Values	Stones of memorial	Joshua 3:14–4:24

PARENTING — STRONG-WILLED CHILDREN — "My daughter always wants to paint outside the lines. She is really a good kid, and I love her a lot, but I don't know what to do. How do you raise a child who was born with a strong will?"

1 — Where Are My Instructions?	Jesus was a strong-willed child	Luke 2:41–52
2 — Born to Be Wild	The devil made me do it	Genesis 3:1–24
3 — Necessary Discipline	Eli: a parent who failed	1 Samuel 3:1–21
4 — Dealing with Anger	Moses faces his critics	Numbers 11:4–34
5 — Your Kids Drive You Crazy	Little Jacob grabs for power	Genesis 25:19–34
6 — Happy Endings	Jacob's strength comes through	Genesis 32:22–32

PARENTING — ADOLESCENTS — "My teenager is about to drive me crazy. The music, posters, clothes; it's outrageous! We can't even talk about it without shouting. How can we make it through adolescence?!"

1 — Stressful Times	Trouble in the family	Luke 15:11–32
2 — Confusing Times	When Jesus didn't come home	Luke 2:41–52
3 — Angry Times	The golden calf	Exodus 32:1–35
4 — Decisions, Decisions!	Samson's dating dilemma	Judges 14:1–20
5 — A Parent's Responsibility	Eli's failure to restrain his sons	I Samuel 3:1–21
6 — Getting Along	Joseph: a kid with an 'attitude'	Genesis 37:1–11

PARENTING — CHALLENGING ISSUES, SPECIAL NEEDS — "God have me a very special child. Now, I need the wisdom to raise this child. I feel somewhat alone and nobody understands."

1 — Adopted Children	Moses: an adopted child	Exodus 1:22–2:25
2 — Children of Divorce	Ishmael: Rejected and dejected	Genesis 21:1–21
3 — Single-Parent Children	Double blessing for a single parent	I Kings 17:1–24
4 — Children With Disabilities	Why was he born blind?	John 9:1–34
5 — Gifted Children	Jesus perplexes his parents	Luke 2:41–52
6 — Substitute Parents	Esther: raised by a relative	Esther 2:1–18

PARENTING — PARENTS IN PAIN — "Where did we go wrong? I never dreamed our son would make the choices he has. Didn't our values sink in at all? And how do we relate to him now? What should or shouldn't we say to him?"

1 — Sharing Your Story	Prodigal: a parable of pain	Luke 15:11–32
2 — Coping With Grief	Eli and his wayward sons	1 Samuel 2:12–26
3 — Dealing With Disappointment	Chaos in David's family	2 Sam. 13:23–39
4 — Knowing How to Relate	David longs for Absalom	2 Samuel 14:1–33
5 — Feeling Their Pain	Peter disowns Jesus	Luke 22:54–62
6 — Believing in Miracles	Jesus forgives Peter	John 21:1–25

Great Commission Disciple Making

YOUTH — DISCOVERING MY REAL IDENTITY — "I know I'm good at some things and no so good at others. I don't want to be weird, but I do want to be myself. What makes me unique? How can I be all that I was meant to be?"

1 — Being Real	A Pharisee and a tax collector	Luke 18:9–14
2 — My Uniqueness	Zacchaeus	Luke 19:1–10
3 — My Personality	Mary and Martha	Luke 10:38–42
4 — My Abilities	Using your 'talents'	Mat. 25:14–30
5 — Strengths and Weaknesses	Gideon's fears	Judges 6:1–40
6 — God's Call	Following Jesus	Luke 5:1–11

YOUTH — FINDING FRIENDS AND FITTING IN — "I always feel out of place. It's so hard to fit in. I don't want to come off like I'm either shy or obnoxious. Can I be myself and still have friends?"

1 — Acceptance	Paul's struggle for acceptance	Acts 9:20–31
2 — Fitting In	"The Lord looks at the heart"	1 Samuel 16:1–13
3 — Being Myself	David can't use Saul's armor	1 Sam. 17:12–50
4 — Feeling Secure	David and Jonathan — Part 1	1 Samuel 18:1–30
5 — Getting Close	David and Jonathan — Part 2	1 Samuel 20:1–42
6 — True Friends	Four friends who cared	Mark 2:1–12

YOUTH — WHAT DO I BELIEVE? — "I've done the church thing. It's easy to let all that teaching go in one ear and out the other. I think it's time to know what I really believe, and really believe what I already know."

1 — God the Father Almighty	Maker of heaven and earth	Genesis 1:1–2:3
2 — Jesus Christ	An angel visits Mary	Luke 1:26–38
3 — Holy Spirit	The Spirit shakes things up	Acts 4:1–31
4 — Christian Church	The cost in "being there"	Acts 4:32–37
5 — Forgiveness of Sins	Jesus: my substitute	Mark 15:1–15
6 — Resurrection and Life	A new day dawns	Matthew 28:1–20

YOUTH — SURVIVING DAY TO DAY — "I have to buy my own clothes. Beg people for a ride. Make a C average in school just to stay on the team. Everybody's on my back. And my best friend didn't call tonight. Life stinks."

1 — Stressed Out	Facing storms	Mark 4:35–41
2 — Daily Grind	Slaving away in Egypt	Exodus 5:1–21
3 — Making the Grade	Parable of the talents	Mat. 25:14–30
4 — Feeling Alone	Jesus in Gethsemane	Mark 14:32–42
5 — Dealing with Disappointment	Jesus is betrayed and arrested	Mat. 26:47–56
6 — Facing Failure	Peter disowns Jesus	Luke 22:54–62

YOUTH — GETTING ALONG WITH PARENTS — "In my parents' eyes, I can't do anything right. I don't look right, act right, study right, spend money right or pick friends right. As long as I'm still at home, will I always be wrong?"

1 — Parental Requests	Jesus and his mom at a wedding	John 2:1–11
2 — Parental Expectations	A mother's dream	Mat. 20:20–28
3 — Family Tension	When Jesus didn't come home	Luke 2:41–52
4 — Dealing with Frustrations	Jesus and his family	Mark 3:20–35
5 — Arguing Over Relationships	Samson and his women	Judges 14:1–20
6 — Making Things Right	A son returns home	Luke 15:11–32